# A Guide to Japanese Art Collections in the UK

# A Guide to Japanese Art Collections in the UK

Gregory Irvine

The Japan Society
FOUNDED 1891

*Publisher*
Hotei Publishing
Imprint of KIT Publishers
Mauritskade 63
P.O. Box 95001
1090 HA Amsterdam
The Netherlands
www.hotei-publishing.com
www.kit.nl/publishers



ISBN 90-74822-74-6
NUR 642

*Editing*
Linda Cook, Amsterdam

*Design*
Qwerty realisatie, Leiden

*Production*
Meester & de Jonge, Lochem

# Foreword

Britain's first contact with Japan came in 1600 with the shipwreck of the English mariner William Adams, a man who went on to become advisor to Shogun Tokugawa Ieyasu. Trade links were established by the setting up of the English East India Company trading post in 1613 and later that same year the first documented examples of Japanese art (two suits of armour) to arrive in this country were sent by the shogun to King James as a diplomatic gift.

During the following centuries Japanese art was treasured by the wealthy classes but it was not until the 19th century that Japan's art began to be fully appreciated by the general public. Most collections of Japanese art to be found in the UK today were formed during the relatively short period from about 1870 to 1920 and there are now many examples of Japanese art in UK collections that cannot be found in Japan at the present time. In recent years, particularly following the UK's nationwide 1991 Japan Festival and the events of Japan 2001, there has been a huge upsurge in the interest in and understanding of Japan's long cultural heritage.

I believe that this guide will greatly benefit all those with an interest in Japan's unique art and culture by identifying the wide range of Japanese art collections to be found throughout the UK - although there are undoubtedly more treasures still to be discovered. I sincerely hope that through the art of Japan we can continue to build bridges between our two cultures and I believe that this guide will contribute to the continuation of the long cultural relationship between our two countries.

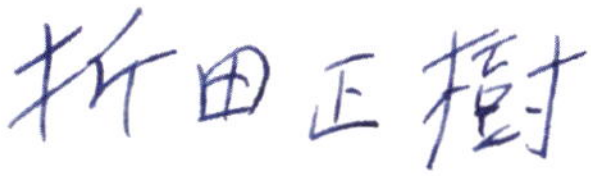

Masaki Orita
Ambassador

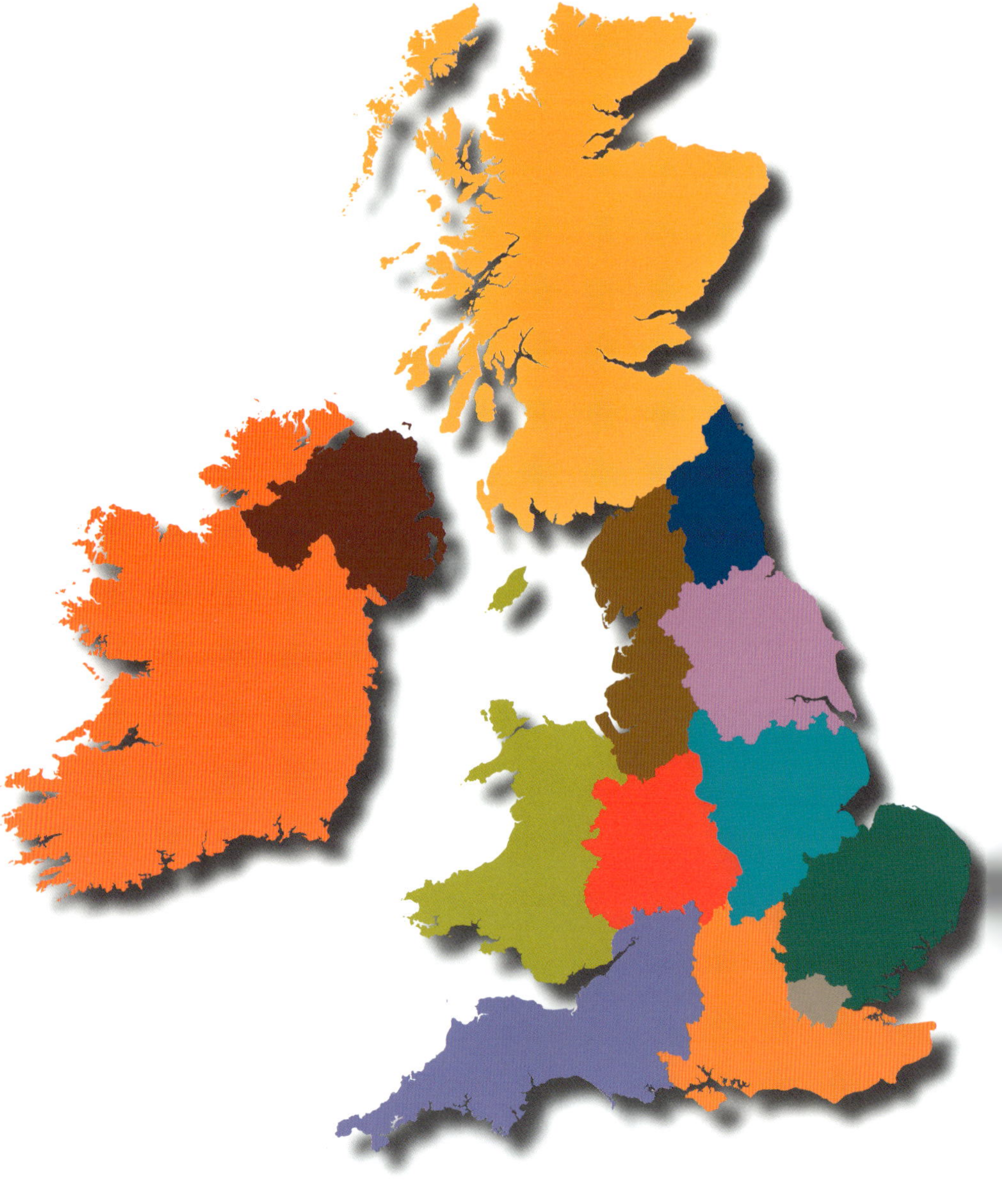

# Contents

# Acknowledgements

My thanks go to the Great Britain Sasakawa Foundation, which generously provided seed money for the project and without whose financial help, unstinting support and faith in the guide we would probably have never got the project off the ground.

My thanks and gratitude go to Françoise White who worked with me in the early stages of the project and helped get the whole thing started. Thanks also to Clare Barclay of the Japan Society for all her help and expert knowledge of publishing and for keeping remarkably calm throughout the project. Thanks to Captain Robert Guy, Executive Director of the Japan Society, who has earnestly supported the idea from the start; also to my colleagues at the Victoria & Albert Museum when my time and work there was interrupted by work on the guide. Lastly to my family, Harriet, Dan and Grace who have supported me with this work and have put up with my seclusion at the keyboard long into the night and at weekends – when of course we should have been out visiting the collections!

# Introduction

The idea for compiling this guide came about during a meeting of the Japan Society Publications Committee, of which I am a member, when I suddenly found myself volunteering to update and expand upon Bowen Pearse's 1991 publication *Companion to Japanese Britain and Ireland*. This slim, useful volume was produced to commemorate the centenary of the founding of the Japan Society in 1891. I quickly became aware of the difficulties Mr. Pearse must have had in compiling his guide. The work on this publication should in reality have been full-time, so juggling my V&A work with the requirements of extracting information and images from the various collections across the UK was challenging to say the least.

In the early part of the project I was fortunate to have the assistance, for a far too short period, of Françoise White. Françoise performed the role of researcher with vigour, and diligently mailed, telephoned and generally chased up the various collections whilst trying to persuade people that this was indeed a worthwhile project that would ultimately be to their benefit, as their collections would become known to a wider audience. I knew where many of the major collections were but otherwise had little idea of precisely what types of Japanese art could be found in the UK's numerous regional museums and other collections. There were many surprises. For example, Bury Museum has a small collection of ivories and examples of the usual types of Japanese objects that were acquired during the late 19th century. It also has a huge, signed Meiji-period bronze standing nearly four metres high! This would seem to be an object that was on show at one of the great world exhibitions of the second half of the 19th century, possibly Paris 1900, but this wonderful piece certainly needs much further research. Curators at the Tokyo University of Fine Art have been looking into the background of this piece for me.

I certainly did not have time to visit all the collections featured in this guide so I have had to rely on available published material and the knowledge of those responsible for their collections to inform me. I particularly wanted the curators of the collections to tell me where they thought the strengths of their collections lay. They could also provide me with good background to the history of their collections. Unfortunately, in a small, but significant number of cases, this proved to be a fairly thankless task. For various reasons, some institutions (even some with well-known nationally important collections) never responded, despite my repeated requests for information. A number of them responded negatively (I am thinking of a particular stately home where I know Japanese collections are held but they effectively told me they were far too busy with their general tourist trade to enter into any correspondence). Other collections were extremely enthusiastic about the whole project and, at times, overwhelmed me with information. Others, without specialist curators for Japanese art, were extremely helpful but did not know what they had; yet others were overwhelmed with work on new galleries and other projects, otherwise they would have been happy to co-operate. There are some known exclusions; for example the Science Museum in London has not been included as I cannot discover any one person responsible for Japanese objects although there are apparently quite a number of interesting Japanese scientific instruments and other relevant objects in their collection.

What has come out of all this research is that there are at least 150 institutions in the UK that have collections of Japanese art and even in the final stages of writing I am discovering a few more. I am sure there are still more to be found and I would be more than pleased to hear about them. The collections range from small, personally collected groups of Japanese objects – such as those at Bateman's, the home of Rudyard Kipling now administered by the National Trust, and the huge, well-documented collections of national museums such as the Victoria & Albert Museum and the British Museum. Yet other collections are held in museums administered by local authorities; others are in university museums and libraries of varying sizes. There are many fine examples of Japanese art in the UK's grand country houses and stately homes – once private collections that are now open to the public. Some are still occupied by the original family and others are administered by local authorities or the National Trust. Such was the vogue for collecting Japanese porcelain and export lacquer during the 17th and 18th centuries, that of the hundreds of large houses from that period there must be few which do not have at least one Japanese object in their collections. I have tried to include as many properties as possible that are known to have Japanese objects but there are bound to be many more and I therefore refer the reader to publications such as *Hudson's Historic Houses and Gardens*, which lists these properties.

Finally, there are the Royal Collections. The royal family has, since the early 17th century, been the recipient of diplomatic and other gifts from Japan and there is a considerable amount of research still to be done in order to establish the full extent of what Japanese art works are held in the collection. A major research programme is currently being carried out on a scale model of the Taitokuin Mausoleum (for Tokugawa Hidetada), which was exhibited at the 1910 Japan-British Exhibition at White City. The City of Tokyo presented the model to King George IV and it was displayed but was then dismantled and stored for many years. This is a fascinating and unique object, not least because the original Taitokuin was destroyed in 1945 and the project aims to restore the model; it may eventually be re-exhibited on the original site in Tokyo.

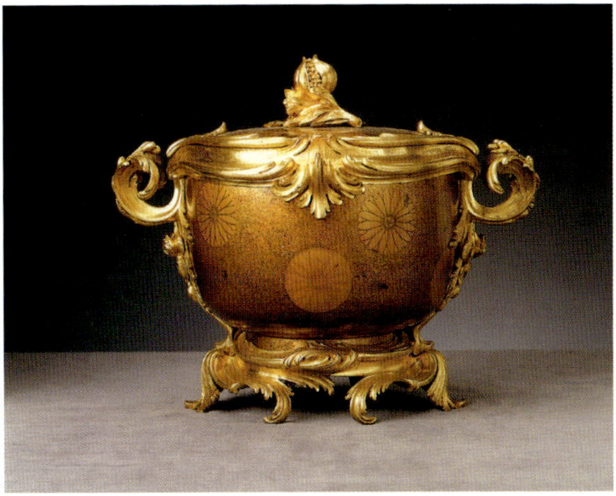

*Lacquer bowl in ormolu mounts*

Many of the finest pieces in the Royal Collection are on display in those royal households that are periodically open to the public, but there are certainly many more Japanese objects held in the reserve collections. The royal family has a long history of generously donating objects to the UK's museums. Some members of the royal family were collectors in their own right; there is documentation in the V&A archives that tells of Queen Mary during the 1920s simply "dropping in" at the V&A with gifts of netsuke and other small items that she had bought especially for the Museum.

At a very early stage in the planning process it was decided to drop the word 'comprehensive' from the title of this guide as it quickly became apparent that all I could do was provide a snapshot at a particular time of the numbers and types of Japanese art held in the UK's superb collections. There is a still a great deal more to discover about the extent of our Japanese collections in the UK. At the time of writing, all the information given in this guide is correct (as far as I can establish) although even during the course of the project I discovered that some telephone numbers, email addresses and website URLs have changed. I would therefore strongly advise checking collections' details before visiting. Some information may be vague depending on what I already knew, was able to discover or from what I was sent by the collections concerned. Some collections are undergoing physical moves or building work and collections open now may be closed by the time the guide is published – and vice-versa.

There was also a deliberate, albeit sometimes difficult, decision not to include Japanese gardens in this guide. I offer no apologies for some of the inclusions in the guide (but certainly for any exclusions) and decided to include some institutions in the Republic of Ireland where there are wonderful collections of Japanese art. The curators of these collections have no problem being included in a guide to Japanese art that is otherwise devoted to UK collections.

The numbers and types of objects on display in the collections mentioned in this guide may vary from time to time, as environmentally sensitive objects such as paper, paintings, lacquer and textiles should not be displayed for long periods. A common characteristic to most of the collections is that a large percentage of their holdings may be in reserve collections and, for the most part, these reserve collections can be seen by prior appointment. I must stress the word prior as, from personal experience, it is unfortunate to have to refuse someone who simply turns up (often from halfway across the world) expecting to be able to immediately see objects in storage that may not even be on the same site as the main collections. That said, the many and varied collections in the United Kingdom contain a vast resource for the study, appreciation and enjoyment of Japan's huge range of arts and manufactures and I hope this guide will serve to increase that understanding and pleasure.

For convenience, the collections featured in the guide have been divided into their respective geographical regions within the UK and the provision of maps and an index of the names of the collections and of the types of objects to be found in the collections themselves should enable the reader to navigate both the written text and the collections themselves.

# Collecting Japanese Art in the UK

In 1613 Captain John Saris arrived in Japan to establish a trading factory on behalf of the East India Company. He carried credentials from King James I (of England) and enlisted the help of Will Adams, an Englishman who had arrived in Japan in 1600 as the pilot of a Dutch trading vessel and who had risen to become Shogun Tokugawa Ieyasu's chief advisor on foreign affairs. Saris did not stay in Japan for very long and endured many frustrations before leaving in December of 1613 remarking that he was "never again to tempt fortune in the East".

He returned bearing gifts from the shogun for King James. These included two suits of armour, a *katana* and a *waggadash* (*wakizashi*) for himself. He also had a large private collection of *shunga* – Japanese erotic prints, which was discovered and burned by the company and he was dismissed for this and for excessive private trading. The armours are in the collections of the Royal Armouries, Leeds (although one is still officially the property of the royal family), but of Saris' *katana* and *waggadash* we have no record. The armours have had a chequered history and in 1660 one of the two armours in the Royal Armouries collection, the "armour sent to his now Majesty, Charles the second, by the great Mogull, consisting of backe, breast, taces, headpiece, vizor and pieces of the greaves' appeared in the *View and Survey of the King's Majesty's Armoury.* It was placed on display and excited considerable public interest.

In July 1662, "many persons of quality went to the armoury in the Tower of London to see that most noble and strong defence for the body, the suit of armour sent from the Emperor Mougul, which suit was presented to His Majesty the King of England," and in 1688, a valuation of £5 was placed upon the armour.[1] From being the first recorded Japanese object to arrive in Britain, the fact that the armour was Japanese was overlooked until the 19th century. The Tower of London remained both an armoury and a visitors' attraction for centuries with little regard to what would today be regarded as curatorship.

It was not until the 1950s that, under H. Russell Robinson (Superintendent of the Armouries, and latterly Keeper of Armour), curatorship began to appear and Russell Robinson actively started to acquire Japanese armour for the Tower's collection. In 1965 he organised the immensely important *Exhibition of Japanese Armour.* This exhibition included pieces from the Tower Armouries, the Ashmolean Museum, Fitzwilliam Museum, Maidstone Museum, National Trust at Snowshill Manor, Royal Scottish Museum (as it was then named) and the Victoria & Albert Museum, as well as objects from private collections and collectors.

Japan had effectively closed her doors to the West from around 1637 but permitted trade through the port of Nagasaki from where examples of fine porcelain and lacquer ware (frequently in the form of furniture, domestic pieces or religious objects) found their way into the great houses of Europe. The export of such material was usually through the Dutch East India Company, although there was a brief, unsuccessful English trading presence in Japan at the English East India Company factory that operated at Hirado from 1613 to 1623. The finer-quality wares were acquired for country houses and palaces for both decorative and utilitarian functions. In England, early inventories, such as the 1688 inventory of Burghley House, detail examples of lacquer and porcelain. Not only the extremely grand houses had such material the inventory of Dunster Castle in rural Somerset (of the slightly later date of 1690) also mentions lacquer cabinets, one of which is still in the castle. The fashion for such objects continued throughout the 17th and 18th centuries and few houses of note did not have some representative collections of Japanese art works decorating their mantelpieces or carefully placed in prominent positions in their rooms.

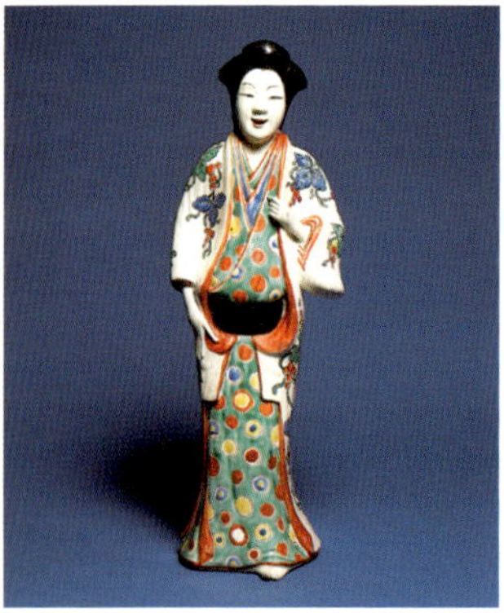

*Bijin figure, Arita porcelain with overglaze enamels, c. 1680-1700, C.3-1961, Given by the Friends of the Fitzwilliam*

Burghley is an excellent example of a private collection in a property now open to the public and Dunster Castle an example of the type of property once privately owned but now administered by the National Trust and open to the public. One significant problem I encountered during the compilation of this guide is that in quite a few instances, the custodians of many of these private or once-private collections did not know whether the objects they have are actually Japanese or otherwise.

The seventeenth and eighteenth centuries in Britain also saw the foundation of what are now large public museums but which at the time were the collections of private individuals. On the 24th May 1683, the Ashmolean Museum in Oxford opened its doors to become the first private collection of 'curiosities' to be opened to the public. Even the use of the term 'Museum' was a novelty in English: a few years later the New World of Words (1706) defined it as 'a Study, or Library; also a College, or Publick Place for the Resort of Learned Men', with a specific entry for 'Ashmole's museum'[2], described as 'a neat Building in the City of Oxford'. The collection of Elias Ashmole was already half a century old having been founded by John Tradescant (died 1638) and displayed to the public (for a fee), first by him and later by his son John (1608-62) in their house at Lambeth in London, at a site roughly on the opposite bank of the River Thames to where the present day Houses of Parliament are located.

The Museum of Eastern Art was formed in 1949 as a subdivision of the Department of Fine Art and was housed in the old Indian Institute which had maintained its own museum of Indian art since 1897. Through a gradual process in the early 1950s and early 1960s the transfer of these combined collections to the Ashmolean's own building formed the Department of Eastern Art. Since this time, under specialist curators, the museum's collections of Japanese paintings and export ceramics have greatly expanded. More recently, the work of artists and craftsmen of the Meiji period has featured prominently in the Ashmolean's Japanese galleries.

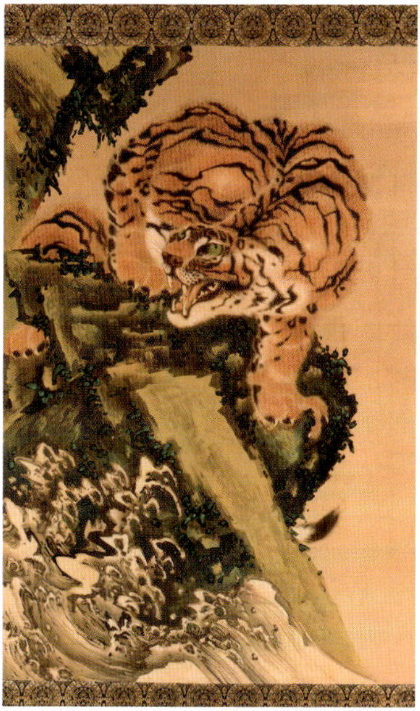

*Tiger by Ganku c. 1784-96, 1931.4-27.01*

In 1753, almost one hundred years after the opening of Ashmole's Museum, the British Museum in London was founded on the original gift of Sir Hans Sloane. Sloane's collection contained Japanese material acquired from the family of the German physician Engelbert Kaempfer who had brought back objects from Japan where he had served from 1690-1692. From this early source the British Museum (BM) has grown to be perhaps the most well know museum in the UK. From around 1860 the BM began to actively collect Japanese art (particularly prints and ceramics) under the keepership of Sir Augustus Wollaston Franks and later acquired considerable numbers of paintings, notably from the collection of one William Anderson. 1913 saw the establishment of the sub-Department of Oriental Prints and Drawings with Laurence Binyon cataloguing the collections. In 1933 the Department of Oriental Antiquities was formed with specialist curators working on Japan: in 1987 a separate Department of Japanese Antiquities was created and in 1990 the BM opened a superb suite of Japanese Galleries.

From this moment the BM began to actively acquire substantial collections of Japanese objects and embarked on an ambitious exhibition programme. Japanese objects flooded in and the BM seemed to be Japan's first choice for donations irrespective of whether the BM had the space to properly store or curatorial expertise to do justice to the objects. Unfortunately, through various measures, in 2003 the Japanese department was subsumed into the 'Department of Asia' with a solitary full-time curator responsible for all the collections which had been so carefully built up over the years and the special exhibition programme has all but disappeared.

Soon after the establishment of an official British presence in Japan in 1859, there was a donation of diplomatic gifts from Shogun Tokugawa Iemochi to Queen Victoria through the offices of Sir Rutherford Alcock, Britain's first Consul General in Japan. In 1865, this gift was donated to the South Kensington Museum (as the Victoria & Albert Museum, or V&A was then called). The gift included a suit of armour, and many polearms and swords as well as fine examples of porcelain. Interestingly, these were the first Japanese swords to enter the Museum's collections and some carry inscriptions that suggest that they were made especially for this diplomatic gift; the armour bears a date that indicates that it had been assembled especially for the gift.

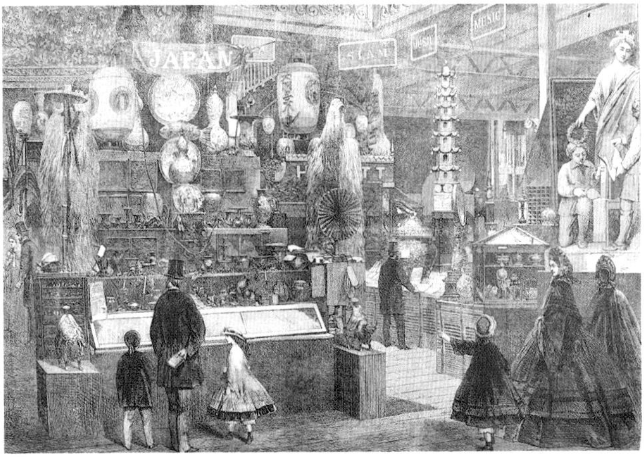


*The Japanese Court at the International Exhibition London, 1862*

Although Alcock was not recalled from Japan until 1864, he had personally accumulated enough Japanese objects to be sent to the International Exhibition of 1862 in London. The catalogue of this exhibition contains over 600 entries relating to Japan. Alcock's introduction refers to Japan's artworks as follows "... others are very costly, and only to be obtained at prices, which in Europe would probably be thought far disproportioned to their value; but these are chiefly specimens of ... swords and armour, of which latter class the armed retainers of the Daimios, and feudal chiefs themselves, are extravagant admirers; and when wealthy, they will give any price for an approved weapon by a maker of great repute". Catalogue entry 492 is of interest: "Short sword of one of the party of assassins which attacked the British Legation on 5th July, 1861".

The Liverpool collector James Lord Bowes formed the core of his extensive Japanese collection from objects acquired from Alcock's exhibited works. Bowes was an ardent Japanophile and philanthropist who, in 1888, had been made Honorary Consul for Japan in Liverpool. He had a private museum built behind his house to exhibit his collection and this was opened to the general public in 1890. Following his death in 1899, his collection was eventually sold off in 1901. He managed to publish many contentious works on Japanese art during the relatively short period of his Japan-related activities.

During the Meiji period (1868 -1912) Japan rapidly began to participate in the major world exhibitions such as those held in Paris (1867), Vienna (1873), Philadelphia

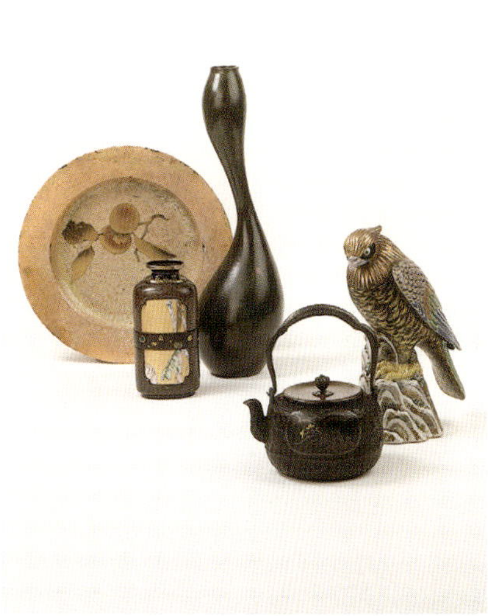

*Japanese objects acquired by the V&A from Siegfried Bing*

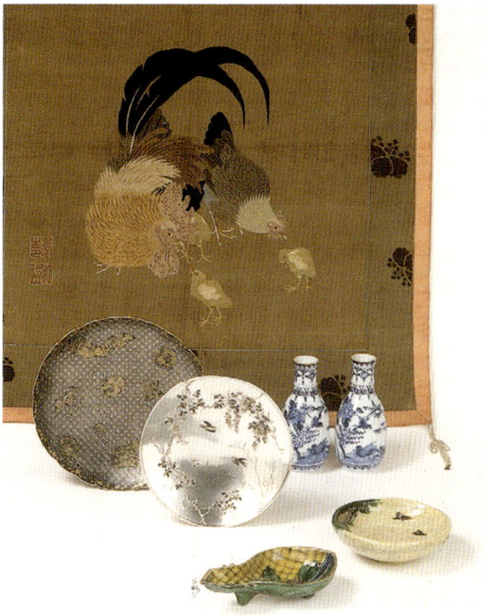

*Japanese objects originally bought by Londos & Co. Christopher Dresser's company, acquired the*

(1876) and again in Paris (1878)[3]. The arts and crafts of Japan were obtainable from private individuals and sold at auctions and in both specialist and non-specialist shops. These shops include Liberty's of Regent Street, Kato of New Oxford Street, and later Yamanaka of Bond Street who had a large staff of Japanese art salesmen. The Victoria & Albert Museum has excellent documentation of many of these transactions including correspondence between the V&A and the dealer Bing in Paris. Private individuals formed wonderful collections of Japanese objects at this time and these were often later sold, given or bequeathed to Museums.

The second half of the nineteenth century was the golden period for collecting Japanese art as the country was 're-opened'. Western travellers flocked to Japan and purchased objects in huge quantities – some of very dubious quality but then they had little previous experience of Japanese art on which to base aesthetic judgments. One such Victorian period traveller to Japan was Merton Russell-Cotes. Very much representative of a man of the period, he and his wife travelled to Japan in 1885 bringing back over one hundred crates full of objects. He opened a 'Japanese Drawing Room' in his hotel, the Royal Bath Hotel in Bournemouth and issued formal invitations to view the collections. Although the hotel remains, sadly the room has gone although photographs exist of the original displays. Russell-Cotes then built a new home, East Cliff Hall, in the grounds of the hotel and included a Japanese-style garden complete with pond, bridge, shrine and incense burners. All that remains now of the original 'Japanese' element in the house is the extraordinary 'Mikado's Room', created around 1920 which incorporates motifs and images inspired by their collections[4].

One particular aspect to the understanding of Japanese art in the early collecting period was how it should be classified. Japan was rapidly emerging from a feudal period, determined to modernise along Western lines and become a world power in the process shaking off its feudal past. Westerners fantasised about 'pure' art from Japan

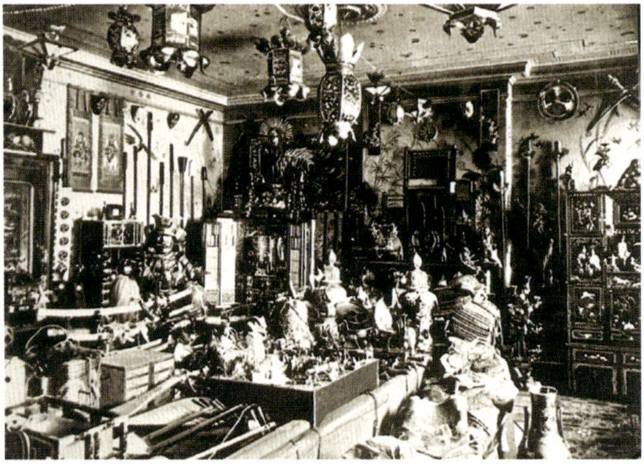

*Japanese Room at the Royal Bath Hotel, Boumemouth*

but the objects brought back from Japan by Western travellers were both 'art' and 'ethnography' – to use both terms loosely. Many 'ethnographic' objects were brought back (particularly in the early years of the twentieth century) particularly by missionaries and form the basis of collections at both national and regional museums.

In Oxford in 1884 the Pitt-Rivers Museum was founded when General Pitt Rivers, an influential figure in the development of archaeology and evolutionary anthropology, gave his collection to the University. The original gift contained more than 18,000 objects but there are now over half a million. Japan has always been well represented in the collections although the original gift from General Pitt Rivers contained only some 300 Japanese objects. Today there are examples of everyday Japanese artefacts - such as bamboo hairpins, a grass snow-cloak as well as many religious items and figures, samurai swords and armour and an interesting collection of Noh masks.

To my knowledge, no major new public collections of exclusively Japanese art were created in the UK during the twentieth century although many museums have benefited from gifts and bequests of Japanese art which had been collected in the late nineteenth and early twentieth centuries. Since then many museums have gone through periods of actively collecting Japanese art, particularly from the nineteenth and twentieth centuries and often with an emphasis on the 'contemporary'. Many collections have, over the years, been rationalised and reassessed with, unfortunately, instances of de-accessioning of their collections, particularly when there has been no specialist curator to advise on the intrinsic value of the collections.

In recent years and particularly following the UK-wide Japan festivals of 1991 and 2001 there has been a growing awareness among the newer generations of curators of Japanese art in the UK of the need to reinterpret our collections and perhaps avoid some of the more rigid classifications of art and ethnography and also to steer clear of the connoisseur-based fixation of some of our predecessors – although the ability to appreciate the aesthetics of a fine object should not be forgotten.

A particular difficulty found in regional museums today is the lack of curatorial specialism and many of the curators in these museums and collections have insufficient knowledge of non-European, let alone Japanese objects. Their job is frequently one of full-time administration with little or no time to research the collections – many of which are of really decent quality. Again, this problem has been emerging through research for this guide and I now have so many invitations to visit and assess collections that I could be kept busy for years to come with work on Japanese art in the UK's many collections. One of the remits which we as curators in national museums are obliged by the government to undertake (time permitting) is to help and assist regional museums with the identification of their collections and I have personally been involved in many projects of this nature.

In recent years there has been the formation of several notable private collections of Japanese art, some of which have been exhibited and published while others have been made readily available to the public. One such is the Robert & Lisa Sainsbury Collection at the Sainsbury Centre for Visual Arts in Norwich. In 1999 Lord & Lady Sainsbury founded 'The Sainsbury Institute for the Study of Japanese Art and Culture' (SISJAC) whose mission statement is 'To promote the study of the material and visual cultures of the Japanese archipelago, and in doing so act as a catalyst for international research in the field'.[5]

In conclusion, in the UK we have an active policy towards promoting the arts and culture of Japan but often find our efforts overwhelmed by the daily running of museum business. Occasionally we do find the time and energy to research and look deeper into the many wonderful collections in our museums and then present this information to the public through publications, lectures, demonstrations or exhibitions. These are the rewarding times.

Japan is more than Mount Fuji, cherry blossom, geisha and samurai – although one might be forgiven for thinking otherwise as this image is often perpetuated even by those Japanese who seek to promote their own art and culture in the West. Too often when we seek help with our Japanese projects, it is these aspects of Japan that are offered to us. It is time for us as curators to move on and re-interpret our Japanese collections in the context of the 21st century where the traditional and modern can co-exist.

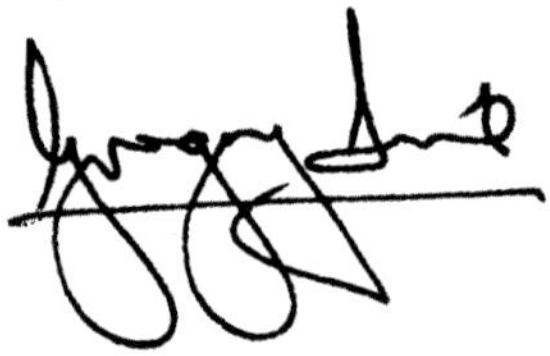

Gregory Irvine

Notes

[1] Thanks to Thom Richardson, Keeper of Arms & Armour at the Royal Armouries for this reference

[2] The Historical Development of the Ashmolean Museum. Ashmolean Museum website www.ashmol.ox.ac.uk/ash/faqs/q003

[3] A useful list of these world expositions can be found at www.lib.csufresno.edu/subjectresources/specialcollections/worldfairs/welcome.html

[4] www.russell-cotes.bournemouth.gov.uk/japcol.htm

[5] www.uea.ac.uk/scva/rlsc

# South-West England

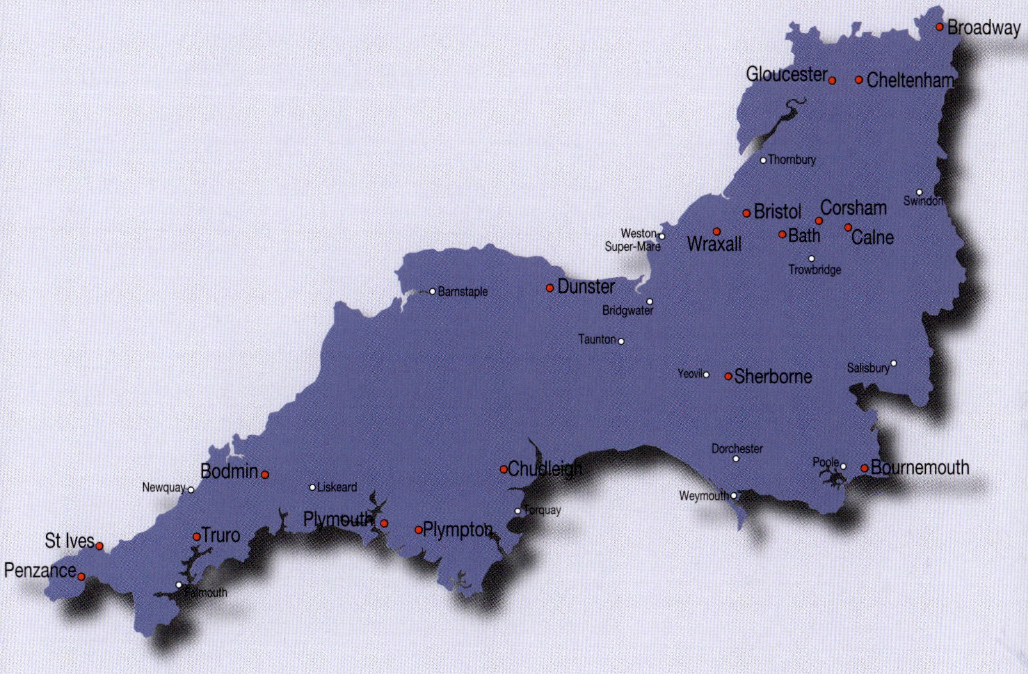

# Bath

## Holburne Museum of Art

This elegant late 18th-century building began life as the Sydney Hotel, which was at the heart of the Sydney Pleasure Gardens; these were visited by Jane Austen from nearby Sydney Place. It became the Holburne Museum in 1916 and houses the superb art collection formed by Sir William Holburne (1793-1874) of English and continental silver, porcelain, majolica, glass and Renaissance bronzes. The Picture Gallery contains works by Turner, Guardi and Stubbs as well as portraits of members of Bath society by Thomas Gainsborough. The Japanese collections of the museum are unusual in that they consist almost entirely of nearly 100 ivory and wood netsuke that were given to the museum by the Reverend Winwood of Bath in 1920. Unfortunately nothing is known of the details of this gift and although the netsuke are not currently on display they are available to view by prior appointment.

**Holburne Museum of Art**
Great Pulteney Street
Bath
Somerset
BA2 4DB

Tel: 01225 466669
Fax: 01225 333121
holburne@bath.ac.uk
www.bath.ac.uk/holburne

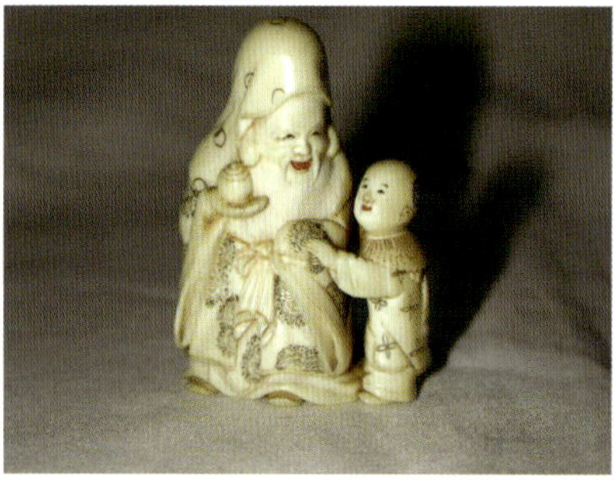

*Ivory okimono*

## Museum of East Asian Art

The Museum of East Asian Art was founded in 1993 as a result of the vision of Brian McElney OBE, a retired solicitor who practised in Hong Kong for over 35 years. Pieces collected by Mr. McElney formed the basis of the collection and today visitors will find ceramics from all the countries of East Asia, bamboo carvings, and one of the UK's most comprehensive Chinese jade collections. There are also fine examples of metalwork and other decorative arts. The Museum pursues an active education and publication programme.

Museum of East Asian Art
12 Bennett Street
Bath
Somerset
BA1 2QJ

Tel: 01225 464640
Fax: 01225 461718

museum@east-asian-art.
freeserve.co.uk
info@meaa.org.uk
www.meaa.org.uk

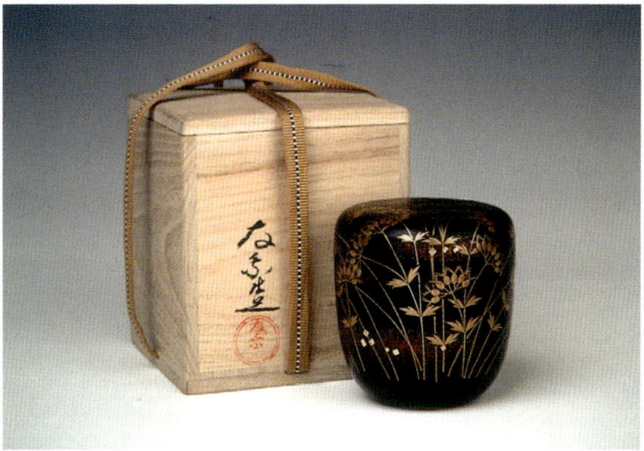

*Natsume and box*

At the time of writing there are some 56 Japanese objects in the collection including Ryukyuan lacquer, inro, lacquer boxes, tea ceramics, 19th-century Hirado-ware, Nabeshima porcelain, Satsuma ware, Kakiemon porcelain, netsuke, a few sword-fittings and several prints.

## Bodmin

### Lanhydrock House

In 1620 Sir Richard Robartes, the son of a successful Cornish moneylender bought the old monastic manor at Lanhydrock and began to build a traditional house around a central courtyard. Many of the owners of Lanhydrock were Members of Parliament and took an active interest in local affairs. Little change was made to the house over the next two centuries, apart from the demolition of the east range in the 1780s. The house remained unoccupied for long periods of time and suffered greatly from neglect. In the mid-19th century, the 1st Baron Robartes of Lanhydrock and Truro came to live at his ancestral home and commissioned George Gilbert Scott to modernise and remodel Lanhydrock.

Unfortunately, 20 years after this work was completed there was a disastrous fire that destroyed much of Lanhydrock. When the house was presented to the National Trust in 1953, it came with few contents, and much of the current furniture represents a similar arrangement to what would have been in use after the rebuilding work. Consequently Lanhydrock is now an excellent example of a later Victorian house although there are parts that survive from the 17th century – not least the superb 30-metre long gallery with decorated plaster ceiling.

Lanhydrock House
Bodmin
Cornwall
PL30 5AD

Tel: 01208 73320
Fax: 01208 74084

lanhyrock@
nationaltrust.org.uk
www.nationaltrust.org.uk

Among the High Victorian furniture and paintings there are about 70 to 80 pieces of Japanese art to be found. These are mostly, but not exclusively, 19th-century and include some extremely good examples of *cloisonné*, Satsuma ceramics, Imari and Arita porcelain and late 19th-century Seto blue and white jardinières. There was also, if memory serves me well, a 'ken' – a Buddhist ritual sword, hanging over a doorway.

## Bournemouth

### Russell-Cotes Art Gallery & Museum

Built between 1897-1907 as both a family residence and museum by John Frederick Fogerty, the Russell-Cotes Art Gallery and Museum embraces a number of architectural styles which reflect the tastes of the period and of the clients, Annie and Merton Russell-Cotes. It is a combination of Italianate villa and Scottish Baronial set in grounds incorporating a Japanese garden situated on the cliff top overlooking Poole Bay, the Isle of Wight and the Purbecks.

Sir Merton and Lady Russell-Cotes (Merton was knighted in 1909) visited Japan in 1885 and returned with over 100 cases of Japanese objects. They displayed these in a specially decorated 'Japanese Drawing Room' in their hotel, the Royal Bath, opening in 1887 and often referred to as a 'Japanese Museum'. Merton enrolled as a member of the Japan Society in 1892, while his wife was elected later in the year. Their collection was later transferred to East Cliff Hall, their residence within the grounds of the hotel, which became the Russell-Cotes Art Gallery & Museum in 1908. The collection was spread throughout the house until 1920 when the Blue Bedroom was converted into 'The Mikado's Room'. The ceiling was painted with Japanese designs and the covings painted with objects and scenes of Japan, as well as portraits of the Emperor Meiji and Empress Haruko. The Russell-Cotes were visited by the Japanese Ambassador, H.E. Katsunosuke Inoue in 1915 and he commented on objects of particular note in their collection; namely a splendid silver elephant by Nakagawa Yoshizane, three works by Komai of Kyoto and an 18th century butsudan which allegedly had once belonged to a daimyo.

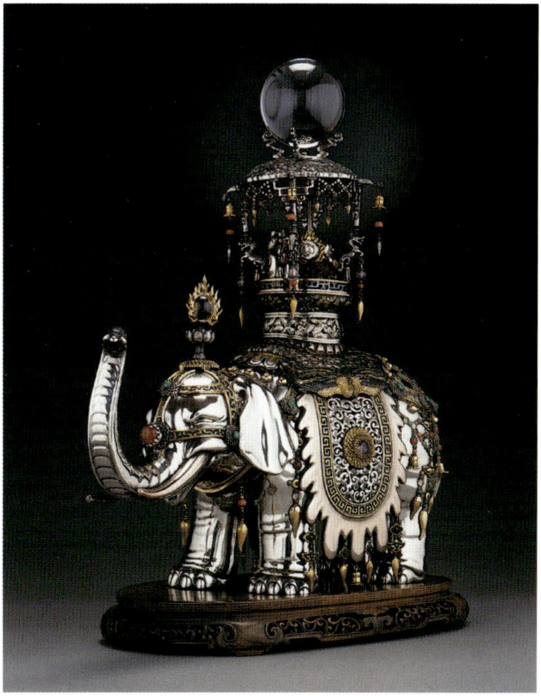

*Silver elephant by Nakagawa Yoshizane*

William Sutherland donated his collection of lacquer to the Museum in 1921 shortly after the deaths of the Russell-Cotes, but before the Museum formally opened as a municipally run gallery on 10th March 1922. Sutherland's collection was made during his time in Japan at the early part of the century and he first offered the collection to the Victoria and Albert Museum (V&A) as early as 1912 on condition they accepted it in its entirety. This was not acceptable and by 1921 the V&A had agreed to only accept those pieces that were not already represented in their collection. Sutherland's move to the Bournemouth area at this time thus proved opportune. Of particular note is a late 19th century lacquerware production set complete with tools, materials and thirty-eight sake cups illustrating the stages of production.

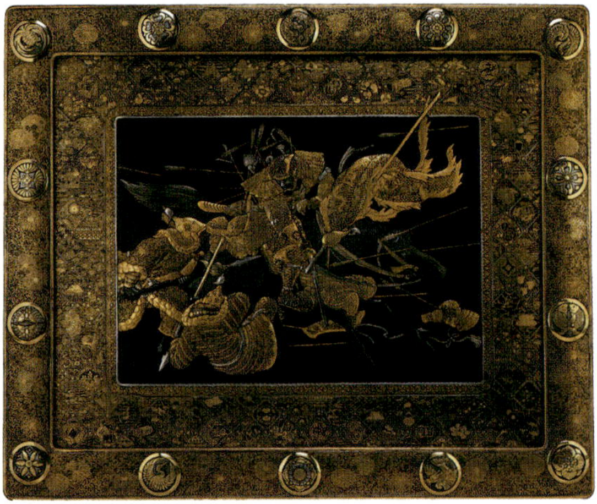

*Plaque by Komai of Kyoto*

Other objects in the collection (which numbers some 2,500 objects) include a few scroll paintings, prints and printed books, Meiji period photograph albums, ceramics, a good and interesting collection of metalwork including arms and armour, sculpture, lacquer, some costume and textiles and Buddhist objects including shrines. The museum is fascinating as it represents the collections of an individual during the period when interest in Japan was at its height in

**Russell-Cotes Art Gallery & Museum**
East Cliff
Bournemouth
Dorset
BH1 3AA

Tel: 01202 451812
Fax: 01202 451851

www.russell-cotes.bournemouth.gov.uk
www.russell-cotes.bournemouth.gov.uk/japcol.htm
(Japanese collections)

the UK and the collections have been sympathetically presented in both contemporary and 'original' displays – including the wonderful 'Mikado's Room'.

The non-Japanese collections include some world-famous pre-Raphaelite paintings by Dante Gabriel Rossetti and Lawrence Alma-Tadema. The feel of the original part of the house (there have been some sympathetic modern additions) is perhaps best summed up in an introduction to the museum from its own web pages: 'On entering the Russell-Cotes Art Gallery and Museum, you are struck by the influence of late 19th century studio houses, reflected in the exotic and eclectic decoration. A plaster rendition of the Parthenon frieze graces the stairs and a Moorish alcove echoes the exotic residences of Leighton and Alma-Tadema'.

## Bristol

### Bristol City Museum and Art Gallery

The City Art Gallery opened in 1905 in a building paid for by the local tobacco magnate, Sir William Henry Wills. The Art Gallery complemented the adjacent Museum that had opened in 1872 and was immediately popular. In the first four months 289,000 people visited the inaugural exhibition. In 1940 incendiary devices hit both the Museum and Art Gallery and the Museum was gutted in the resulting fire. Since then both institutions have been housed together in the Art Gallery building. The Eastern Art Department, originally called Oriental Art, was formed in 1965 to look after material from China, Japan, India and the Islamic world. Since that time it has been staffed by one curator. There are currently some 8,000 objects in the collection. In 1998 it was recognised by the Museums and Galleries Commission as being of outstanding national importance and awarded 'designated' status.

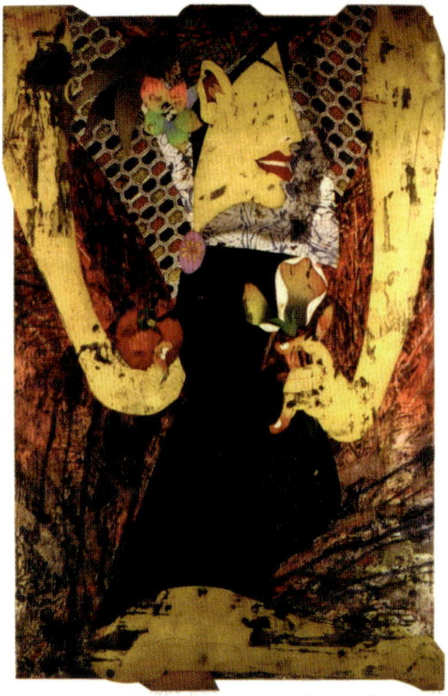

*Fashion Produce (L), Yuji Hiratsuka*

The main strength of the Eastern Art collection lies in its Chinese ceramics and glass. However there is also a significant collection of over 1,000 Japanese objects; these include some 500 woodblock prints, 300 netsuke and *okimono* and 100 sword-fittings, together with ceramics, textiles, lacquer and books. This emphasis on prints, netsuke and sword-fittings mirrors the interests of many late 19th- and 20th-century British collectors who were, for the most part, obsessed by the taxonomy of objects.

The first Japanese acquisition, recorded in the Ethnography register, was made by the Museum in 1894 with the gift from a Mrs. Browne of some "Old satin damask, from Yedo". This was followed by the acquisition of a photograph of Japanese "Stone Celts, Knives & Arrow-heads" and a kimono. The opening of the Art Gallery in 1905 appears to have encouraged further gifts and bequests, for example a "wooden mask" and some porcelain wine cups. The first active purchase of Japanese items took place in 1906 when a group of 13 netsuke was bought from the London dealer Arthur Knapp.

Japanese material was collected slowly during the first half of the 20th century. Some of the earliest Japanese objects to enter the collection were a group of netsuke acquired in 1906 and a pair of bronze incense burners acquired in 1917. The Museum began to collect woodblock prints in the late 1940s and continued to do so during the 1950s and 1960s. The collection includes an outstanding group of woodblock prints of the mid-18th to early 19th century. It contains examples of the work of famous artists such as Hokusai and Utamaro as well as less well-known artists such as Kiyomitsu (1735-85).

Although Bristol's collection of 18th- and 19th-century Japanese material is substantial, there are, as with so many museums in the UK, comparatively few 20th-century or contemporary pieces. The present curator is trying to redress this balance and the Museum recently purchased a collection of 16 contemporary Japanese prints and six paper fans from an exhibition, *Made in Japan,* held at Bristol City Museum in 2001. The exhibition showed the work of 30 or so contemporary Japanese printmakers and paper sculptors. At the same time a display was mounted of 80 *ukiyoe* prints from the Museum's permanent collection, selected to establish links between the techniques and subject matter of the historic and contemporary works. Both shows were part of the nationwide Japan 2001 programme.

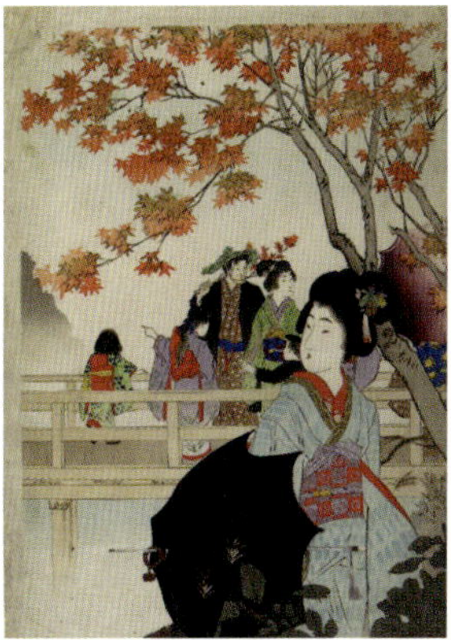

*Viewing autumn maple leaves, c. 1890-1900. Mb4391-10*

The contemporary works purchased for the collection include a set of four large drypoint prints: *A Daydream of Insects*, by Toshio Fujita, a brightly coloured lithograph by Yasuhiro Sobajima, *Cats Smiling*, and *Fashion Produce Left*, a *chine collé* work by Yuji Hiratsuka. Works by Koen Sakamoto and Haruko Cho demonstrate the experimentation currently underway with digital images.

**Bristol City Museum and Art Gallery**
Queen's Road
Bristol
Gloucestershire
BS8 1RL

Tel: 0117 922 3571

www.bristol-city.gov.uk/museums

The Museum generally has a good representative selection of its Japanese collections on display at any one time and there are frequent special themed displays both from the collections and using loaned objects. The Museum has an excellent educational programme and works closely with Japan 21 (www.japan21.org.uk), an offshoot of the Japan Festival Education Trust that promotes Japan through its art and culture.

## Broadway

### Snowshill Manor

Although the manor house of Snowshill displays some classical details of around 1720 the main part of the house is from approximately 1500 but was much altered and extended in the 17th century. By 1919 the manor was a semi-derelict farm when it was bought and restored by the collector Charles Paget Wade, once described by J.B. Priestly as "my eccentric, but charming friend of the fantastic manor house".

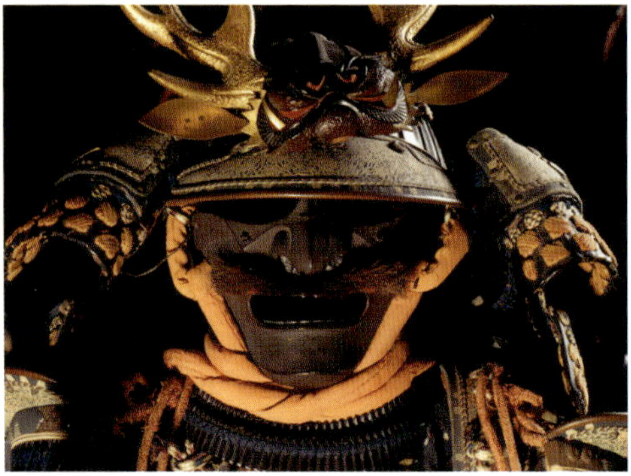

*Japanese armour at Snowshill Manor*

Wade was an architect and craftsman who inherited sugar estates in the West Indies from his father thus enabling him to devote his life to amassing his enormous and varied collection of craftsmanship. Wade collected from around 1900 to 1951 when he gave the collection and the manor to the National Trust. Wade mostly acquired his objects from antique shops and dealers in the UK. There are some 22,000 items in the collection, which includes musical instruments, clocks, toys, bicycles, weavers' and spinners' tools, arms and armour, porcelain and paintings as well as nautical instruments. There is also a 2,000-piece costume collection.

The Green Room at Snowshill also boasts an extraordinary collection of some 26 suits of samurai armour all arranged theatrically together with weapons and other military accoutrements such as stirrups and many totally unrelated Japanese objects (shrines, lacquer etc.). The items have all been arranged personally by Wade to give the impression of a *daimyo*'s encampment in the twilight. The armours mostly date from the 17th to the 19th century. These armours were, on the whole, acquired from various parts of England between the years 1940 and 1945 when such items were far from fashionable, so much so that it is documented that Wade bought some suits by weight, much like bags of coal. Having spent several days personally working on the collection (in January when the heating was off!) I know how important and interesting some of the armour pieces are. The 'best' armours are not on display but are held in reserve storage (as is some of the lacquer and costume collection). Many of the armours are mounted on lifelike mannequins made in Japan in the late 19th century; these *ningyo* present an area of considerable interest and research in Japan at the moment with some particular scholars of the Meiji period.

There are no precise figures available for the numbers of objects in the Japanese collections at Snowshill but the numbers must surely run into the hundreds. As well as the arms and armour, the Japanese collection includes lacquer (cabinets, boxes, picnic sets, inro, a palanquin and some bowls), *tsuba* and other sword-fittings, other metalwork (including bronzes, *cloisonné*, temple bells, folding screens, carvings (including netsuke), pillar clocks, musical instruments, personal and domestic accessories, clothing and two wonderful, miniature yet lifelike, Meiji-period models of a basket maker and a carver of Noh masks.

**Snowshill Manor**
Nr. Broadway
Gloucestershire
WR12 7JU

Tel: 01386 852410
Fax: 01386 842822

snowshillmanor@
nationaltrust.org.uk
www.nationaltrust.
org.uk/places/
snowshillmanor

Most of the objects at Snowshill manor will be unavailable to view throughout much of 2004 as essential cleaning, electrical rewiring and lighting work is done. It will also be a period to carry out conservation and documentation of the collection. It is hoped that by Easter 2005 all the essential work will have been completed and the house can re-open with all the objects back on display in an improved environment. Snowshill is truly one of the most original collections of Japanese art in the UK and is also unique in that the collection is, as far as I am aware, intact and is displayed in the fashion which the collector, Charles Paget Wade intended.

## Calne

### Bowood House

Bowood House has been the home of the Lansdowne family since 1754. It was here in 1901 that Ito Hirobumi, the principal architect of the reform and changes under the Meiji government, was entertained at Lord Lansdowne's stately seat in Wiltshire. The 5th Marquess of Lansdowne was the UK's Foreign Secretary at that time and what was eventually to become the Anglo-Japanese Treaty was negotiated in London during 1901 by Lansdowne and the Japanese Ambassador, Hayashi Tadasu.

Bowood House
Derry Hill
Calne
Wiltshire
SN11 9QP

Tel: 01249 812102
Fax: 01249 821757

houseandgardens@bowood.org
www.bowood-house.co.uk

The treaty was duly signed on January 30th 1902 and was considered a triumph in Japan, where it had a powerful influence in boosting national pride. For the first time ever a European country had allied with an Asiatic power; in effect, the British had sanctioned Japanese aggression in Korea and strengthened the Japanese eagerness to challenge the Russians successfully in the Russo-Japanese War of 1904-05.

The only Japanese items of note on display at Bowood are the objects that constitute a splendid five-piece garniture of Arita vases that date back to around 1700. The tops of these objects have ormolu mounts.

## Cheltenham

### Art Gallery & Museum

In 1898 the 3rd Baron de Ferrieres, a former mayor and MP for Cheltenham, gave 43 important paintings to the town, together with £1,000 towards the building of a gallery in which to house them. This gallery was opened in 1899. In 1905 the Schools of Art and Science left the premises they occupied next door to the Art Gallery, and the Museum was opened in these rooms two years later. The first real increase in space and visitor facilities came in 1989 with the opening of an extension to the Art Gallery & Museum.

The collections cover local themes as well as art and archaeology, costume and jewellery and world cultures. The Japanese collections contain about 80 objects including ceramics, prints by artists such as Hokusai, Hiroshige, Kunisada and Kuniyoshi, 19th-century metalwork, armour, swords and firearms and some costume. One sword in the collection is believed to be from the 17th century and is signed Munenaga which, if it is by the Munenaga who was a pupil of Umetada Myoju, would make it extremely interesting indeed. The sword was surrendered to Lord

Louis Mountbatten who presented it to General Lord Hastings, Lionel Ismay, who had local connections and the sword was given to the Museum in 1946.

**Art Gallery & Museum**
Clarence Street,
Cheltenham
Gloucestershire
GL50 3JT

Tel: 01242 237431
Fax: 01242 262334

ArtGallery@cheltenham.gov.uk
www.cheltenhammuseum.org.uk

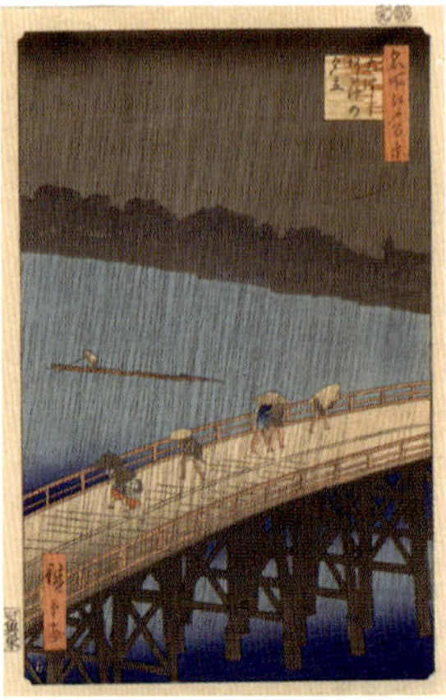

*Sudden shower on the Ohashi, Ando Hiroshige*

## Chudleigh

### Ugbrooke House

Ugbrooke Park has been the home of the Lords Clifford of Chudleigh for over 300 years and is the present Clifford family's private home. In Tudor times a manor house had been built around the earliest house on the site. Robert Adam remodelled the present house in the 1760s and Ugbrooke Park is a good example of the work of Capability Brown. There are really very few Japanese objects in the collection but there are some examples of weaponry, pictures and some undefined examples of 'clothing'. As with all private collections it would be best to first check what might be on display.

**Ugbrooke House**
Chudleigh
Devon
TQ13 0AD

Tel: 01626 852179
Fax: 01626 853322

## Corsham

### Corsham Court

Corsham Court, based on an Elizabethan house dating from 1582, has been the home of the Methuen family for some 300 years. It was bought by Paul Methuen in the mid-18th century to house

Corsham Court
Corsham
Wiltshire
SN13 0BZ

Tel: 01249 701610

enquiries@corsham-court.co.uk
www.corsham-court.co.uk

his collection of 16th- and 17th-century Italian and Flemish paintings. Capability Brown and John Nash made various alterations to the house and gardens. Further additions were made to the collection of paintings and furniture in the 19th century.

The collections that can be seen today are principally paintings, 18th-century English furniture and Chinese porcelain. Within the collection, however, are some 25 Japanese objects including export lacquer chests, porcelain and a few prints.

## Dunster

### Dunster Castle

There has been a castle on top of the wooded hill in Dunster since at least Norman times and a 13th-century gatehouse still survives. The Jacobean house built in 1617 was remodelled in 1868-72 by Antony Salvin for the Luttrell family, who have lived here for six centuries and turned the property from coastal fortress to secluded country seat. It retains superb plasterwork and a fine carved staircase that was installed in the late 17th century, and a unique set of leather hangings.

The only Japanese object noted at Dunster Castle is an interesting Japanese export lacquer chest that may date from around 1630. The chest is inlaid with mother-of-pearl and decorated with *mon* (family crests); unfortunately the back of the chest has suffered light damage. There may be reference to this piece in an inventory of the late 17th century.

Dunster Castle
Dunster
Nr. Minehead
Somerset
TA24 6SL

Tel: 01643 821314
Fax: 01643 823000

dunstercastle@nationaltrust.org.uk
www.nationaltrust.org.uk

## Exeter

### Royal Albert Memorial Museum and Art Gallery

The idea for the Museum was originally proposed by Sir Stafford Northcote as a practical memorial to Prince Albert and an appeal fund was launched in 1861 with the first stages of the Museum being completed by

1868. Originally known as the Devon and Exeter Albert Memorial the building provided an integrated museum, art gallery, library, reading room, school of art and school of science in the approach to culture long encouraged by the late Prince Albert. In 1899 the York Wing was opened by the Duke and Duchess of York, (later King George V and Queen Mary) and the title of Royal Albert Memorial was adopted. The building has changed little since that time and the library moved out of the museum buildings in 1930. The school of science became Exeter University and the school of art is now Plymouth University's Faculty of Art & Education.

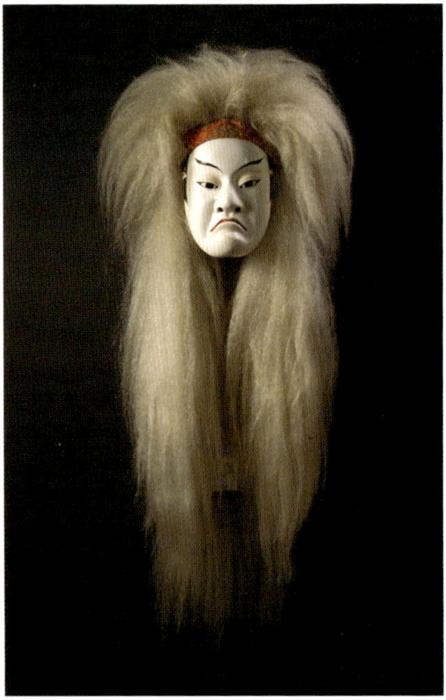

*Kagura mask*

The Museum has a wide-ranging collection of local history, archaeology, ceramics, natural history and world cultures; it is in the latter category that most of its 300 or so Japanese objects can be found. Fifty-eight objects classified as decorative art are found on the Museum's database; 193 under ethnography with a further 54 specifically classified as Ainu. The collections include religious and ceremonial objects, theatrical accessories, graphic works (prints and paintings) lacquer ware, textiles (including everyday wear), personal accessories, arms and armour ceramics (including tea ware). At the time of writing only a suit of Japanese armour is on display but the Museum is, along with so many other in the UK, planning major redevelopment.

Some of the earliest objects were acquired in the 1870s and it is believed that some others were given by the firm of James Veitch and Sons, originally an Exeter-based firm of nurserymen who, between 1840 and 1880 sent plant collectors all over the world who also brought objects back, carefully packed between their plant specimens. In 1853 the firm moved to the Kings Road, Chelsea, London, and in the 1880s some objects were sent back to Exeter to be given to the Museum.

Royal Albert Memorial
Museum and Art Gallery
Queen Street
Exeter
Devon
EX4 3RX

Tel: 01392 665858
Fax: 01392 421252

ramm@exeter.gov.uk
www.exeter.gov.uk/residents/arts/museums/ramm/index.xml

### Castle Drogo

Castle Drogo was designed by Sir Edwin Lutyens for the self-made millionaire Julius Drewe and was built between 1910 and 1930. Sir Julius' main business interests were in the hugely successful Home and Colonial Stores and he was able to retire in 1899 at the age of 33. He discovered that a Norman baron named Drogo de Teigne had been an ancestor and was therefore determined to build a castle on the land that had once belonged to the baron. Lutyens skilfully combined a medieval atmosphere (created by the bare granite, exposed timbers and tapestry-hung walls) with comfortable and stylish rooms fitted with the latest conveniences of the day. These included central heating and elaborately appointed bathrooms.

The only Japanese objects noted at Castle Drogo are two very similar 18th-century Japanese export lacquer cabinets on English giltwood stands from about 1730.

Castle Drogo
Drewsteignton
Nr. Exeter
Devon
EX6 6PB

Tel: 01647 433306
Fax: 01647 433186

castledrogo@nationaltrust.org.uk
www.nationaltrust.org.uk

# Penzance

## St Michael's Mount

St Michael's Mount, accessible by causeway at low tide, was originally the site of a Benedictine priory, and the dramatic castle on top of this famous island dates from the 12th century when a group of Prince John's supporters seized the Mount to hold as a fortress. The buildings reverted to monastic use but again became a stronghold in the Wars of the Roses and during the Cornish Rebellion against Edward VI. During the Civil War the Mount was held for the King but surrendered to the Parliamentarians in 1646. In 1659 the Mount was bought by Sir John St. Aubyn and since that time it has had a peaceful existence. The castle today contains fascinating rooms including an armoury, a rococo Gothic drawing-room and, at the highest point, a 14th-century church.

The remarkable Victorian apartments are decorated with fine plaster reliefs and contain some Chippendale furniture; there are also collections of paintings and armour. The Mount remained in the ownership of the St. Aubyn family until 1954 when it was given to the National Trust by the 3rd Lord St. Levan. The St. Aubyn family retained a lease for part of the castle, garden and grounds while safely preserving the Mount for the future in the care of the National Trust.

There are a few interesting Japanese objects in the castle: a suit of armour that was given to the 2nd Lord Levan when he was ADC to the Governor of Hong Kong in 1904; a bow (and some unrelated arrows); a signed 16th-century *katana* (Tadamitsu of Osafune in Bizen) with an unsigned *wakizashi* and a *sodegarami* (sleeve-entangler, used by Japanese policemen).

St Michael's Mount
Marazion
Nr. Penzance
Cornwall
TR17 0EF

Tel: 01736 710507
Fax: 01736 719930

godolphin@manor-office.co.uk
www.stmichaelsmount.co.uk/
www.nationaltrust.org.uk

# Plymouth

## Plymouth City Museum & Art Gallery

The first municipal Museum & Art Gallery in Plymouth was opened in 1899. The current building on North

Hill was established in 1910 and is the administrative headquarters of the city's Museums Service. Since its inception the Plymouth City Museum & Art Gallery has maintained a collection that reflects the history and taste of the local population. The 18th-century Cottonian Collection, the most important of the Museum's art collections, is a further example with its remarkable collection of prints, other *objets d'art* and its library. Its collection comprises small groups of ceramics, bronzes and paintings, several hundred old masters and English drawings and watercolours, as well a substantial body of several thousand fine and rare prints.

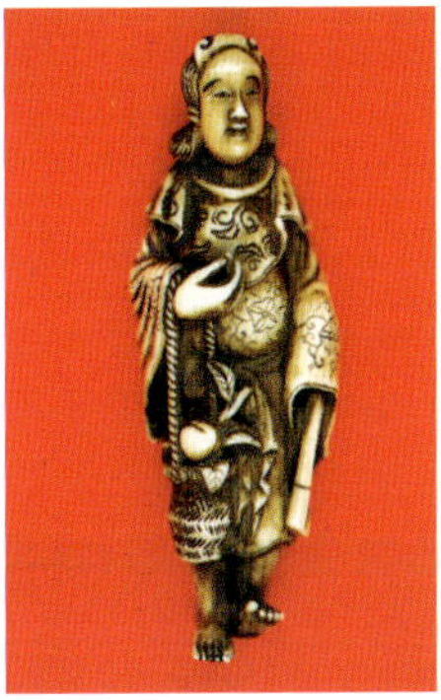

*Ivory netsuke of a foreigner*

The Museum also has important fine and decorative art collections; the former includes easel paintings, watercolours, drawings and prints, the latter a fine collection of ceramics (especially Plymouth and Bristol porcelain) and a good representation of ceramics by the Martin Brothers.

The Human History collections encompass archaeology, social history and ethnography objects. The collections are the result of over 100 years of collecting and public donations. The ethnographic collections contain objects from all over the world and include over 100 Japanese items, some 30 of which were given by the pioneering explorer Gertrude Benham. Gertrude was a doughty traveller who not only travelled the world for over 30 years but also

**Plymouth City Museum & Art Gallery**
Drake Circus
Plymouth
Devon
PL4 8AJ

Tel: 01752 304774
Fax: 01752 304775

enquiry@
plymouthmuseum.gov.uk
www.plymouthmuseum.
gov.uk

is the first woman known to have climbed Mount Kilimanjaro, in Tanzania. The objects include carvings (including netsuke), weapons, food containers, lacquer items, personal accessories and games and pastimes. Unfortunately little if any of the Japanese collections are currently on display.

## Plympton

### Saltram

Saltram has been home to the Parker family for generations and was built in the middle of the 18th century, incorporating parts of an earlier Tudor building. It is complete with many of its original contents including splendid State Rooms by Robert Adam. There are exquisite plasterwork ceilings and four rooms are decorated with 18th-century Chinese wallpaper. The collections include period furniture, porcelain and paintings including many portraits by Sir Joshua Reynolds and Angelica Kauffmann. The house was given to the National Trust in 1957.

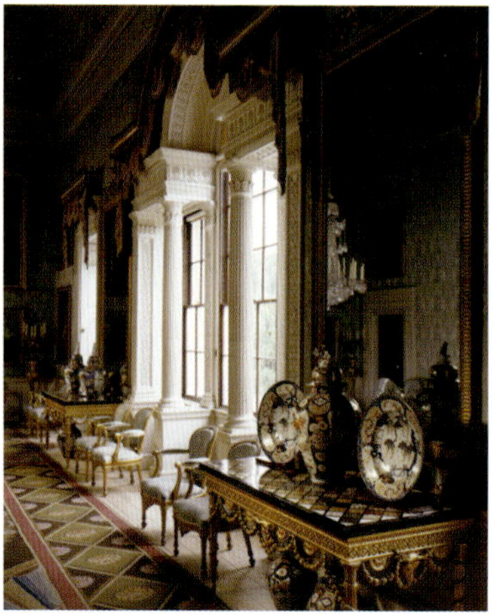

*Porcelain at Saltram*

The Japanese collections include two groups of Imari large covered jars and plates arranged on Adam pier tables. It is believed that this display may date back to an original arrangement of the 1770s.

**Saltram**
Plympton
Plymouth
Devon
PL7 1UH

Tel: 01752 333500
Fax: 01752 336474

saltram@nationaltrust.
org.uk
www.nationaltrust.org.uk

# St. Ives

## The Leach Pottery

Bernard Leach (1887-1979) was born and brought up in the Far East where his father was a colonial judge in China. His mother died in childbirth so he was sent to Japan and spent the first four years of his life with his grandparents who were working there as missionaries. In 1897 he was sent to England to be educated but in 1903 he persuaded his father to allow him to study at the Slade School of Art. When his father died in 1904, Leach joined the Hong Kong and Shanghai Bank but left in 1906 and enrolled at the London School of Art. Leach returned to Japan in 1909, built a house and studio in Abiko, then a remote suburb of Tokyo, and began to study the Japanese language.

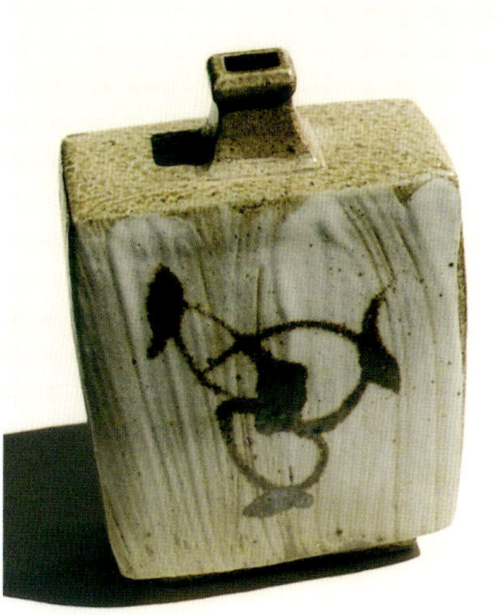

*Rectangular slab vase by Hamada Shoji*

Leach was accepted into the Shirakaba (White Birch) group of artists and intellectuals and developed a great friendship with Soetsu Yanagi and Tomitomo Kenkichi. In 1911 a chance encounter with a group of artists and a raku firing ensured that ceramics were from then on to take a central role in his life. He began to study under Kenzan VI, heir to a great and famous tradition of pottery.

In 1920 Bernard Leach returned to England and settled in St. Ives where, with the help of his friend Hamada Shoji he started the St. Ives pottery. A cottage and a studio were built and with local workmen, Leach and Hamada constructed a wood-burning climbing kiln, the first of its type to be built in the West. Due to many technical problems Hamada eventually arranged for a kiln engineer, Matsubayashi, to come from Japan in order to reconstruct the kiln. The kiln was then used (with various modifications) until the mid-1970s. Bernard Leach had become an active member of the St. Ives artistic community; in the late 1920s the St. Ives Society of Artists was set up and in 1949 the Penwith Society of Arts was formed with Barbara Hepworth, Ben Nicholson and Bernard Leach among its members.

The Leach Pottery
Higher Stennack
St. Ives
Cornwall
TR26 2HE

Tel/Fax: 01736 796398

leachpottery@aol.com
www.leachpottery.com

In 1999, Leach Pottery Ltd. (including the workshop, showroom and cottage) was bought by Alan and Sally Gillam. There had been a small exhibition of the work of Bernard Leach and Hamada Shoji at the Leach Pottery for many years, but it was decided to expand the exhibition to include some of the many potters, students and apprentices who had passed through the pottery over the years since its establishment.

## Salisbury

### Salisbury & South Wiltshire Museum

In among the Stonehenge and archaeology galleries at the Salisbury museum are three woodcut prints by Yoshijiro Urushibara (1888-1953) of Stonehenge. Urushibara is well-known for two prints of Stonehenge – one by moonlight and one by daylight - but one of the prints in the museum collection fits neither of these two categories.

Urushibara was born in Tokyo but lived in England and France until the late 1930s. At the age of 19, Urushibara travelled to London to demonstrate Japanese printmaking at the Japan-British Exhibition of 1910. He was then hired by a Japanese printing firm that was making print copies of the famous Chinese scroll *Admonitions of the Instructress*, for the British Museum. He taught Japanese woodblock printing techniques and collaborated with artists such as Frank Brangwyn.

**Salisbury & South Wiltshire Museum**
The King's House
65 The Close
Salisbury
Wiltshire
SP1 2EN

Tel: 01722 332151
Fax: 01722 325611

museum@
salisburymuseum.org.uk
www.salisburymuseum.
org.uk

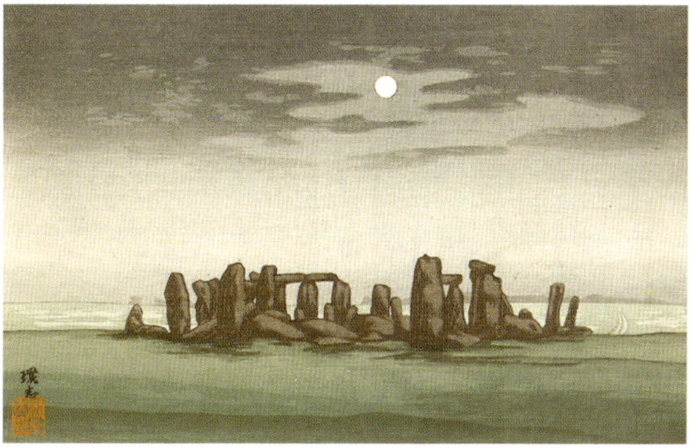

*Stonehenge, by Yoshijiro Urishibara*

## Sherborne

### Sherborne Castle

The first building on the site of the present building was a medieval hunting lodge that belonged to Sherborne Old Castle. Having been given the lease to the old castle, Sir Walter Raleigh decided to build a new home rather than try to modernise the old castle. He named the new building Sherborne Lodge. After Raleigh was executed for treason the property was eventually sold by James I to Sir John Digby in 1617 and his family has lived here ever since.

During the English Civil War the old castle was destroyed by the Parliamentary forces and the name Sherborne Castle came to be applied to the new building. In the 19th century the last Earl Digby died without heir and Sherborne Castle was left to his Wingfield Digby nephew in whose family the care of the castle is today entrusted.

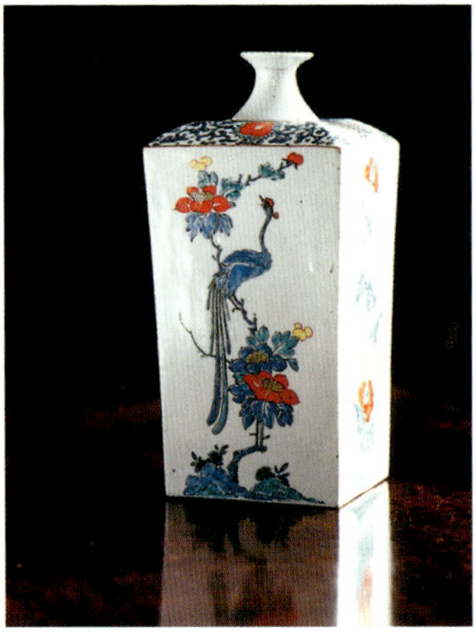

Kakiemon bottle

Sherborne Castle
Sherborne
Dorset
DT9 5NR

Tel: 01935 813182
Fax: 01935 816727

enquiries@
sherbornecastle.com
www.sherbornecastle.com

It would seem from documentation and archive material that the Digby family has been collecting Japanese porcelain since around 1680 and the collection today contains an impressive collection of about 50 pieces of Kakiemon porcelain, some 20 pieces of Arita porcelain, export lacquer chests and other examples of lacquer ware. Most of the collection is on display in the public rooms and other pieces can be seen by special arrangement.

## Truro

### Royal Cornwall Museum

The Royal Cornwall Museum has good collections of local minerals, archaeology and local history, paintings and drawings of the Newlyn School of artists as well as a good collection of drawings from the Italian, French, Dutch and English schools. British artists represented include Hogarth, Romney, Gainsborough, Constable, Turner, Blake, Rossetti, Burne-Jones and Augustus John. The Museum also has a substantial (some 800 objects) collection of Japanese art. A report on the Japanese collection at the museum, written by Mr. F.A. Turk in 1984, describes the collection as "probably one of the best of its kind in any provincial museum in Britain.... some of the pieces would be desirable ones for a national collection". Following a survey of the Museum's Japanese collections in 1998 (by Gregory Irvine) it was realised that the extent and quality of the Museum's collection of Shibayama lacquer ware made it unique in terms of European collections of such objects.

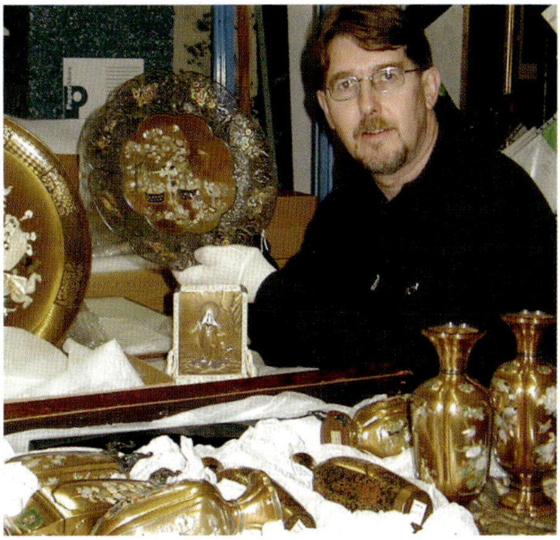

*The Shibayama collection at the Royal Cornwall Museum, Truro*

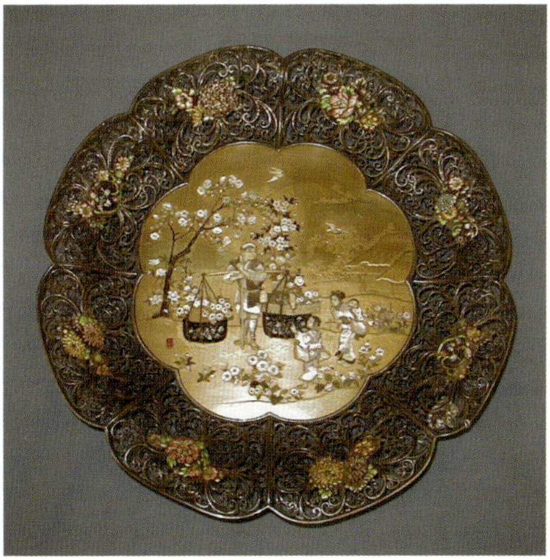

*Metal dish with Shibayama-style decoration*

The Japanese collection had been formed by a number of bequests: the 1913 bequest of C.H.T. Hawkins' extensive collection of ivories, *tsuba*, lacquer, inro and screens, the 1915 and 1923 bequest from Alfred de Pass of sword furniture, arrows, inro and some ivory carvings (mostly netsuke and *okimono*) and finally, the 1934 Allen bequest of 97 fine ivory carvings.

The Hawkins collection was possibly formed on the advice of Henri Joly and from information contained in a largely indecipherable letter it may be that some of the considerable number of Shibayama pieces had been specially commissioned by Hawkins.

The collection includes nearly 300 carvings (*okimono* and netsuke), dating mostly from the 18th and 19th centuries, sword-fittings including *tsuba* (with one acquired from Samuel Bing), *fuchi-kashira*, *menuki*, *ojime*, arrow-heads, personal accessories (such as hair ornaments), lacquer (including boxes and some 74 inro) and bronzes. The bronzes include a rather wonderful life-size bronze eagle that had been acquired in Kobe around 1890 by a Mr. Thomas Bunt of Falmouth. The eagle was originally offered to a local church for use as a lectern before being accepted by the Museum.

Most of the Museum's collections can be found online at www.chain.org.uk a searchable database for Cornwall's museums; searching on 'Japan' under 'Royal Cornwall Museum' produces around 800 items.

**Royal Cornwall Museum**
River Street
Truro
Cornwall
TR1 2SJ

Tel: 01872 272205
Fax: 01872 240514

enquiries@royal-cornwall-museum.org.uk
www.royalcornwallmuseum.org.uk

## Twigworth

### Nature In Art

Nature in Art's collection reflects the diversity of artistic work that has been produced by artists from all over the world who have been inspired by nature through the centuries. The collection includes work from over 50 countries and spans a time period of over 1,500 years. The range of work also represents the many different approaches to the subject that artists have used. Styles vary from hyper-realist to abstract (pictures, sculptures and objects), with oils, watercolours, acrylics, mixed media, ceramics, glass, wood, fabrics and many others. The Museum holds many changing themed exhibitions so it is not uncommon for visitors to see pictures by artists as diverse as Picasso or Audubon together with Byzantine mosaics or objects by Gallé, Lalique and 18th- and 19th-century British or Japanese ceramists.

There are 54 Japanese objects in the permanent collection including carvings (wooden and ivory netsuke), *cloisonné* enamels (including two by Ando Jubei), prints (by artists such as Koson and Hokusai), sword-fittings, ceramics, and lacquer inro and cast figurative bronzes. Although there is no specific Japanese display there are usually some Japanese objects to be found in the thematic exhibitions.

**Nature In Art**
Museum and Art Gallery
Wallsworth Hall
Twigworth
Gloucester
GL2 9PA

Tel: 0845 450 0233
Fax: 01452 730937

ninart@globalnet.co.uk
www.nature-in-art.org.uk

## Wraxall

### Tyntesfield

Tyntesfield was inspired and remodelled by John Norton around 1864 for William Gibbs, a successful merchant. The mansion is an extraordinary Gothic Revival extravaganza complete with towers and turrets and survives with much of its original Victorian interior intact together with an unrivalled collection of Victorian decorative arts. Tyntesfield was saved for the nation by the National Trust in June 2002 with funding from the National Heritage Memorial Fund, other heritage partners and a £3-million public appeal.

Conservation and restoration work of the fabric of the building at Tyntesfield is ongoing but the principal rooms that are currently open include a library with a large collection of blue and white oriental porcelain above the bookcases. There are examples of Japanese porcelain and metalwork in the collection but as the acquisition of the property happened relatively quickly the curators are still working on cataloguing and creating inventories of the collections.

**Tyntesfield**
Wraxall
Bristol
North Somerset
BS48 1NT

Infoline: 0870 458 4500
www.nationaltrust.org.uk/places/tyntesfield

# South-East England

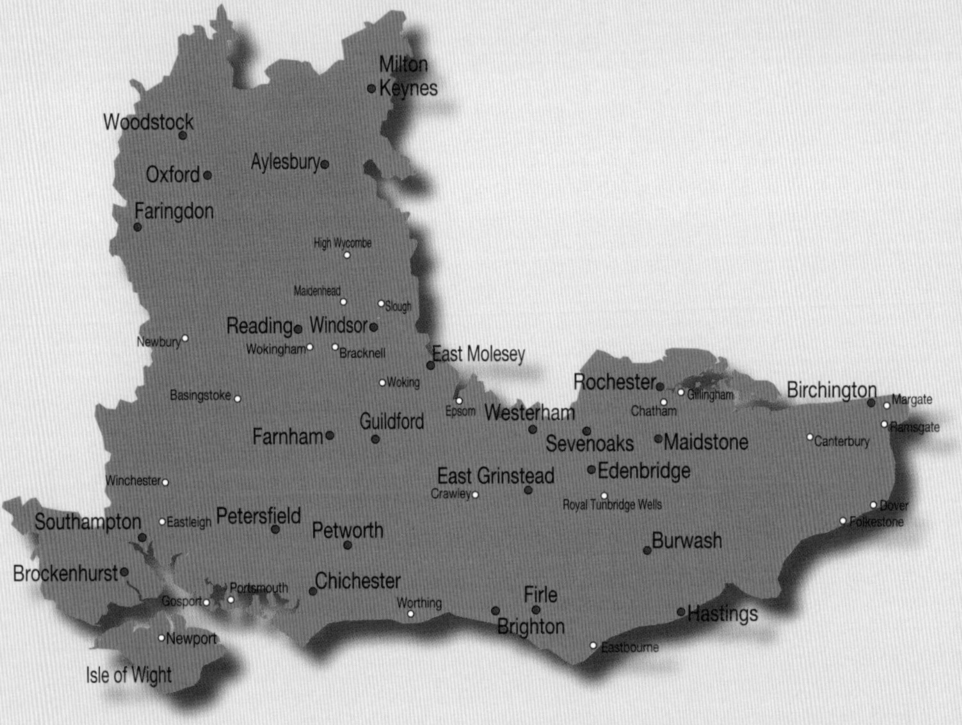

# Aylesbury

## Waddesdon Manor

Waddesdon Manor was built between 1874 and 1889 for Baron Ferdinand de Rothschild in order to entertain his many distinguished guests who included Queen Victoria and Lord Rosebery. The manor was also designed to display his vast collection of art treasures. Baron de Rothschild had a great knowledge of French 18th-century art and the house is designed in the style of a French 16th-century château. It contains a remarkable collection of French 18th-century decorative arts. The furniture, Savonnerie carpets and Sèvres porcelain are of international importance and rank with the collections of some of the best museums in the world. There are outstanding portraits by Gainsborough and Reynolds, other works by 17th-century Dutch and Flemish masters, and a spectacular silver dinner service made for George III.

The Baron's sister, Alice de Rothschild, lived at Waddesdon Manor after him and added to the collections, principally a great deal of the Sèvres porcelain. She left the property to her great nephew James de Rothschild who brought over from France the collection of furniture, china and pictures that he had inherited from his father Baron Edmond de Rothschild of Paris.
When James de Rothschild died in 1957 he left Waddesdon Manor and its contents to the National Trust although the de Rothschild family is still involved in the running of Waddesdon Manor through a family charitable trust. The family has carried out an extensive restoration programme and has lent more works of art to extend the collection.

There are some 60 Japanese objects in the collection and much of it is on display in the public rooms. The collection includes ceramics (some of which were acquired in the 1870s), lacquer (incorporated into western furniture and small objects such as vases and trays), textiles, arms and armour and photographs.

**Waddesdon Manor**
Waddesdon
Aylesbury
Buckinghamshire
HP18 0JH

Tel: 01296 653203
Fax: 01296 653237
Infoline: 01296 653211

waddesdonmanor@
nationaltrust.org.uk
www.waddesdon.org.uk

# Birchington

## Powell-Cotton Museum

The Powell-Cotton Museum was founded in 1895 by Major P.H.G. Powell-Cotton to hold his collections, which were eventually acquired over 25 expeditions to Africa and five to South-East Asia between 1885 and 1939. Three are galleries of animal diorama displays that depict more than 250 African and Asian mammals against their natural habitats. There are five galleries devoted to a huge collection of African ethnographic artefacts, European firearms, European and Asian cutting weapons, European porcelain and Chinese export porcelain as well as important local archaeological finds. A further six rooms include oriental and English furniture as well as other miscellaneous objects.

Much of the Japanese material was acquired by Major Powell-Cotton on his world trip of 1887 although the splendid shrine was apparently bought through an advertisement in *The Times*. The collections include arms and armour, furniture and a large collection (circa 170) of netsuke, most of which are not on permanent display.

**Powell-Cotton Museum**
Quex Park
Birchington
Kent
CT7 0BH

Tel: 01843 842168
Fax: 01843 846661

powell-cotton.
museum@virgin.net

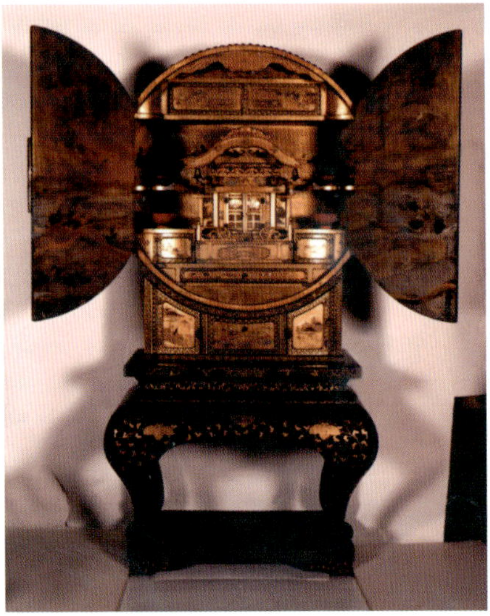

*Meiji period shrine*

# Brighton

## Brighton Museum & Art Gallery

The Brighton Museum & Art Gallery reopened in May 2002 with a complete re-display of its splendid and varied collections. This project was part of a larger regeneration scheme in and around the famous Royal Pavilion estate in the heart of Brighton. Vibrant and original new galleries provided greatly improved access to the Museum's nationally and locally important collections. Objects are now displayed in stimulating contexts with a wide range of interpretative techniques, including the latest interactive information technology.

The Japanese collections in Brighton are divided between those that fall into the categories of fine arts and decorative arts, and those that are covered by the category of 'world art'. Fine art includes a small holding of Japanese prints including examples by Hokusai, Hiroshige, Eisen and Eizan. The decorative arts category includes ceramics (stoneware and porcelain) and metalwork – mostly small decorative bronzes and some interesting iron tea kettles. Unfortunately there is not a huge number of Japanese objects currently on display except in the World Art Galleries. The World Art holdings include carvings (ivories, wooden objects and stone carvings), figures (including bronze religious objects), clothing (including a fireman's helmet), personal and domestic items as well as military equipment (including armour and swords and daggers). There is also an interesting collection of Noh masks.

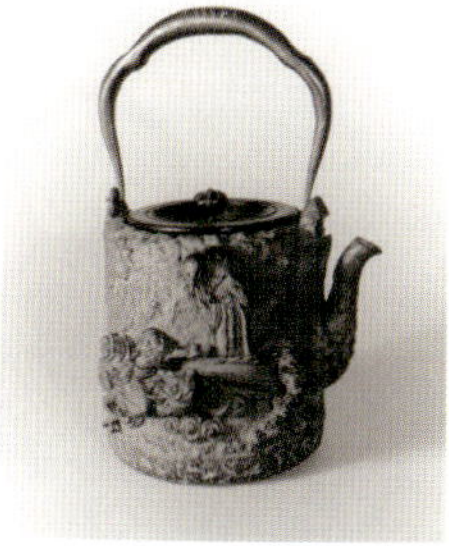

*Iron teakettle, 19th century*

Brighton Museum & Art Gallery
4/5 Pavilion Buildings
Brighton
East Sussex
BN1 1EE

Tel: 01273 290900

museums@brighton-hove.gov.uk
www.brighton.virtualmuseum.info

# Brockenhurst

## Beaulieu Palace

The Palace House was formerly the 14th-century Great Gatehouse of Beaulieu Abbey and is set in glorious grounds and gardens with immaculate lawns and walkways that overlook the Beaulieu River. The House has been in the ownership of the current Lord Montagu's family since 1538, when Sir Thomas Wriothesley, who later became the First Earl of Southampton, bought the estate after the Dissolution of the Monasteries. Lord Henry Scott, the first resident owner of Palace House, extended it in the 1870s and the architect was Sir Arthur Blomfield. The house as it is today is an extraordinary mixture of Victorian Gothic, medieval Gothic and 18th-century fortification styles.

Although perhaps more famous for its National Motor Museum, (which certainly contains examples of Japanese motorcycles), the visitor to Palace House will find a few examples of 19th-century Japanese *cloisonné*, ivories and lacquer boxes on display in the public rooms. The current Lord Montagu believes that these may have been collected by John, 2nd Lord Montagu of Beaulieu on his visit to Japan in 1888.

Beaulieu Palace
Brockenhurst
Hampshire
SO42 7ZN

Tel: 01590 612345
Fax: 01590 612624

info@beaulieu.co.uk
www.beaulieu.co.uk

# Burwash

## Bateman's

This elegant Jacobean house was the home of the author Rudyard Kipling from 1902 to 1936. Many of the objects in the house reflect the author's strong associations with the East. There are numerous oriental rugs and artefacts and most of the rooms have been kept much as Kipling left them. The house is set in beautiful grounds that run down to a small river with a water-mill. Kipling's Rolls Royce can also be seen.

In 1889 Kipling left India and travelled to Burma, Singapore, Hong Kong and Canton, Japan, and San

Francisco and then crossed America. In Japan he criticized the Japanese middle class for its eagerness to adopt western fashions and values. "... I was a barbarian, and no true Sahib," he wrote. Chapters 11 to 13 of his 1899 book *From Sea to Sea* contain some interesting observations on Japan. It may have been during this visit in 1889 that Kipling collected the few interesting objects that can be found at Bateman's. They all seem to be have been made in the second half of the 19th century and therefore contemporary with his visit. The objects include a Shibayama-style inro, some ivory carvings, bronze vessels, tobacco pouch, a gold *nashiji* lacquer box and a couple of small shrines.

Bateman's
Burwash
Etchingham
East Sussex
TN19 7DS

Tel: 01435 882302
Fax: 01435 882811

batemans@nationaltrust.org.uk
www.nationaltrust.org.uk/main

## Canterbury

### Canterbury Royal Museum & Art Gallery

This small museum has, according to the response to our request for information about their Japanese holdings, a collection of about 35 Japanese objects including some ivory carvings, a Noh mask, a few examples of ceramics and a collection of swords and fittings, which are usually on display. Unfortunately little is known about these collections.

Canterbury Royal Museum & Art Gallery
High Street
Canterbury
Kent
CT1 2RA

Tel: 01227 452747

museums@canterbury.gov.uk
www.canterbury.gov.uk

## Chichester

### Goodwood House

Goodwood House started out as a gentleman's residence with the original elements built during the reign of James I. The 1st Duke of Richmond was visiting the house as early as 1689 and in 1697 he purchased the Jacobean house. This "old house" as it is referred to is now the section to be found at the rear of the current configuration of the house. The house was added to and developed throughout the 18th century and the Main Hall was classicised in 1730. Between 1747 and 1750 a handsome Palladian-style south wing was added. Goodwood House is presently home to the Earl and Countess

**Goodwood House**
Chichester
West Sussex
PO18 0PX

Tel: 01243 755000
Fax: 01243 755005

curator@goodwood.co.uk
www.goodwood.co.uk/house

of March; the earl is heir to the present Duke of Richmond whose excellent art collections the house contains.

There is small number of interesting pieces of Japanese porcelain to be found throughout the house – as well as some examples of export furniture that one typically expects to find in a house of this period that has been owned by the same family since the 17th century. It is believed that these pieces were acquired during the mid-18th century by the 3rd Duke and Duchess of Richmond as part of the fashion for collecting such objects at that time.

## East Grinstead

### Standen

Standen was built between 1891 and 1894 by the architect Philip Webb, a friend of William Morris, for the Beale family. Webb, along with William Morris, was an important member of the Arts and Crafts movement whose purpose was to promote craftsmanship over the mass manufacturing processes in the late Victorian period. The house is decorated with William Morris carpets, wallpapers, fabrics and paintings that are contemporary with the furnishings, some of which were in fact designed by Webb himself. Standen is also set in rather beautiful gardens with views over the Sussex countryside. There are also ceramics created by William de Morgan.

Standen has a small but interesting collection of Japanese art including 34 prints (about 20 are generally on display at any one time) and ten ceramics (including a teaset). Some of the objects might have been acquired by the original owners, the Beale family, on a trip to Japan in the late 19th century. The gardens at Standen include a small Japanese-style garden surrounded by bamboo.

**Standen**
West Hoathley Road
East Grinstead
West Sussex
RH19 4NE

Tel: 01342 323029
Fax: 01342 316424

standen@nationaltrust.org.uk
www.nationaltrust.org.uk
www.nationaltrust.org.uk/places/standen

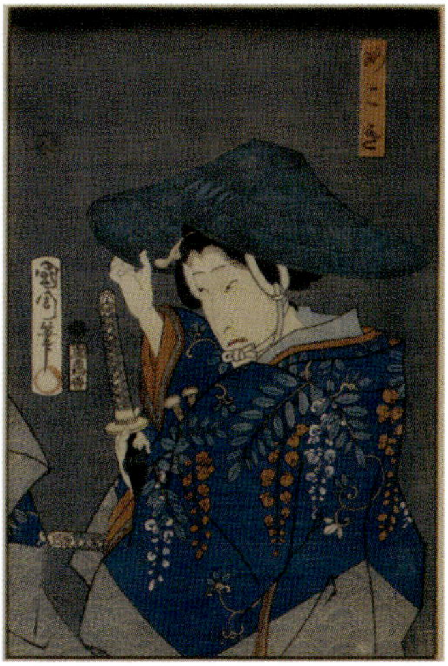

*Print from the collection at Standen*

## East Molesey

### Hampton Court Palace

Hampton Court Palace was built between 1514 and 1525 for Thomas Wolsey, Cardinal and Lord Chancellor of England. By 1528, Wolsey had fallen from favour and was forced to hand over Hampton Court to King Henry VIII who, within six months, began his own building operations. By around 1540 when the king had finished his modifications, Hampton Court Palace was one of the most modern, sophisticated and magnificent palaces in England and had tennis courts, bowling alleys, pleasure gardens for recreation and a hunting park of more than 1,100 acres.

**Hampton Court Palace**
East Molesey
Surrey
KT8 9AU

Infoline: 0870 752 7777

www.hrp.org.uk/webcode/home.asp
www.hrp.org.uk/webcode/hampton_home.asp

Successive monarchs have made changes to Hampton Court, notably those carried out in the 1690s by King William III and Queen Mary, who had apartments added to the palace from designs by Sir Christopher Wren. In the King's State Apartments (notably in the Little Bedchamber) there is a group of 17th-century Japanese decorative porcelain from the collection of Queen Mary (d.1694) including the lidded hexagonal Arita porcelain jars that have become known as 'Hampton Court jars'.

# Edenbridge

## Chiddingstone Castle

In 1803 the original building of Chiddingstone Castle (originally known as High Street House) was converted into a romantic castle on the instruction of its then owner Henry Streatfield. The result was an unusual mixture of styles. In 1955 the 'castle' was extremely run-down but was bought by Denys Eyre Bower (1905-1977), an eccentric collector who was once described as the modern William Beckford (but without his wealth). On his death he left his home and its contents to the nation; both the house and its collections are now administered by a private charitable trust.

The Castle has about 250 Japanese objects and there are extensive collections of arms and armour on display in two rather aging cases; the best swords are not actually on display. There are also many Japanese Buddhist images on view in a room devoted to Eastern religion. There is a small room displaying archaeological material including *haniwa* figures; the same room has other military accoutrements including saddles and stirrups as well as iron articulated animals. The main room of the house is almost totally full of Japanese objects including ceramics, masks and superb lacquer from early periods through to the late 19th century.

The principal treasure of Chiddingstone Castle is, however, on loan to, and on display at the Ashmolean Museum in Oxford. This is the Japanese export lacquer box known as the Chiddingstone Casket. The box was probably made around 1635 and is most likely to have been crafted by the same workshop as the superb contemporary export lacquer box in the collection of the V&A that is inscribed with the name of Maria Van Diemen, wife of the Governor General of the Dutch East Indies from 1636-1645. William Beckford was known to have owned the Van Diemen box at one point, leading to speculation that he may also have once owned the Chiddingstone Casket.

**Chiddingstone Castle**
Near Edenbridge
Kent
TN8 7AD

Tel: 01892 870347

www.chiddingstone-castle.org.uk

# Faringdon

## Buscot Park

Edward Loveden Townsend built Buscot Park between 1779 and 1783. The house is an imposing example of late 18th-century Italianate country houses that were inspired by the architecture of Andrea Palladio. A subsequent owner, Robert Tertius Campbell, died bankrupt in 1887; Buscot was then sold to Sir Alexander Henderson, later 1st Lord Faringdon who acquired paintings by Rembrandt, Gainsborough, Murillo, Reynolds and the Pre-Raphaelites including Rossetti and Millais but especially Burne-Jones, thereby establishing the Faringdon Collection. Gavin Henderson, the 1st Lord Faringdon's grandson and heir, was also an enthusiastic collector of pictures and many of the paintings to be seen at Buscot today were acquired by him.

The collections at Buscot include Japanese Imari porcelain and an interesting late 17th-century heavy bottle of Arita ware with Dutch decoration in Japanese style, which has the initials 'IC' on the base; these may stand for Johannes Camphuys, the principal Dutch merchant at Deshima from 1671 to 1675.

**Buscot Park**
Faringdon
Oxfordshire
SN7 8BU

Tel: 01367 240786
Fax: 01367 241794
Information:
0845 345 3387

estbuscot@aol.com
www.buscot-park.com

# Farnham

## Crafts Study Centre

In August 1970 a pioneering group of six craftspeople and educationalists set up a charity called the Crafts Study Centre. The group had in mind to collect and exhibit the works of artist/craftsmen, to collect and publish books, magazines and periodicals in connection with such works and to establish and maintain museums, libraries and study centres for these purposes.

The Crafts Study Centre originally opened in 1977 in rooms within the Holburne Museum, Bath. The remarkable collection of 18th-century fine and decorative arts housed at the Holburne could be juxtaposed in surprising ways with modern craft collections. The Crafts Study Centre then relocated from the Holburne Museum of Art in Bath in 2000 to The Surrey Institute of Art & Design, where a purpose-built museum and study centre (that should open in the summer of 2004) now houses the collection.

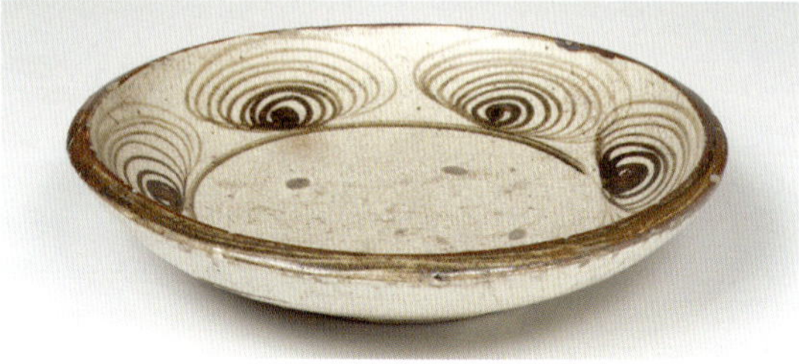

*Seto oil dish, Bernard Leach Source Collection, P.79.52*

**Crafts Study Centre**
The Surrey Institute of Art & Design
University College
Falkner Road
Farnham
Surrey
GU9 7DS

Tel/Fax: 01252 719550

craftscentre@surrart.co.uk
www.craftscentre.surrart.ac.uk

The centre holds 18 pots made by Hamada Shoji and 14 Japanese pots from the Bernard Leach source collections. In addition, the centre has a Bernard Leach archive of some 14,000 items, many of which relate to Leach's time in Japan, and details some of his early connections between the UK and Japan. The archive holds many drawings and sketches made by Leach while in Japan.

## Firle

### Firle Place

Firle Place, set in an ancient park, has been the home of the Gage family for over 500 years and is currently owned by the 7th Viscount Gage. The original Tudor building has been modified over the years, notably during the 18th century. The house has a good collection of 18th-century French furniture and a painting collection of Dutch and Flemish schools that contains works by Rubens and Reynolds. There are examples of Chinese porcelain but apparently only one example of Japanese art; this is a rather splendid pair of Kakiemon figures of hounds. Unfortunately it is not known when and from where these wonderful beasts were acquired.

**Firle Place**
Firle, Lewis
East Sussex
BN8 6LP

Tel: 01273 858335

gage@firlplace.co.uk
www.firleplace.co.uk

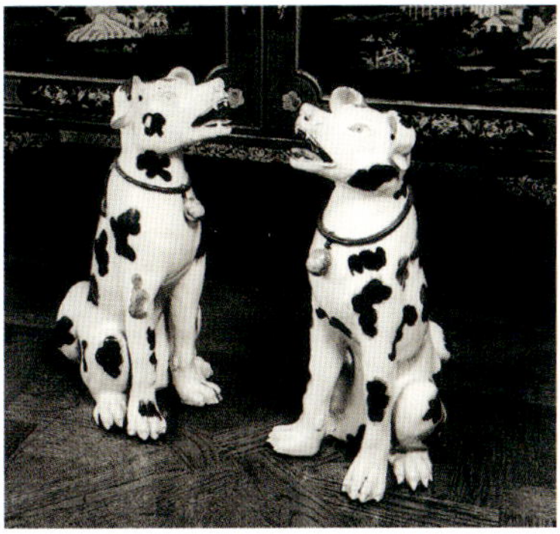

*Pair of Kakiemon hounds*

## Guildford

### Clandon Park

Clandon Park has been the home of the Onslow family since 1641 when Sir Richard Onslow bought the house. The Elizabethan house was rebuilt around 1731 by his great grandson Thomas, 2nd Baron Onslow. The house was designed by the Venetian architect Giacomo Leoni.

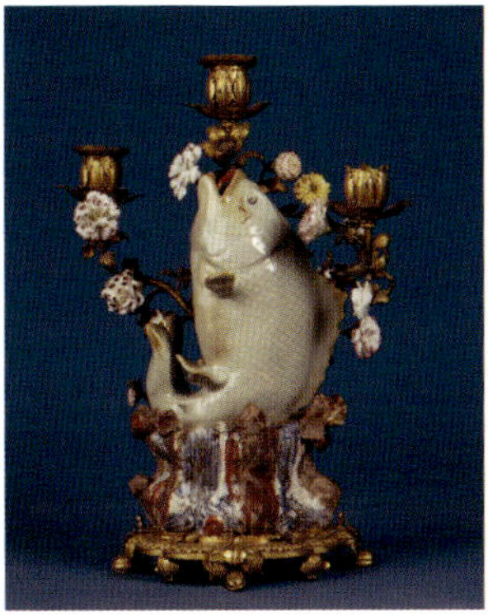

*Export porcelain in ormolu mounts at Clandon Park*

Many of the original contents of Clandon have been sold over the years, beginning with a great sale of 1781. Today the collection at Clandon includes a famous collection of furniture, carpets, porcelain and needlework, together with the Mortlake Tapestries, many Onslow family paintings and a collection of Italian comedy figures.

**Clandon Park**
West Clandon
Guildford
Surrey
GU4 7RQ

Tel: 01483 222482
Fax: 01483 23479

clandon@nationaltrust.org.uk
www.nationaltrust.org.uk/main/
www.nationaltrust.org.uk/places/clandonpark

The Japanese collections include some exquisite Arita animal figures in Louis XV ormolu mounts as well as a pair of Arita jars with Regency ormolu mounts. These objects can be found on display in the rooms open to the public.

## Hastings

### Hastings Museum and Art Gallery

The Japanese collections at the Hastings Museum are interesting as they mostly come from the collection of Lord and Lady Brassey who travelled around the world in their yacht Sunbeam during the years 1876 and 1877.

Lord Brassey had been one of the commissioners for the Colonial and Indian Exhibition held in South Kensington, London, in 1886. One of the most popular features of the exhibition was the full-sized reproduction of an Indian palace that was intended to represent a typical Indian royal residence. On the upper storey the Durbar Hall was used for the Prince of Wales' official receptions. At the close of the exhibition Lord Brassey acquired the Durbar Hall for use as a smoking room and museum at the back of his house at 24 Park Lane, London. The museum housed the collection of ethnographic material acquired by Lady Brassey on their earlier world travels.

From 1889 to the death of Lord Brassey in 1918, the Lady Brassey Museum in the Durbar Hall was open to visiting groups by arrangement. In 1919 the second Lord Brassey presented the building and its contents to the town of Hastings where, in 1931, it was re-erected as an extension to the existing museum. Today the lower Durbar hall has objects relating to the Indian subcontinent and has displays of Lady Brassey's jewellery and costume collection, metalwork, and models of everyday life in 19th-century India. The upper Durbar Hall has displays relating to the life of the Brassey family, including a model of its

**Hastings Museum and Art Gallery**
Johns Place
Bohemia Road
Hastings
Sussex
TN34 1ET

Tel: 01424 781155
Fax: 01424 781165

museum@hastings.gov.uk
www.hmag.org.uk

yacht Sunbeam as well as objects collected on the family's voyages around the world.

Although numbering only about 50, the Japanese objects collected by the Brasseys include a suit of armour, edged weapons (including *katana*, *wakizashi* and *naginata*), saddles and stirrups as well as sword-fittings. There are also some interesting prints (Kuniyoshi, Toyokuni, Sadahide, and Kunisada), some ceramics (including tea ware) and small ivory carvings (including netsuke). The armour and examples of netsuke, lacquer and ceramics are generally on display at the museum.

## Isle of Wight

### Osborne House

Overlooking the sea on the north coast of the Isle of Wight the Osborne Estate was purchased in 1845 by Queen Victoria and Prince Albert as a private home; the original house was not substantial enough to accommodate a large family so Prince Albert designed a replacement and by 1851 the new Osborne House had become a substantial ornate house in the Italian Renaissance style. Prince Albert was greatly involved with the highly successful Great Exhibition of 1851 and many exhibits relating to this event can be seen at Osborne. Also displayed throughout the house are numerous gifts to the Queen from around the world.
Queen Victoria's role as Empress of India is celebrated in the decoration of the Durbar Room that was constructed between 1890 and 1891 and served as an elaborate banqueting hall. The completion of the room coincided with the introduction of electricity and so the Indian-influenced lamp stands were designed to take full advantage of this emerging technology. Osborne House now comprises several wings, apartments and buildings; the grounds also contain a summer-house, Swiss Cottage, and a museum that contains a number of gifts from Japan including a group of ceramic figures presented to the Duke of Gloucester by the Governor of Shiga prefecture.

**Osborne House**
East Cowes
Isle of Wight
PO32 6JY

Tel: 01983 200 022
Fax: 01983 281 380

www.english-heritage.org.uk

# Maidstone

## Maidstone Museum and Bentlif Art Gallery

The Museum in Maidstone has collections of local history and the fine and decorative arts. It also has an extensive collection of Japanese art that includes over 1,000 woodblock prints and printed books, a comprehensive collection of sword-fittings (*tsuba*, *kozuka*, *kogai*, *fuchi-kashira*), lacquer (including inro, boxes and *suzuribako*), carving and figural pieces (including bronzes, netsuke and *okimono*), other metalwork (including incense burners, vases and religious objects), ceramics (including porcelain and stoneware with an interesting selection of incense boxes), personal accessories, small items of 19th-century furniture, and many other miscellaneous objects.

The Museum has benefited from many gifts from local collectors such as "the Hon. Henry Marsham who retired from the army in the 1870s to collect ceramics in Japan which he bequeathed to the museum in 1908" and the Hon. Walter Samuel who by the 1920s had built up a collection of sword-fittings, netsuke, lacquer, woodblock-printed books and prints (over 650 items), which were given to the Museum in 1924. Samuel's father, Lord Bearsted (founder of the Shell Company) financed a new wing for the Museum, which was constructed between 1919 and 1924.

Maidstone Museum and Bentlif Art Gallery
St. Faith's Street
Maidstone
Kent
ME14 1LH

Tel: 01622 754497
Fax: 01622 602193

museum@maidstone.gov.uk
www.museum.maidstone.gov.uk

# Oxford

## Ashmolean Museum

On the 24th May 1683, the Ashmolean Museum in Oxford opened its doors to become the first private collection of 'curiosities' to be opened to the public. Even the use of the term 'museum' was a novelty in the English language. A few years later the *New World of Words* (1706) defined 'museum' as "a Study, or Library; also a College, or Publick Place for the Resort of Learned Men" and included a specific entry for "Ashmole's Museum" described as "a neat Building in the City of Oxford". The collection of Elias Ashmole was already more than 50 years old, having been founded by John Tradescant (died 1638) and displayed to the public (for a fee), first by him and later by his son John (1608-62) in their house at Lambeth in London. The house was situated roughly on the opposite bank of the River Thames to where the present day Houses of Parliament are located. The Tradescant collection laid the foundations of Oxford University's oriental collections as it contained a number of examples of orientalia; for example a Burmese Buddha, some Chinese storage jars, Indian and Turkish weapons, Moroccan spurs as well as tourist trinkets from the Holy Land. In 1845, the Ashmolean moved to its present building, an impressive neo-Grecian edifice designed by C.R. Cockerell.

The Museum of Eastern Art was formed in 1949 as a subdivision of the Department of Fine Art and was housed in the old Indian Institute that had maintained its own museum of Indian art since 1897. Through a gradual process in the 1950s and early 1960s the transfer of these combined collections to the Ashmolean's own building formed the Department of Eastern Art. Since that time, under specialist curators, the Museum's collection of Japanese paintings and export ceramics has greatly expanded. More recently, the work of artists and craftsmen of the Meiji period has featured prominently in the Ashmolean's Japanese galleries.

The collections of the Ashmolean Museum are surpassed only by those of the British Museum and the Victoria & Albert Museum. The Japanese collections have, over the years, benefited from many gifts such as the Japanese ceramics given by Gerald Reitlinger. Reitlinger's collection of Japanese export porcelain, along with purchases from a special fund (the Story Fund that is used exclusively for Japanese objects) have created an extremely comprehensive collection.

The Ashmolean Museum's Japanese collection numbers around 5,000 objects plus some 3,000 pot sherds. These items include paintings and screens (470 in total), prints (around 2,000), Buddhist and secular sculpture, carvings (including netsuke), archaeological material (including *haniwa* and kiln-site objects), most types of ceramics – especially porcelain (some 500 examples of export porcelain), one suit of armour, a few swords and many examples of sword furniture (around 2,000), a few textiles and around 100 examples of Meiji-period art objects including *cloisonné*, bronzes and ceramics. There is a small but well-displayed gallery devoted to Japanese art and other Japanese works can be found in adjacent galleries.

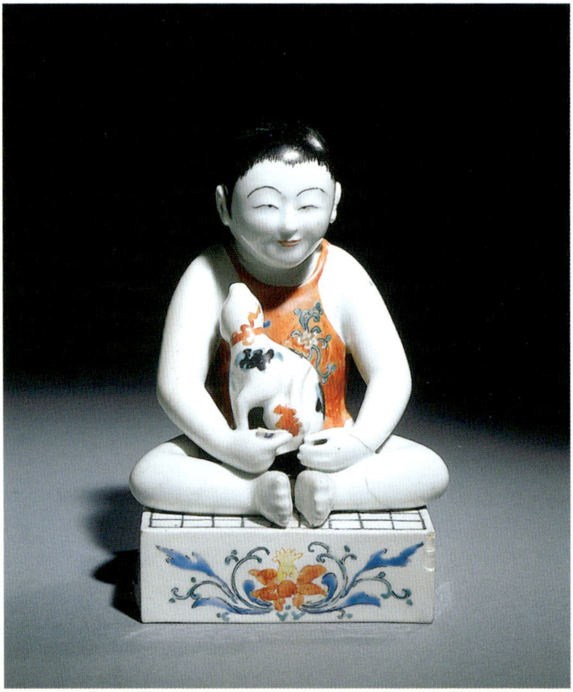

*Kakiemon figure of a boy with a dog. Gift of Gerald Reitlinger, 1978.670*

**Ashmolean Museum**
Beaumont Street
Oxford
OX1 2PH

Tel: 01865 278000
Fax: 01865 278018

eastern-art@ashmus.ox.ac.uk
www.ashmol.ox.ac.uk
ashweb.ashmol.ox.ac.uk/PotWeb/HomePage.html
ashweb.ashmol.ox.ac.uk/PotWeb/PotProsp-Japan.html

### Bodleian Japanese Library

The Bodleian Library in the University of Oxford is one of the oldest libraries in Europe, and in the UK is second in size only to the British Library. Its history dates from 1602 but even then this was a library re-founded on the site of an even earlier library. The Bodleian Japanese Library was opened in 1993 in the newly constructed Nissan Institute of Japanese Studies in the precincts of St. Antony's College. The library is an open-access library, with seating space for 32 users at any one time. The Library, combining Bodley's extensive holdings on Japan with the residual collection of the Nissan Institute Library, houses the University's principal collections relating to Japan. The collections transferred from the central Bodleian site remain for reference only but members of the University may borrow the residual Nissan holdings.

The Bodleian's historical collections in Japanese are small but there are some unique treasures that were acquired in the early years of its foundation; these include *Saga-bon*, *Kirishitanban* and Ieyasu's *shuinjo*. The first known accession of Japanese printed material was three volumes of *Saga-bon* presented to the Library in November 1629 by Robert Viney, who studied at Oxford in 1621-25. *Saga-bon* refers to a group of luxury editions of Japanese literary works printed by Hon'ami Koetsu's press at Saga, Kyoto, c.1608-15. The Bodleian's copies are texts of the Kanze school of Noh plays.

Various kinds of missionary literature of the Jesuit Mission Press in Japan (known as *Kirishitanban-ban)* were produced from 1590 until the expulsion of the missionaries from Japan in 1614. The press used both Japanese and European typefaces, of both wood and metal. Many of these books were destroyed when the country was closed and the priests expelled. The Bodleian is fortunate in possessing six titles of these great rarities, including *A Compendium of the Acts of the Saints*, the first book printed from movable types in Japan, which came within the collection of John Selden, received in 1659.

The original *shuinjo* (vermilion seal document) of 1613 was issued by Shogun Tokugawa Ieyasu to grant the English Company trade privileges in Japan. The Bodleian's *shuinjo* is believed to be one of the two copies given to John Saris, the commander of the eighth voyages of the Company. The exact date of its acquisition by the Library is not known, but it was already included in the list of the Bodleian manuscripts that was probably compiled in 1680. Dated the 28th day of the 8th month, the 18th year of the Keicho period (12 October 1613), the document, bearing Ieyasu's seal in vermilion, was issued to the captain of an English ship, to whom it grants privileges for trade in Japan and concomitant terms including jurisdiction rights in seven articles.

Bodleian manuscripts in Japanese are few, numbering about 100 titles. Many of them were added to the stock by donation or purchase in the early years of the 20th century, when rare books were not too expensive to buy in Japan. The collection includes *Nara ehon* (Nara picture books), such as a very decorative scroll of Urashima.

**Bodleian Japanese Library**
27 Winchester Road
Oxford
OX2 6NA

Tel: 01865 284506
Fax: 01865 284500

japanese@bodley.ox.ac.uk
www.bodley.ox.ac.uk/dept/oriental/bjl.htm
www.bodley.ox.ac.uk/dept/oriental/allegro.htm

### Pitt Rivers Museum

The Pitt Rivers Museum displays archaeological and ethnographic objects from all areas of the world. The Museum was founded in 1884 when General Pitt Rivers, an influential figure in the development of archaeology and evolutionary anthropology, gave his collection to Oxford University. The original gift contained more than 18,000 objects but today the collection numbers over half a million. In the Pitt Rivers Museum the collections are arranged 'typologically' (according to type); musical instruments, weapons, masks, textiles, jewellery, and tools are all displayed in groups to show how the same problems have been solved at different times by different peoples. The Pitt

Rivers Museum still retains its Victorian atmosphere with cluttered cases and the original small handwritten labels.

Japan has, from the outset, been well represented in the Museum's collections. There were only some 300 Japanese objects in the original gift, which contained examples of everyday Japanese artefacts as well as samurai armour and a remarkable set of 52 Noh masks. These masks were all made in the north-east of Japan during the Edo Period, with dates ranging from the early 17th to the early 19th century. It is believed that they comprise a set used by a particular Noh theatre company in the mid-19th century. The collection includes cloth pouches used for storing the masks, which seem to be of textile fragments from old Noh costumes.

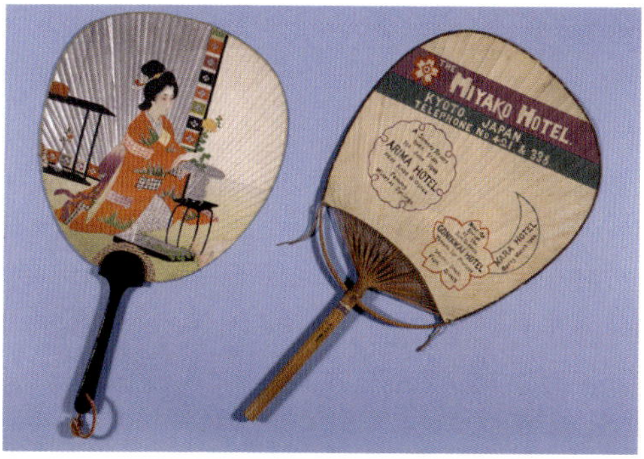


*Advertising material for the Miyako Hotel, Kyoto, 1908*

One of the most significant collectors of Japanese material on behalf of the Museum was Basil Hall Chamberlain, Professor of Japanese and Philology at the Imperial University of Tokyo. From 1888 to 1908, Chamberlain acquired (on behalf of the Museum) everyday artefacts, musical instruments, kites and several hundred religious items. He also obtained two large funeral urns from the Ryukyuan (Okinawa) Islands. Chamberlain also commissioned the Revd. J. Rousseau to acquire objects from the Ainu of Hokkaido, amongst whom he was working as a missionary. Within this remarkable collection is a decorated bear-skull memorial pole.

The Japanese collections have increased over the years with the most significant recent addition arriving in 1996 when John Lowe donated more than 600 artefacts, including both unique works of high aesthetic value and everyday objects he had bought to furnish his homes in Japan. In his words, he was "tipping into the Museum's lap the contents of four Japanese households". The Japanese photographic collections include a set of portrait photographs of the Japanese ambassador and his delegation taken in Paris in the early 1860s, whilst amongst the music collection is a koto once played by the celebrated Japanese actress Sadayakko.

The breakdown of the collection today is as follows: 6,664 objects on the database (500 archaeology, 4,000 ethnography, and 1,500 historical photographs). These include archaeological and ethnographic material comprising arms and armour, weapons, toys and games, musical instruments, netsuke, clothing and textiles, a large number of everyday objects and ephemeral items such as fans and fire-making equipment, historical photographs of Japan and Japanese people. Approximately 30% of the Japanese collections is on display including cases of Samurai objects (armour and weapons), 54 Noh masks, toys and games, Ainu costume, religious items, musical instruments, charms and a few prints.

**Pitt Rivers Museum**
South Parks Road
Oxford
OX1 3PP

Tel: 01865 270927
Fax: 01865 270943

prm@prm.ox.ac.uk
www.prm.ox.ac.uk
www.prm.ox.ac.uk/japan.html

## Petersfield

### Uppark

Uppark was built around 1690 for Forde, Lorde Grey of Warke, and later 1st Earl of Tankerville in the then fashionable domestic style of architecture derived from the Netherlands. His descendants sold the house in 1747 to Matthew Fetherstonhaugh. Sir Matthew and his wife redecorated the house extensively and brought in their collection of furniture and pictures, many of which had been purchased on their Grand Tours of the Continent between 1749 and 1751.

Their only son Sir Harry, who lived an extravagant life at Uppark entertaining the Prince Regent among his frequent guests, enlarged the collection. When aged over 70 he married his dairymaid and on his death in 1846 he left her the entire estate. She then left it to her unmarried sister and eventually the estate passed to the second surviving son of another friend and neighbour, the 4th Earl of Clanwilliam, on the condition that he should assume the name of Fetherstonhaugh. Lady Meade-Fetherstonhaugh, whose husband inherited as Lord Clanwilliam's son in 1931, gave the house to the National Trust in 1954.

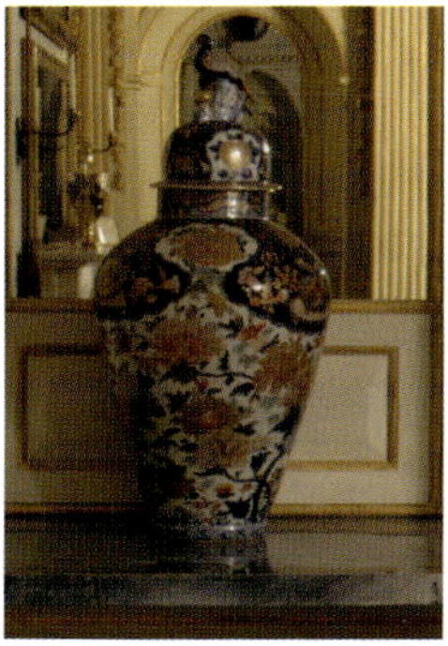

*Imari porcelain at Uppark*

Uppark
South Harting
Petersfield
Hampshire
GU31 5QR

Tel: 01730 825415
Fax: 01730 825873

uppark@nationaltrust.org.uk
www.nationaltrust.org.uk/places/uppark

In 1989, Uppark was severely damaged by fire and the Meade-Fetherstonhaugh family's personal collections were destroyed. The National Trust has endeavoured to restore Uppark to the condition it was in before the fire. There are four large Imari vases and covers (from the National Trust collection rather than that of the family) to be seen at Uppark.

## Petworth

### Petworth House

There has been a house on the present site of Petworth since the Earls of Northumberland had a house there in the 13th century. Around 1690 Charles Seymour, 6th Duke of Somerset, began to remodel the house. His collection of art was also the foundation for the splendid collection which can be seen at Petworth today.

On the Duke's death in 1748 the house passed by marriage to the Wyndham family and Charles Wyndham, the 2nd Earl of Egremont, employed Capability Brown to landscape the park. He added his own taste in art to the collection of French, Italian and Dutch and amassed a large quantity of ancient sculpture from Rome and Greece. His son, the 3rd Earl, collected contemporary British paintings and was a patron of Turner; he acquired work from artists such as Gainsborough, Reynolds, Zoffany and Fuseli. The interiors of the house include work by Grinling Gibbons and the carvings he executed here are considered to be the finest he ever produced.

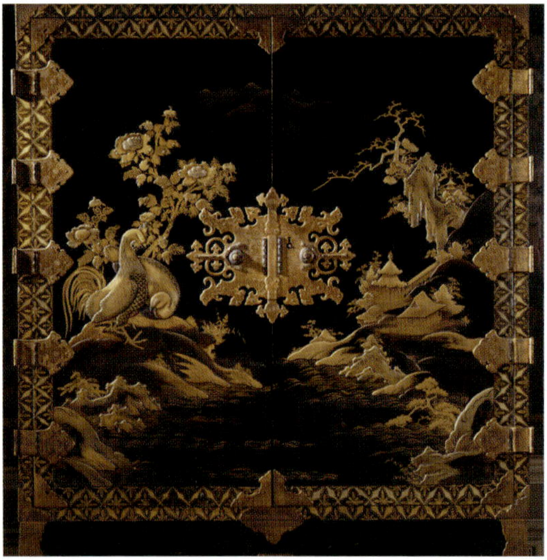

*Lacquer chest at Petworth House*

Petworth House and park were given to the National Trust in 1947 although the house is still the home of Lord and Lady Egremont. There are some interesting examples of Japanese porcelain to be seen in most of the rooms open to the public at Petworth and at least one example of export lacquer furniture. There are fine Kakiemon dishes and figures of hawks, many Arita dishes, bowls and vases as well as an impressive Imari ware in the form of a garniture together with examples of Imari vases and bowls.

**Petworth House**
Petworth
West Sussex
GU28 0AE

Tel: 01798 342207
Fax: 01798 342963

petworth@nationaltrust.org.uk
www.nationaltrust.org.uk/places/petworth

# Reading

## The Museum of Reading

In 1879 the foundation stone was laid for the Reading Free Library and Museum although since 1786 there had been an earlier museum in the Town Hall. The current museum opened in 1883. The collections today are varied and include British and contemporary paintings, Roman art and archaeology, local history and a collection of sculpture and decorative art. This ranges from early 12th-century Romanesque stones from Reading Abbey to sculpture by 19th- and 20th-century artists such as Rodin and Epstein.

Among this wide-ranging group of objects are about 100 Japanese items including a large collection (more than 40) of 19th-century ivory *okimono*. There are also some prints, ceramics (mostly 19th-century, including Satsuma, Kutani, Kyoto ware and one contemporary piece), and miscellaneous pieces loosely classified as 'ethnographic' (amour parts, clothing and personal accessories). Improvement of the documentation of these collections is one of the Museum's current priorities and little if anything is, at present, on display.

**The Museum of Reading**
The Town Hall
Blagrave Street
Reading
Berkshire
RG1 1QH

Tel: 0118 939 9800
Fax: 0118 939 9881

curator@readingmuseum.org.uk
www.readingmuseum.org.uk

# Rochester

## Guildhall Museum

The Guildhall Museum in Rochester was built in 1687 and is one of the finest 17th-century civic buildings in Kent. The main staircase and main chamber have marvellously decorated plaster ceilings. The building now houses the museum of Medway's history and its Roman history and maritime links. The centrepiece of the Museum is a two-tier gallery recreating a prison hulk of the Napoleonic period. There is also an interesting collection of objects from the Victorian and Edwardian eras. Within the collection is an interesting group of Japanese arms and armour, which includes helmets and their accessories and a good matchlock gun.

**Guildhall Museum**
High Street
Rochester
Kent
ME1 1PY

Tel: 01643 848717
Fax: 01643 832919

guildhall.museum@medway.gov.uk
www.medway.gov.uk/index/leisure/museums/2465.html

# Sevenoaks

## Knole

Knole is one of the largest private houses in England and is a splendid example of medieval architecture with Jacobean embellishments on the site of an original palace built between 1456 and 1486 for Thomas Bourchier, Lord Chancellor and Archbishop of Canterbury. In 1566 Queen Elizabeth I granted Knole to her cousin Thomas Sackville, 1st Earl of Dorset, whose descendants, later Dukes of Dorset, have lived here ever since. Between 1603 and 1608 the 1st Earl made extensive alterations and additions, transforming the interior. He added panelling and plasterwork in the Great Hall and other principal rooms and installed the magnificent Great Staircase.

At the same time he began the collection of Jacobean furniture for which Knole is notable today. The collection of 17th-century furniture and textiles at Knole was mostly acquired by the 6th Earl. As Lord Chamberlain to William III the Earl was entitled to take away furnishings discarded from the royal palaces. As a result the galleries at Knole are filled with state beds, chairs, stools and tapestries that once adorned Whitehall, Kensington and Hampton Court. The King's Room contains a beautiful silver looking-glass, table and candle holders. The splendid bed is embellished with cloth of silver and gold with matching chairs and stools.

Although there are collections of fine Chinese porcelain at Knole (some in ormolu mounts), the fashion for collecting Japanese export lacquer and porcelain seems to have been overlooked by this splendid house; there are only two pieces of Imari porcelain (a dish and a leaping carp) and a 17th-century ewer.

**Knole**
Sevenoaks
Kent
TN15 0RP

Tel: 01732 462100
Fax: 01732 465528

knole@nationaltrust.org.uk
www.nationaltrust.org.uk/places/knole

# Southampton

## Southampton City Art Gallery

Southampton City Art Gallery has a good collection of 20th-century British Art; also on display is a 14th-century Italian renaissance altarpiece, Burne-Jones' *Perseus* series and 17th-century Dutch landscapes and French Impressionist paintings. There is an interesting collection of British studio ceramics with a representative collection of works by Bernard Leach and Hamada Shoji. There are few other Japanese objects but there is an interesting late 19th-century Komai-style necklace of 'Kyoto damascene' work and two swords, one of which was reputedly surrendered to Lord Louis Mountbatten.

Southampton City Art Gallery
Civic Centre
Commercial road
Southampton
Hampshire
SO14 7LP

Tel: 02380 832277

www.southampton.gov.uk/art

# Westerham

## Squerryes Court

The present house at Squerryes was built around 1680 by Sir Nicholas Crisp, a London merchant. In 1700, Edward Villiers, 1st Earl of Jersey bought Squerryes and in 1731 the 3rd Earl sold the property to John Warde (1682-1746) in whose family the house has since remained. Warde was the son of Sir John Warde, Lord Mayor of London, one of the first governors of the Bank of England, and had direct connections to the Honourable East India Company.

The house has a good collection of paintings from the Italian, 17th-century Dutch and 18th-century English schools as well as furniture, porcelain and tapestries that were all acquired or commissioned by the Warde family in the 18th century. The Japanese pieces in the collection include some fine Imari porcelain (a garniture as well as bowls and jars) and a splendid Arita lidded vase. There are also two fine Japanese export lacquer chests – which rest on the floor without European stands – in the same room as two japanned chests.

Squerryes Court
Westerham
Kent
TN16 1SJ

Tel: 01959 562 345
Fax: 01959 565 949

enquiries@squerryes.co.uk
www.squerryes.co.uk

# Windsor

## Windsor Castle

Windsor Castle is one of the official residences of Her Majesty The Queen and was first established in 1087 by King William I; the castle has been occupied by the royal family since that time but has been remodelled over the centuries. The most significant changes to the castle were carried out by Henry II, Edward III, Charles II, George III and George IV.

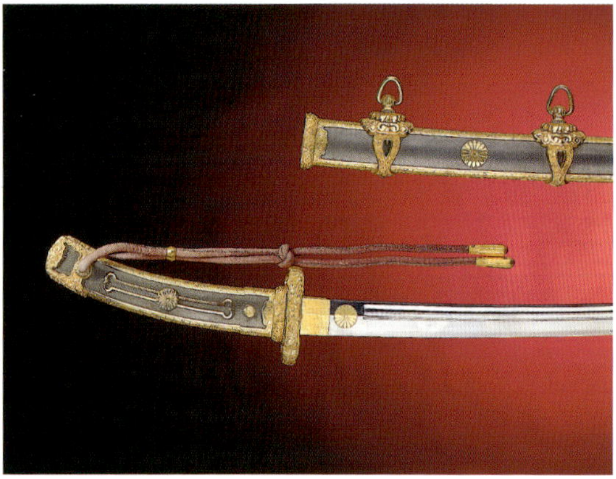

*Detail of tachi and scabbard*

There are extensive displays of arms and armour in the State Entrance, Grand Vestibule and Queen's Guard Chamber; these collections include the *domaru* presented to Queen Victoria in 1869 by her son Alfred, Duke of Edinburgh along with important swords dating from the 16th to 19th centuries that were all gifts from the Japanese Emperor Meiji. In the State Apartments there are extensive displays of 17th-century Japanese porcelain, some of which may be from the collection of Queen Mary II; other examples are probably from the collection of George IV in the early 19th century or from Queen Mary in the early 20th century. The State apartments also contain superb examples of 17th-century export lacquer cabinets mounted on English giltwood stands as well as 18th-century French furniture, which incorporates older Japanese lacquer panels.

Windsor Castle
Windsor
Berkshire

Contact:
The Official Residences of
The Queen
London
SW1A 1AA

Tel: 020 7766 7304
Fax: 020 7930 9625

bookinginfo@
royalcollection.org.uk
www.royal.gov.uk

# Woodstock

## Blenheim Palace

Blenheim Palace covers seven acres of ground and is one of the largest private houses in England. The Manor of Woodstock and the money for building the palace were given as a gift by Queen Anne and a grateful nation to John Churchill, 1st Duke of Marlborough in appreciation of his victory over the French in 1704 at the Battle of Blenheim. The palace was designed in the baroque style by Sir John Vanbrugh and built between 1705 and1722. Capability Brown re-landscaped the park in 1764 and created the lake; the great bridge designed by Vanbrugh was then half under water.

Blenheim Palace houses a fine collection of paintings including works by Reynolds and Van Dyck. There are also wood carvings by Grinling Gibbons, splendid furniture and bronzes. Sir Winston Churchill, a cousin of the 9th Duke, was born at Blenheim Palace in 1874. It is currently home to the 11th Duke of Marlborough. There are only five examples of Japanese porcelain to be seen at Blenheim: Imari beakers and vases and a splendid Kakiemon jar.

**Blenheim Palace**
Woodstock
Oxfordshire
OX20 1PX

Tel: 08700 60 20 80
Fax: 01993 810 570

administrator@
blenheimpalace.com
www.blenheimpalace.com

# London

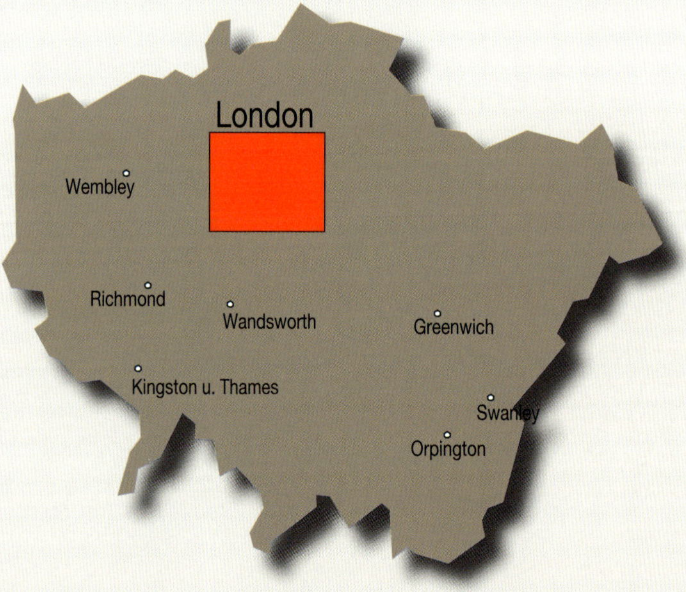
London
Wembley
Richmond
Wandsworth
Greenwich
Kingston u. Thames
Swanley
Orpington

## Bethnal Green Museum of Childhood

The Bethnal Green Museum of Childhood is a branch museum of the Victoria & Albert Museum (V&A) and began life as a prefabricated building at South Kensington at the time of the 1851 exhibition. The original iron frame that is still visible inside the Museum was brought to Bethnal Green in the 1860s, re-erected and finished with its distinctive red brick to the designs of J.W. Wild. The outside of the building was decorated with murals depicting the arts, sciences and agriculture and the marble mosaic floor was put together by women prisoners from Woking gaol.

In June 1872, The Bethnal Green Museum was opened by the Prince and Princess of Wales (the future King Edward VII and Princess Alexandra). Among its first displays were the Animal and Food products collection from the Great Exhibition of 1851 and 1,600 works of art belonging to Sir Richard Wallace (now the Wallace Collection). In the 1920s, the Museum started to focus on children. Keeper Arthur Sabin encouraged local schools to visit, established a classroom, and gave child-friendly lectures. One of the galleries was dedicated to childhood, childhood material was actively collected, and objects transferred from the V&A. Finally, in 1974, the Director of the V&A, Roy Strong, re-defined Bethnal Green as a Museum of Childhood, and it was later officially recognised as the National Museum of Childhood.

Although there is no dedicated curator for the Japanese collections at the Bethnal Green Museum of Childhood there is an interesting and varied collection of Japanese children's toys and games that range from Meiji-period wooden toys to Bandai transformers! A basic search on the Museum's database brings up over 1,500 Japanese objects in the BGM collections. These include boys' festival material, dolls and other figures, mechanical toys (mostly 1950s to 1970s), costume, dolls' houses and furniture (including miniature tea services), military toys (1960s to 1970s), costume (1850 to 1999), some early 20th-century Bunraku puppets as well as miscellaneous toys, many made for the Western market.

**Bethnal Green Museum of Childhood**
Cambridge Heath Road
London
E2 9PA

Tel: 020 8980 2415

bgmc@vam.ac.uk
www.vam.ac.uk/vastatic/nmc/index.html

## British Library

The Japanese Section of the British Library holds around 80,000 volumes of Japanese books, about 1,500 serials and official publications and some 350 manuscripts. Of the printed books around 3,500 titles are pre-Meiji.

The history of the Japanese collections began around 1723-25 when Sir Hans Sloane purchased 45 Japanese works that had been collected by Engelbert Kaempfer (1651-1716), a German physician and traveller who had stayed in Japan from 1690 to 1692. These works passed into the collections of the British Museum in 1753. Further acquisitions came from Philipp Franz von Siebold (1796-1866) who had travelled in Japan from 1823 to 1829 and again from 1859 to 1862. Later significant collections came from Western scholars of Japan such as Sir Ernest Satow (1843-1928) who gave some rare specimens of early printing and a superb collection of around 2,000 volumes of illustrated woodcut books from William Anderson (1842-1900), a British surgeon and early devotee of Japanese art. Many Japanese books, primarily of artistic rather than textual, interest, were transferred to the Department of Oriental Antiquities of the British Museum.

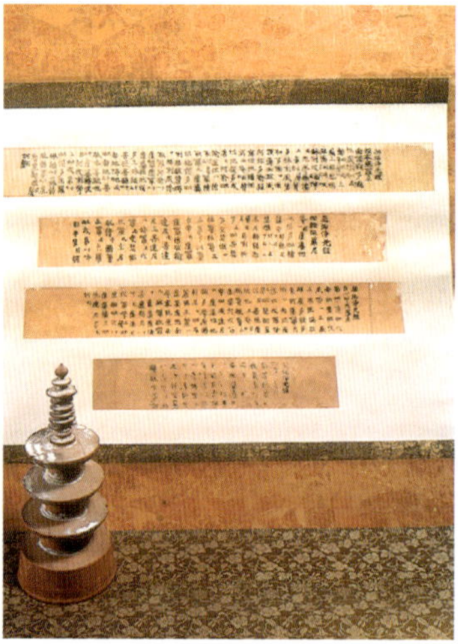

*Hyakumanto: Or.78.a.11*

**British Library**
Japanese Section
Asia/Pacific & Africa
Collections
96 Euston Road
London
NW1 2DB

Tel: 020 7412 7662
Fax: 020 7412 7641
Tel: 020 7412 7000
(British Library general number)

www.bl.uk/collections/japanese.html
www.bl.uk/collections/japanese.html#history
(history of collections)

Since Satow's time, the Japanese collection has been further increased by the acquisition of various items of major significance such as the unique set of eight *Hyakumanto Darani* (Million Pagoda Charms) printed between 764 and 700 AD on the orders of Empress Shotoku (718-770). They are among the earliest printed documents from anywhere in the world with authenticated dates to have survived to the present day. The oldest Japanese printed book in the possession of the British Library is entitled *Joyuishikiron Jukki* and is a Buddhist commentary printed around 1170-80. The British Library also has examples of *Kirishitanban*, missionary literature of the Jesuit Mission Press in Japan that was produced from around 1590 until the expulsion of the missionaries from Japan in 1614. The press used both Japanese and European typefaces, of both wood and metal. Many of these books were destroyed when the country was closed and the priests expelled. A small number of Japanese items are included in the permanent exhibition in the British Library Ritblatt Gallery and other items may occasionally be on display in special exhibitions.

### British Museum - department of Ethnography

The Japanese holdings of the ethnographic collections of the British Museum also have their origins in the objects acquired by Sir Hans Sloane from the family of Engelbert Kaempfer. With the appointment in 1886 of A.W. Franks as Keeper of the Department of British and Medieval Antiquities, (which then embraced the ethnographic collections), a fresh incentive was brought to the collection and display of ethnographic material.

Today there are in excess of 1,500 Japanese objects in the collection including ceramics, metalwork, basketwork, lacquer ware, textiles and costume. The majority of the collections relate to everyday life and include many objects acquired by missionaries who travelled to Japan in the late 19th and early

20th centuries. There are Ainu objects from John Anderson who travelled to Hokkaido in the 1880s and further Ainu material from Dr. Neil Gordon Munro, a physician who lived and worked in Hokkaido between 1930 and 1942. There is also an interesting collection of tourist ephemera, notably that which was collected on a special visit in 2001 by a curator from the department. This visit, entitled *Collecting souvenirs in Japan: a diary* can be accessed via the 'Tours' tab of the Museum's 'Compass' site at: http://www.thebritishmuseum.ac.uk/compass/ and makes fascinating reading.

British Museum
Department of Ethnography
Great Russell Street
London
WC1B 3DG

Tel: 020 7323 8041
Fax: 020 7323 8013

ethnography@thebritishmuseum.ac.uk
www.thebritishmuseum.ac.uk
www.thebritishmuseum.ac.uk/ethno/ethhome.html
www.thebritishmuseum.ac.uk/compass/ (online exploration of the British Museum collections)

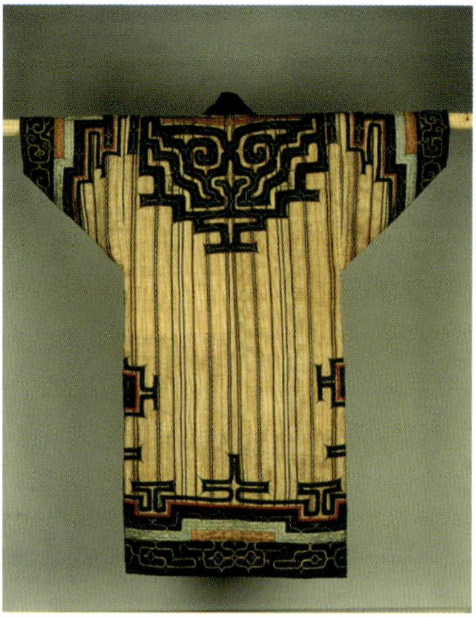

*Ainu embroidered coat, donated by Dr John Anderson FRS, 1885, 12-19*

### British Museum - department of Asia

The Japanese collections of the British Museum (perhaps the most well-known museum in the UK) number nearly 30,000 objects and include archaeological material, the arts of Buddhism and Shinto, paintings and woodblock prints, woodblock-printed books, swords and armour, metalwork (including a large collection of sword-fittings), lacquer, pottery and porcelain and sculptural and carved works in different media (including a large collection of netsuke). There is also a little-documented collection of textiles, mostly everyday wear from the 1920s to the 1950s.

The British Museum's original gift from the collection of Sir Hans Sloane contained Japanese material that had been acquired from the family of the German physician Engelbert Kaempfer (1651-1716) who had brought it back from Japan. The Museum also acquired Japanese objects from the great world exhibitions in Vienna, Paris, and London and from specialist and non-specialist shops in London such as Liberty's of Regent Street, Kato of New Oxford Street, and Yamanaka of Bond Street, (which had a large staff of Japanese art salesmen). The appointment in 1886 of A.W. Franks as Keeper of the Department of British and Medieval Antiquities brought about an enthusiastic new approach to the collecting of Japanese art. Franks was a collector himself and many of the objects in the collection today are from his own private collection.

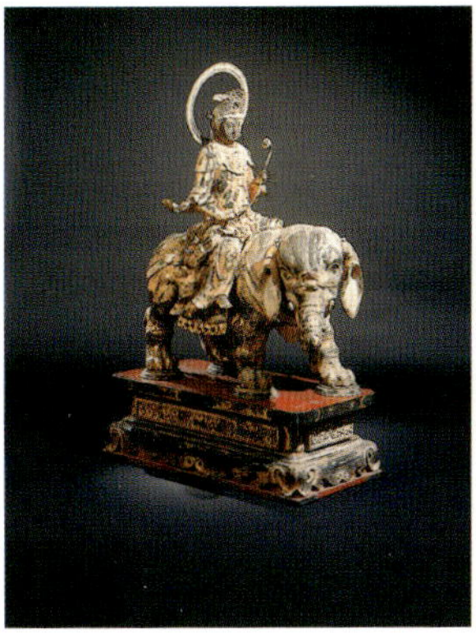

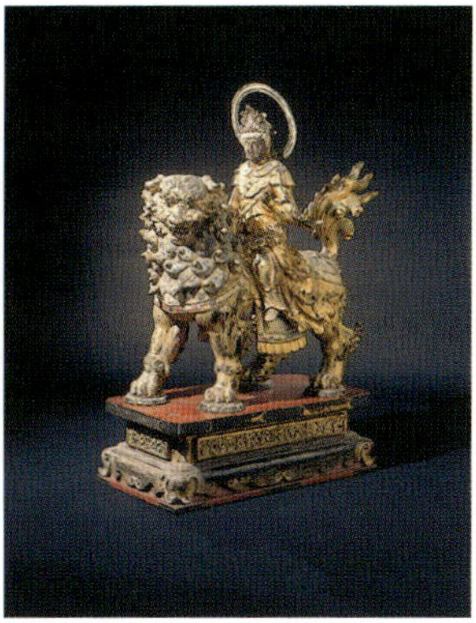

*Bodhisattva Monju by Koyu, c.1680, 1988.3-14.2 (left)*

*Bodhisattva Fugen by Koyu, c.1680, 1988.3-14.1 (right)*

The Japanese paintings in the Museum number around 4,500 and include many fine pieces from the Kamakura period and later. The collection of *ukiyoe* prints and paintings numbers about 7,000 and includes works by all the important artists. There is an especially good collection of Sharaku prints. Since the early 1980s an aggressive collecting policy has seen the collection of 20th-century prints brought from almost nothing to comprehensive holdings. Printed illustrated books – mainly from the Edo period but including a good selection of Taisho and early Showa-period works amassed over the past two decades – are now the most important holdings in Europe.

Archaeological material includes a significant group of 366 objects from the Kofun period collected in Japan by William Gowland (1842-1927). The collection of swords, largely a result of the R.W. Lloyd bequest, contains a number of significant blades of exceptionally high quality. In 1999 103 swords were taken to Japan to be polished by the traditional method with a generous grant from the Peter Moores Foundation. The pre-Meiji period ceramics collection includes many fine pieces of tea ceremony ware, and fine export porcelain of the 17th century and later. There are also very good examples of early lacquer in the collection.

British Museum
Department of Asia
Great Russell Street
London
WC1B 3DG

Tel: 020 7323 8560
Fax: 020 7323 8874

japanese@
thebritishmuseum.ac.uk
www.thebritishmuseum.
ac.uk
www.thebritishmuseum.
ac.uk/ja/jacoll.html
(link to history of the
Japanese collections)
www.thebritishmuseum.
ac.uk/compass/ (online
exploration of the British
Museum collections)

An important gift (the British Museum benefits greatly from gifts and bequests) was the private collection of rare ritual masks donated by Mr. Nobutaka Oka in 1999. The gift from Mr. Shibata Akihiko of around 500 pieces of domestic-style porcelain from the Edo period makes the collection the most comprehensive outside Japan.

In 1987 a separate Department of Japanese Antiquities was formed and in 1990 a new suite of special galleries devoted to Japanese art was opened. Since that time the numbers of staff has been greatly reduced and today the department has been subsumed into the larger department of Asia. Unfortunately there are no permanent displays of the collections but themed exhibitions are periodically mounted.

### Buckingham Palace

In 1761 King George III bought Buckingham House (owned from the beginning of the 18th century by the Dukes of Buckingham) as a comfortable family home close to St. James' Palace where court functions were held. Buckingham House became known as

**Buckingham Palace**
London
SW1A 1AA

Contact:
The Official Residences of
The Queen
London
SW1A 1AA
Tel: 020 7766 7304
Fax: 020 7930 9625

bookinginfo@
royalcollection.org.uk
www.royal.gov.uk

'the Queen's House' and in 1762 work began on remodelling the house to the king's requirements. On his accession to the throne in 1820, King George IV decided to reconstruct the house and with the assistance of his architect John Nash, he set about transforming the house into a palace. Buckingham Palace has been the official London residence of Britain's sovereigns since 1837.

Although in use for the many official events and receptions held by The Queen, some areas of Buckingham Palace are open to visitors. The State Rooms, open each year during August and September, hold some of the finest examples of mostly 17th-century Japanese porcelain and lacquer – mounted in France in the 18th century and purchased by King George IV at the beginning of the 19th century. These include two pairs of 17th-century lacquer bowls with French gilt bronze mounts of around 1760 that were originally purchased for Brighton Pavilion.

## Fan Museum

The Fan Museum is devoted entirely to fans and fan-making and now has a collection of more than 3,500 fans from around the world, dating from the 11th century to the present day. The Museum's own fan collection (together with fans on loan from other collections) is displayed in changing themed exhibitions in which fans are presented in their historical, sociological and economic contexts. A new exhibition is shown at The Fan Museum approximately every four months.

Although the collection is particularly strong in 18th- and 19th-century European fans it also has a collection of some 200 Japanese fans of different types, styles and periods from Edo through to Taisho. The earliest fans in the collection date from around 1700 and were painted in the style of the Kano school; the collection also has a *kanban* (shop sign) in the form of a fan.

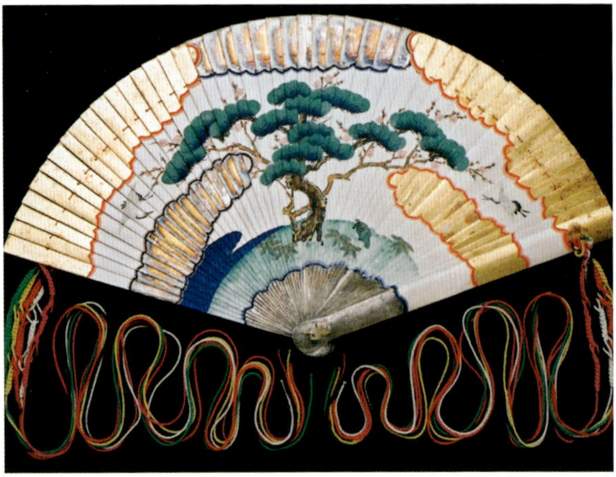

*Court fan, 19th century*

Fan Museum
12 Crooms Hill
Greenwich
London
SE10 8ER

Tel: 020 8305 1441

admin@fan-museum.org
www.fan-museum.org

Fenton House
Windmill Hill
Hampstead
London
NW3 6RT

Tel/Fax: 020 7435 3471

fentonhouse@
nationaltrust.org.uk
www.nationaltrust.org.uk

## Fenton House

This late 17th-century house contains an outstanding collection of European and oriental porcelain, 17th-century needlework pictures and Georgian furniture, and the Benton Fletcher collection of early keyboard instruments, most of which are in working order. There are at least five examples of Japanese porcelain within the collection.

Firepower
The Royal Artillery
Museum
Royal Arsenal
Woolwich
London
SE18 6ST

Tel: 020 8855 7755
Fax: 020 8855 7100

www.firepower.org.uk

## Firepower

A Royal Warrant issued to Captain William Congreve RA by King George III formally established the Royal Military Repository, the forerunner to the Royal Artillery Museum, on the Royal Arsenal site in May 1778. The original museum building was destroyed by fire in 1802 and the surviving artefacts housed in the Old Royal Military Academy. In 1820 the main collection was moved to the Rotunda on Woolwich Common.

The collection includes Japanese firearms from the 19th century to early 20th century as well as a number of Second World War 'surrender' swords and captured flags. There are also two large Japanese early 19th-century engraved bronze cannons on display. The provenance for these two objects is not totally clear.

## Ham House

Ham House was built in 1610 for Sir Thomas Vavasour, Knight Marshall to King James I. In 1626 it became the home of William Murray who, between 1637 and 1639, remodelled the interior of Ham. The decoration from this remodelling is largely intact in most of the rooms, which still contain part of Murray's art collection thus giving a rare picture of fashions under Charles I. On his death in 1655 Ham passed it on to his eldest daughter, Elizabeth. Her father's titles were conferred upon her in 1670, when she became Countess of Dysart.

In 1648 she married Sir Lionel Tollemache, 3rd Baronet, of Helmingham Hall in Suffolk, a wealthy and cultivated squire. Even before Tollemache's death in 1669, Lady Dysart was rumoured to have formed an attachment to the ambitious John Maitland, 1st Duke of Lauderdale, Secretary of State for Scotland. Following their marriage in 1672, they extended and refurnished Ham as a palatial villa reflecting the Duke's status as one of the most powerful ministers of Charles II. Much of this luxurious interior decoration survives, together with pictures, furniture and textiles.

**Ham House**
Ham Street
Ham
Richmond-upon-Thames
TW10 7RS

Tel: 020 8940 1950
Fax: 020 8332 6903

hamhouse@nationaltrust.org.uk
www.nationaltrust.org.uk/places/hamhouse

Elizabeth died at Ham House in 1698 and the house and the Dysart title then passed to her eldest son from her first marriage, Lionel Tollemache, 3rd Earl of Dysart (1649-1727). Eventually in 1935 Ham House passed to Sir Lyonel Tollemache and both he and his son, Cecil, gave Ham to the National Trust in 1948.

There are only four Japanese objects at Ham House: cabinets of Japanese lacquer inlaid with mother-of-pearl and mounted in European style. They are quite superb and were possibly acquired as early as 1650 as at least one appears in the inventory of 1677.

## Horniman Museum

In the 1860s Victorian tea trader Frederick John Horniman began collecting specimens and artefacts from many parts of the world. Horniman opened his family house to the public so that they could view the treasures he had collected but as the collections increased they outgrew the family home. In 1898 Horniman commissioned Charles Harrison Townsend to design a new museum, which opened in 1901. The original collections consisted of natural history specimens, cultural artefacts and musical instruments. Today the collections have greatly increased so that Horniman's original collections account for only some 10% of the ethnography and musical instrument holdings.

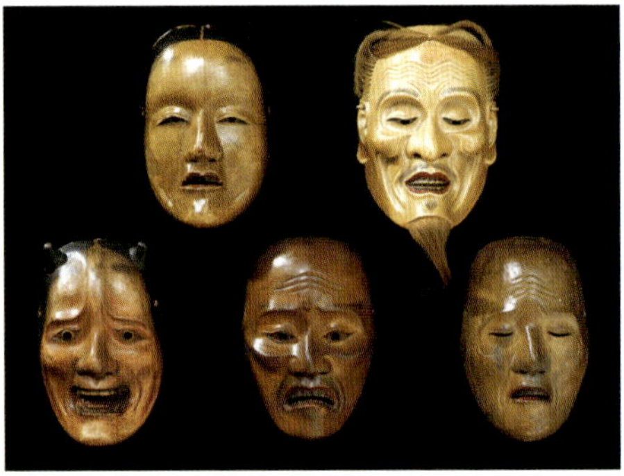

*Masks for Noh performance*

In 1898, the Museum's first curator, Richard Quick (one of the original members of the Japan Society) made a list of material in Frederick Horniman's collections. The Japanese material in the collection then included shrines, porcelain figures, bronze mirrors, vases, incense burners, Buddha images, weapons, ceramics and netsuke. In some cases the acquisition source was recorded, but not in every case. Much had been bought in sales. Although there is no reference in the register to either the 1851 Great Exhibition or the 1862 International Exhibition it is highly likely that some of the Museum's original Japanese collections came from these sources.

There have been further acquisitions over the years such as the Morten bequest of 1909 that consisted of a miscellaneous collection of objects, unlabelled

**Horniman Museum**
100 London Road
Forest Hill
London
SE23 3PQ

Tel: 020 8699 1872
Fax: 020 8291 5506

enquiries@horniman.ac.uk
www.horniman.ac.uk

and without data; the greater proportion of the Japanese part of the collection consisted of 75 ivory carvings. The Museum acquired around 35 items from the 1910 Japan-British Exhibition at White City. These are mostly examples of ethnographic material from the Ainu and included agricultural implements, domestic utensils, weaving equipment and hunting weapons. The Japanese collection today numbers around 2,500 objects and covers a wide range of ethnographic material with some objects (such as Noh masks), which some other collections would classify as 'art'. The lines between art and ethnography have long been blurred.

### Imperial War Museum

The Imperial War Museum is unique in its collections and coverage of conflicts, especially those involving Britain and the Commonwealth from the First World War to the present day. The exhibits and themes of the displays are always thoughtfully and often provokingly displayed and do not attempt to glorify warfare. The Museum has been included in this guide as there is a huge collection of material there that may be of interest to anyone interested in Anglo-Japanese relations and there are indeed many objects that could be categorised as 'art'.

The Department of Art has some 30 objects, including prints, lithographs, childrens' sketch- and scrapbooks, and a poster collection. The Department of Printed Books has a collection of some 50 Japanese Second World War aerial propaganda sheets, some of which are cartoon-illustrated, as well as a small number of Japanese picture postcards, mostly in poor condition.

The Department of Exhibits and Firearms contains approximately 1,400 examples of aircraft (including a section of a Zero cockpit), communications equipment, currency, edged weapons (many 'surrender' swords), ephemera & miscellanea, field equipment, firearms,

**Imperial War Museum**
Lambeth Road
London
SE1 6HZ

Tel: 020 7416 5320
Fax: 020 7416 5374

mail@iwm.org.uk
www.iwm.org.uk
www.iwmcollections.
org.uk

flags, munitions, optical equipment, ordnance, personal equipment, photographic equipment, small arms ammunition, uniforms & head-dress. There is also material in the departments of Documents, Film and Photograph Archive and in the Sound Archive.

The earliest Japanese items acquired by the Museum are probably a gold Peace Commemorative medal and five sets of Peace Commemorative stamps, received, according to Central Files, between 6th January and 13th February 1920 from the Japanese Government via the Foreign Office.

### Japan Society

The Japan Society is the longest established and principal organisation involved in Anglo-Japanese relations in Britain. It has a wide basis of membership and no sectarian interests; membership is open to all as individuals or as companies. Its primary objective is the dissemination, to the British audience, of the knowledge and understanding of Japanese culture and it seeks to provide a forum for social and cultural exchanges between the Japanese living in Britain and the local community.

The Japan Society probably has a longer history than any other of its kind in the world. It grew out of a meeting of the International Congress of Orientalists held in London on 9th September 1891, when a resolution was passed calling for the formation of a society "for the encouragement of Japanese studies and for the purpose of bringing together all those in the United Kingdom and throughout the world who are interested in Japanese matters". The Society's centenary was marked by The Japan Festival, the largest and most successful event of its kind ever to be staged, and its 110th anniversary saw 'Japan 2001'. The Patron of the Society is His Royal Highness, The Duke of Gloucester and the ex-officio President is His Excellency The Japanese Ambassador.

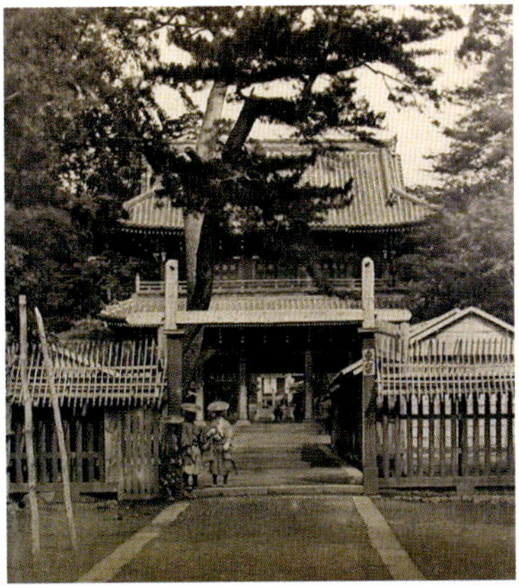

*The British Legation at Tozenji in Edo, Felice Beato, c.1863*

The Society has maintained excellent archives of its meetings since its foundation when the understanding of Japanese art was in its infancy but its members were full of the late Victorian spirit of learning through art and science. There is documentation from the early members, many of whom were influential in the promotion of Japanese culture. The archive and library also hold original material in the form of woodblock-printed books and photographs as well as fascinating early printed travellers' accounts of life in Japan in the latter half of the 19th century. There are approximately 4,000 volumes of books and 2,500 photographs, mostly in their original covers.

Sir Ernest Satow and Arthur Diosy donated a significant number of books. In smaller quantities, other luminaries in Japanese studies such as Basil Hall Chamberlain and Lafcadio Hearn donated books. Sir Francis Piggott donated his draft copy of the first Japanese Constitution of 1889. The French Japanophile and collector Hugues Krafft donated two albums of photographs, one taken during his visit to Japan in 1882 and the other illustrating his private Japanese garden, while the descendants of Lieutenant Alexander Douglas (RN) donated one of the earliest known albums of photographs taken in Japan in 1863 by Felice Beato.

Japan Society
Swire House
59 Buckingham Gate
London
SW1E 6AJ

Tel: 020 7828 6330
Fax: 020 7828 6331

info@japansociety.org.uk
www.japansociety.org.uk

## Linley Sambourne House

Linley Sambourne's artistic career ran from 1867 to 1909. He had many drawing styles but excelled at fanciful caricature of people and animals. In 1867 the editor of the popular satirical magazine *Punch* was shown a sketch of Sambourne's and decided to employ him for freelance work. He continued to work for *Punch* until his death in 1910. The 1880s were Sambourne's busiest years.

In 1874 Sambourne married Marion Herapath, the daughter of a wealthy stockbroker and, helped by her father, the couple acquired an 89-year lease on 18 Stafford Terrace, which had been built in the classical Italianate style in the 1870s as part of a new development of houses. The couple decided to furnish their home in the fashionable 'aesthetic' or artistic style of the period and lived there until Sambourne died in 1910 and his wife in 1914. Their only son Roy inherited the house, making only minimal changes.

In 1980 the house and its contents were sold to the Greater London Council, and the Victorian Society agreed to run it as a museum. It opened to the public in autumn 1980 and ownership of the house later passed to the Royal Borough of Kensington and Chelsea. Following a major restoration project the house re-opened in 2003.

Entering the house one steps back into a late Victorian 'aesthetic- style' interior complete with furnishings and decoration. There are some interesting Japanese objects scattered throughout the house including *fukusa* used as drapes, framed Japanese prints, Imari porcelain, Kutani ware and some interesting large Meiji-period ceramic plates.

**Linley Sambourne House**
18 Stafford Terrace
Kensington
London
W8 7BH

Tel: 020 7602 3316
– extension 305

museums@rbkc.gov.uk
www.rbkc.gov.uk/
linleysambournehouse

## Marble Hill House

Marble Hill House is a magnificent Palladian Thames-side villa situated within 66 acres of parkland. The house was built for Henrietta Howard, Countess of

Suffolk and one-time mistress of King George II. The area was very popular with the aristocracy and, as a consequence, attracted the foremost artists of the time. A great patron of the arts, Henrietta Howard regularly entertained celebrated poets and wits of the day at the house, including Pope, Swift and Gay. Marble Hill House is furnished with some of its original contents as well as with a wealth of fine paintings and objets d'art to reflect its first owner's tastes. The Great Room has lavishly gilded decoration and architectural paintings by Panini. There is also an important collection of early Georgian paintings and furniture. There is currently only one Japanese object on display: a large round lacquer food box bearing the Tokugawa family crest.

**Marble Hill House**
Richmond Road
Twickenham
TW1 2NL

Tel: 020 8892 5115
Fax: 020 8607 9976

www.english-heritage.org.uk

### Royal Botanic Gardens

Kew Gardens is justifiably famous for its huge collections of the world's plant forms and Japan is well represented at Kew. What are perhaps not so well-known are Kew's other Japanese collections. The Economic Botany Collection numbers over 77,000 objects, including some 1,700 Japanese items. The collection illustrates useful plants and contains both plant specimens (about 1,250 of the Japanese objects are wood samples and other plant parts) and artefacts made from plants. The Japanese items include: lacquer ware, paper and paper artefacts, drawings on pith paper/rice paper, paintings on wood, utensils, clothing and food.

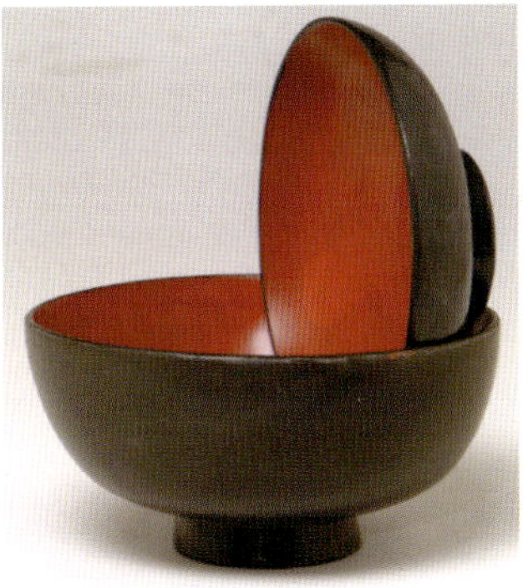

*Rice bowl, EBC 67821*

There are 30 objects collected by Sir Harry Parkes, head of the British Legation in Japan from 1865 to 1883; these include bark, paper samples and paper artefacts. Many more samples of Japanese paper collected by Parkes are held in the Victoria & Albert Museum. There are also 170 objects collected by John James Quin, an employee of the British Foreign Office in Japan (1867-1896). This collection includes lacquer ware and associated artefacts, some dating back to the 1760s. Some of these Japanese objects are on display in Museum No.1 at Kew; the rest can be seen by prior arrangement.

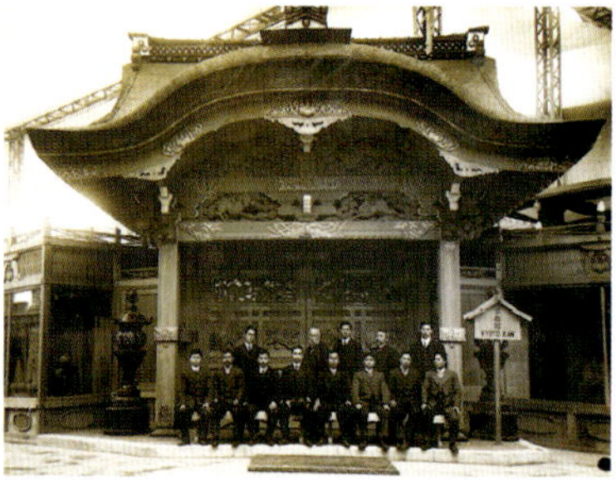

*Copy of the Chokushi-mon at the 1910 Anglo-Japanese Exhibition: now at the Royal Botanic ardens Kew*

**Royal Botanic Gardens**
Kew
Richmond
Surrey
TW9 3AB

Tel: 020 8332 5655 (24 hr)
Fax: 020 8332 5197

info@kew.org
www.rbgkew.org.uk
www.kew.org/collections/ecbot/JapaneseLacquerware.htm (Japanese lacquer)
www.kew.org/collections/ecbot/Paper.htm – paper objects

Within the grounds of Kew Gardens there are also Japanese gardens and a very important reproduction of a Japanese gateway. The Chokushi-Mon (Gateway of the Imperial Messenger) is a four-fifths replica of the Karamon of Nishi Hongan-ji, a famous temple in Kyoto. The replica was created for the Japan-British Exhibition held in London in 1910, and after the exhibition closed it was offered to the Victoria & Albert Museum. The Museum turned down such an enormous object and the gateway was dismantled and reconstructed in the Royal Botanic Gardens, Kew. Built in the architectural style of the Momoyama period the Chokushi-Mon has finely carved woodwork, depicting stylised flowers and animals. The most intricately carved panels portray an ancient Chinese legend depicting the devotion of a pupil to his master. In 1998 the Chokushi-mon underwent a full restoration programme and was re-incorporated into the landscape of Kew.

## Tate Britain

Tate Britain holds the national collections of British Art and international modern art but has been included here for one enigmatic painting in the collection. This is a work of around 1680 by John Michael Wright and is a portrait of Sir Neil O'Neill (?1658-1690). Both and the artist and subject were Catholics and in 1679, as a result of anti-Catholic legislation, Wright had been exiled from London to Dublin where this painting presumably had been executed.

Sir Neil O'Neill is shown standing in the ornately decorated (although somewhat over-romanticised) costume of an Irish chieftain. Beside him is an Irish wolfhound and at his feet is a suit of Japanese armour. This may be seen as a symbolic victory over the persecutors of Catholicism, the religion having been banned from Japan by 1640 after a series of severe persecutions and martyrdoms. The suit has been accurately depicted and has distinctive decoration yet has still to be positively identified. There cannot have been many such pieces in Britain at that time.

Details of the painting can be found under the artist's name in the Tate's excellent online database of the collections. Simply typing in the word 'Japan' brings up some interesting works of contemporary art in Tate Modern either by Japanese artists or by artists with Japanese connections.

**Tate Britain**
Millbank
London
SW1P 4RG

Tel: 020 7887 8000

www.tate.org.uk

## Victoria & Albert Museum

The Japanese collection at the Victoria & Albert Museum is extensive and varied, numbering in excess of 42,000 objects. The items are predominantly from the Edo period but there are some good representative earlier objects and a well-documented collection of pieces acquired from the great exhibitions of the late 19th century. For example the Museum acquired from the Philadelphia Centennial Exposition of 1876 a huge collection of ceramics chosen to represent the entire history of Japanese ceramics. The collections also hold, particularly following a period of active collecting over the last 15 years, a good representative collection of contemporary works in many varied media. The collections today therefore range in period from Heian to the contemporary and include metalwork (arms and armour, mirrors, decorative inlay, figurative works, religious items and over 5,000 sword-fittings), graphic works (including some 28,000 prints and printed books, as well as a few paintings, scrolls and screens), textiles (including court wear, country textiles, textiles for performance, religious items and textile samples), ceramics (of all types), wooden objects including furniture, lacquer ware (including inro and some world-famous examples of export lacquer) and sculpture pieces (that include masks for performance as well as carvings such as *okimono* and netsuke).

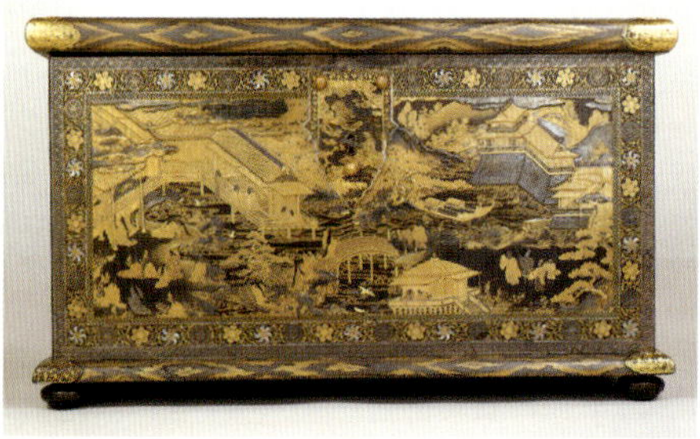

*The Mazarin Chest, c. 1600, 415-1882*

The South Kensington Museum (renamed the Victoria & Albert Museum in 1899 and generally referred to as the V&A) was created on the profits realised from the Great Exhibition of 1851. From the outset, the aims of the Museum were to form collections that would "exhibit the practical application of the principles of design in the graceful arrangement of forms, and the harmonious combination of colours for the benefit of manufacturers, artisans and the general public". The Museum began an active programme of collecting objects from many cultures and the first Japanese item to come into the collections was a group of modern Nagasaki lacquer ware acquired in 1852 and purchased from the company Hewitts and Co. of Fenchurch Street, London.

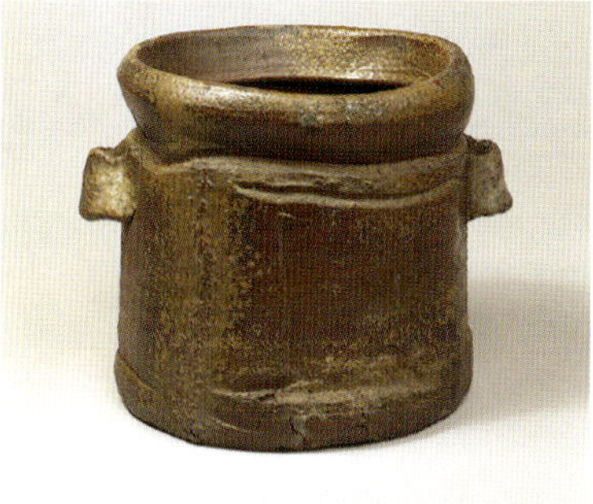

*Bizen water jar c. 1600, 191-1882*

In 1860, Queen Victoria gave the Museum a collection of Imari porcelain formerly in the Japanese Palace at Dresden. In 1865, Queen Victoria donated another group of objects. This comprised items from the diplomatic gift given to her in 1860 from Tokugawa Iemochi and consisted of swords, splendid Oyoroi armour as well as textiles, lacquer ware and ceramics. Sir Rutherford Alcock, the British Consul General in Japan at that time and later the organiser of the Japanese display at the 1862 London International Exhibition, negotiated with the Japanese authorities over the gift. Many of these objects given to the V&A by Queen Victoria were in turn given to what was then the Royal Museum in Edinburgh (now the National Museums of Scotland).

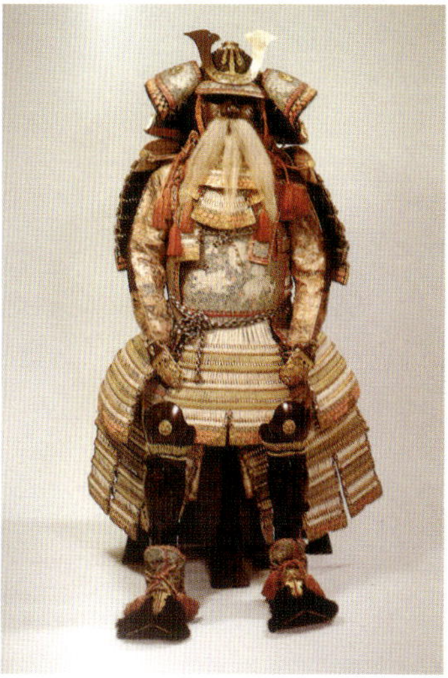

*Oyoroi armour presented to Queen Victoria by Tokugawa Iemochi in 1860: 362-1865*

Royal and diplomatic connections were to prove extremely beneficial to the Museum at many stages throughout its history of collecting. The V&A Japanese collections include many fine items that had been given as gifts and then passed on the Museum. For example there is a sword by Tomomitsu, dated equivalent to 1335, which was especially mounted for presentation to Sir Harry Parkes, Britain's first accredited minister in Japan, by the Emperor Meiji at a private audience in 1872 and which has a dedicatory inscription on the ō-zeppa. Another sword given by the widow of Sir Claude MacDonald, Britain's first full Ambassador in Japan (1905-1912), bears an inscription that indicates that the blade was made literally in front of MacDonald by Sugawara Kanenori, one of the Emperor Meiji's *Teishistu Gige'in* – Imperial Craftsmen.

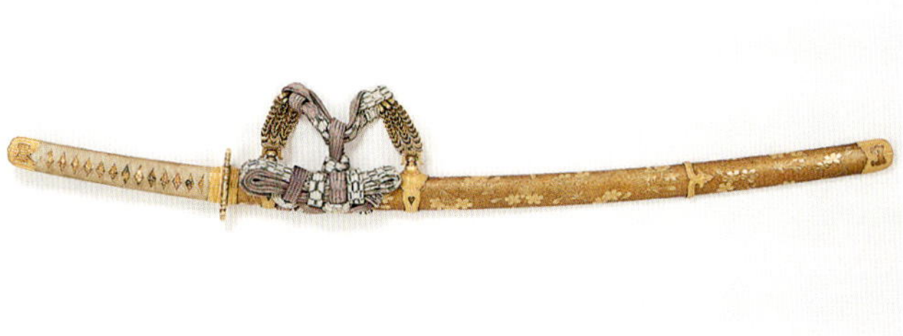

*Tachi presented to Sir Harry Parkes by Emperor Meiji, M.13-1949*

In the early 20th century two specialist curators were appointed to the V&A. The first, Edward Strange, specialised in, wrote extensively on and developed the collections of Japanese prints and printed books and in later years he worked on the V&A's lacquer collection. Albert Koop published very little but taxonomically catalogued and displayed the V&A's collection of several thousand *tsuba* and specialised in Japanese metalwork. This was a time when the V&A benefited from many significant gifts and bequests of Japanese objects, most notably the Salting bequest of metalwork and sword-fittings, lacquer ware and netsuke and in 1931 the extraordinary Hildburgh gift of over 2,500 items of Japanese metalwork, which consisted mostly of sword-fittings.

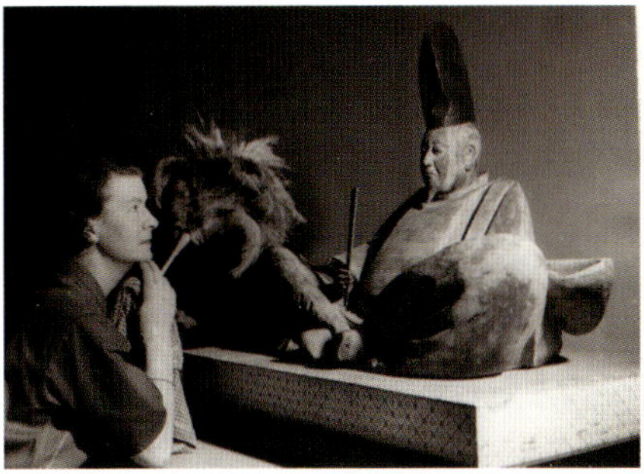

*Art treasures from Japan: Exhibition at the Victoria & Albert Museum, 1958*

The collections at the V&A had traditionally been divided according to material such as woodwork, metalwork, ceramics and textiles. It was not until the creation of the Far Eastern Department in 1970 that the Japanese collections were at last united under one culturally based department where specialist curators could work on objects within a clearly defined context. There was a gallery dedicated to Japanese art but in 1986 the Toshiba Gallery of Japanese Art opened (the first of the V&A's sponsored galleries) and the collections were presented for the first time in both material and themed displays. The display is a permanent one although sections are redisplayed from time to time. The Museum's collections were again restructured and the Japanese collections now fall under the auspices of the Asian Department.

Victoria & Albert Museum
Asian Department
Cromwell Road
London
SW7 2RL

Tel: 020 7942 2244
Fax: 020 7942 2252

far.east@vam.ac.uk
www.vam.ac.uk
iimages.vam.ac.uk – online image database of the collections

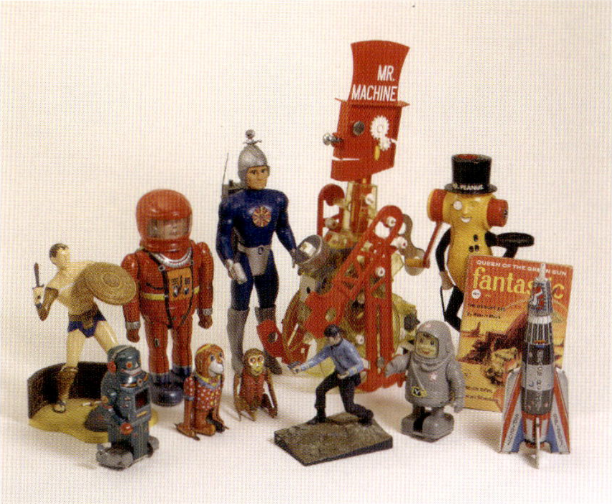


*Toys from the collection of the National Archive of Art & Design at the Victoria & Albert Museum*

## Wallace Collection

Hertford House was originally built as Manchester House in 1776-88 for the 4th Duke of Manchester. The house was leased as the French Embassy in 1836-50. After 1850, under the 4th Marquess of Hertford, it became little more than a store for his ever-growing collection of works of art. Major alterations, including purpose-built top-lit display galleries on the first floor, were carried out between 1872 and 1875 and then between 1897 and 1900 the house was converted into a public museum.

In 1890 Sir Richard Wallace bequeathed all his property to Lady Wallace (1818-97). It was almost certainly the loyal desire to fulfil her husband's wishes that led her to leave the Hertford House collection to the nation on her death. By the terms of Lady Wallace's bequest, the collection is named The Wallace Collection and it remains together "unmixed with other objects of art". Because nothing may therefore be loaned or added it enshrines an Anglo-French 19th-century taste. Among its many treasures is one of the finest collections of French 18th-century pictures, porcelain and furniture outside Paris, a remarkable display of 17th-century paintings and a superb armoury.

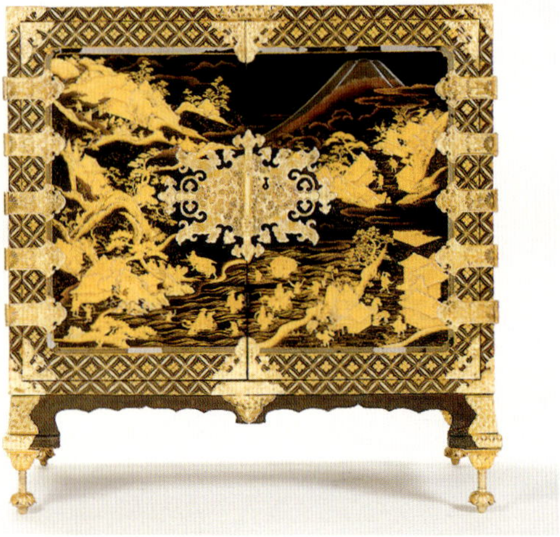

*Japanese lacquer cabinet and French stand, c.1680*

**Wallace Collection**
Hertford House
Manchester Square
London
W1U 3BN

Tel: 020 7563 9500
Fax: 020 7224 2155

www.wallacecollection.org

The Wallace Collection is perhaps best known for its magnificent French 18th-century paintings, miniatures and works of art (furniture, Sèvres porcelain, sculpture and gold boxes). The collections of old masters and 19th-century paintings, European and Oriental arms and armour, and medieval and renaissance works of art are also among the finest in the world.

Included in the collection are 21 Japanese objects, amongst which are fine lacquer ware (including boxes and cabinets, some with panels of Japanese lacquer mounted in Europe to European taste), weapons (including a very good *daisho*) and other examples of smaller furniture as well as incense burners.

### William Morris Gallery

The William Morris Gallery was opened by Prime Minister Clement Attlee in 1950 in what was the Morris family home from 1848 to 1856. Previously the Water House, it is a substantial Georgian dwelling of about 1750, set in its own extensive grounds. The collections illustrate William Morris' life, work and influence and there are permanent displays of printed, woven and embroidered fabrics, rugs, carpets, wallpapers, furniture, stained glass and painted tiles designed by Morris himself and by Edward Burne-Jones, Dante Gabriel Rossetti, Ford Madox Brown and others who together founded the firm of Morris, Marshall, Faulkner & Company in 1861.

**William Morris Gallery**
Lloyd Park
Forest Road
London
E17 4PP

Tel: 020 8527 3782
Fax: 020 8527 7070

W.Morris.Gallery@al.lbwf.gov.uk
www.lbwf.gov.uk/wmg

Sir Frank Brangwyn (who had worked with Urushibara Yoshijiro, the Japanese woodblock printmaker) donated a collection of his own work to the Gallery. This included a collection of between 20 and 30 Japanese woodblock prints by artists such as Hiroshige and Hokusai. These prints are held in the reserve collections of the Morris Gallery.

# Eastern England

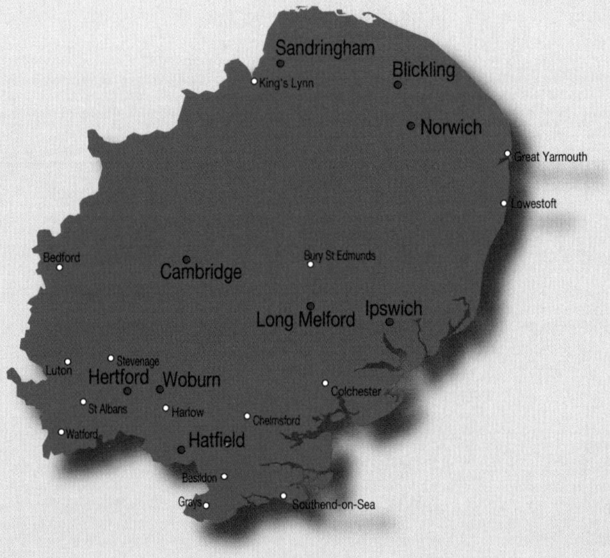

## Blickling

### Blickling Castle

Blickling Castle was built in the early 17th century for Sir Henry Hobart and is regarded as one of England's greatest Jacobean houses. Blickling is famous for its impressive long gallery with splendid plasterwork ceilings and a fine collection of furniture, pictures, books and tapestries. There are formal gardens and extensive parkland with a lake and woods. Blickling was left to the National Trust in 1940 and has been administered by it ever since.

There are few Japanese objects to be found at Blickling but, as may be expected in a grand house of this date, there are some interesting examples of Japanese export cabinets and some wonderful pieces of export Imari to be found throughout the house. There are also some significant examples of japanned European furniture and a Chinese-style bedroom.

Blickling Castle
Blickling
Nr. Norwich
Norfolk
NR11 6NF

Tel: 01263 738030
Fax: 01263 731660

blickling@nationaltrust.org.uk
http://www.nationaltrust.org.uk/places/blickling/

## Cambridge

### Fitzwilliam Museum

The Fitzwilliam Museum owes its foundation to Richard, 7th Viscount Fitzwilliam of Merrion who, in 1816, bequeathed to the University of Cambridge his works of art and library together with funds to house them in order to further "the Increase of Learning and other great Objects of that Noble Foundation". A noble wish indeed and one which many museums founded during the 18th and 19th centuries espoused. Fitzwilliam's bequest included 144 pictures, among them Dutch paintings he had inherited and masterpieces by artists such as Titian and Veronese that he had acquired at sale in London. His library included 130 medieval manuscripts and a collection of autographed music by many composers including Handel and Purcell. In 1848 the Founder's Building opened to the public.

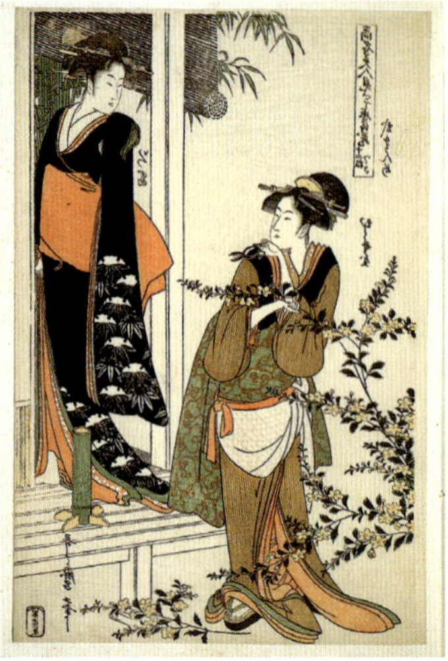

Kitagawa Utamaro, Act two from "The Chushingura parodied by famous beauties", P.349-1945, given by the Friends of the Fitzwilliam

Throughout the 19th and 20th centuries the collections have grown steadily by gift, bequest and purchase; their growth traces the history of collecting in this country over the last 200 years. The Japanese collections of the Fitzwilliam are divided between the Department of Paintings, Drawings and Prints and the Department of Applied Art. The former has a superb collection of some 2,500 prints (including 480 *surimono* and some fan prints), 400 drawings, 36 woodblock books and eight paintings that are all believed to be fakes or pastiches; the first acquisition of prints came in 1896. There are some extremely good impressions of prints by Hokusai and Hiroshige as well as a unique complete album of Utamaro's Chushingura (from the Edmond de Goncourt collection).

The Department of Applied Arts has some 1,300 Japanese objects in the collections plus about 300 objects on long-term loan from two private English collectors. The collections are extensive and of a high quality and include pottery and porcelain, lacquer (including inro), netsuke, textiles, fans, sculpture, swords and armour, sword furniture – including *tsuba*, sculpture and examples of metalwork. The strength of the collection lies in its ceramic holdings (including Sir Frank Brangwyn's collection of pottery and stoneware which was given by, and purchased from, Oscar Raphael) and in its lacquer collection. Although the collections are mostly from the Edo period, there is at least one example of early art to be found in a rather splendid Kofun-period (6th century) Haniwa figure. Interestingly the first recorded Japanese object in the Fitzwilliam's collection was a portable shrine of Manjusri (Monju Bosatsu) "brought from the temple at the British Embassy Jedo in 1860" and given to the Fitzwilliam in 1863.

**Fitzwilliam Museum**
Trumpington Street
Cambridge
CB2 1RB

Tel: 01233 332900
Fax: 01233 332933

fitzmuseum-enquiries@lists.cam.ac.uk

www.fitzmuseum.cam.ac.uk
www.fitzmuseum.cam.ac.uk/opac/public/info.htm (online database of the collections)
www.fitzmuseum.cam.ac.uk/japan/gallery/KUN/kunisada/intro/main.htm (online exhibition of Kunisada actor prints)

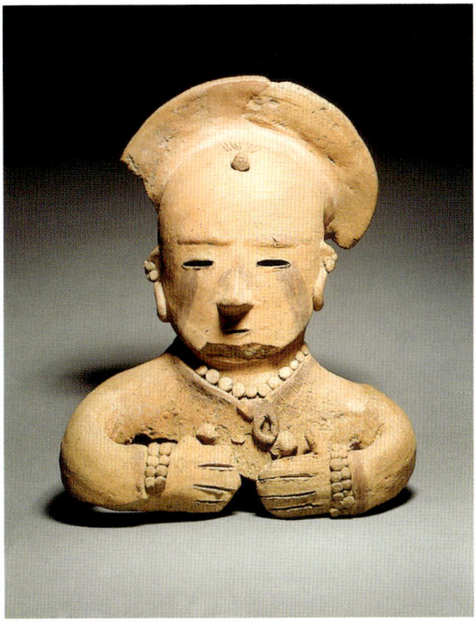

*Haniwa figure, Kofun period, C.397-1991, given by Mr & Mrs Conrad Abrahams-Cureil, in memory of their daughter, Eleanora*

### Museum of Archaeology and Anthropology

Established in 1884, the Museum displays prominent archaeological and anthropological collections from around the world. The ground-floor gallery displays collections of world prehistory and local archaeology; the first-floor gallery offers an historical and geographical display of the social anthropology collection. The top-floor galleries host special exhibitions reflecting current research interests in the faculty.

**Museum of Archaeology and Anthropology**
University of Cambridge
Downing Street
Cambridge
CB2 3DZ

Tel: 01223 333516
Fax: 01223 333517

museum-server.archanth.cam.ac.uk

A quick search on the Museum's database reveals some 876 Japanese artefacts that include prints, scrolls, writing equipment, netsuke, musical instruments, masks, personal items including clothing and accessories, domestic items and tools, armour and weapons, toys and games, smoking equipment and a large selection of religious and ceremonial equipment. There are, of course, also a large number of archaeological pieces including stone implements. Some objects in the collections were collected by explorers, missionaries and travellers such as the famous Scotsman, Dr. Neil Gordon Munro.

## Hatfield

### Hatfield House

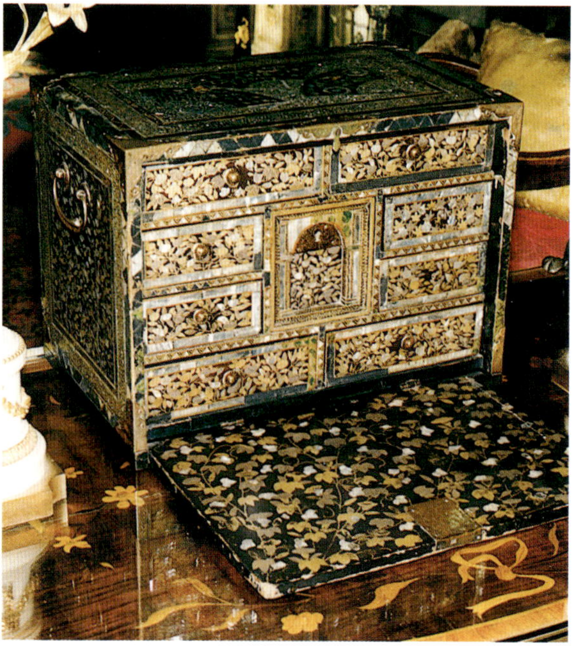

*Seventeenth century export lacquer cabinet*

Hatfield House was built for Robert Cecil, 1st Earl of Salisbury and Chief Minister to King James I, in 1611. This eminent Jacobean house has been in the Cecil family ever since, and is the home of the Marquess of Salisbury. The State Rooms are rich in world-famous paintings, exquisite furniture, fine tapestries and historic armour. Superb examples of Jacobean craftsmanship can be seen throughout Hatfield house, such as the Grand Staircase, with its wealth of lively detail carved in wood, and the rare stained-glass window in the private chapel.

**Hatfield House**
Hatfield
Hertfordshire
AL9 5NQ

Tel: 01707 287010
curator@hatfield-house.co.uk

www.hatfield-house.co.uk

The house contains a few good pieces of Imari porcelain and also has an interesting small, drop-front export lacquer cabinet in typical Namban style that may have been acquired in the early 17th century.

## Hertford

### Hertford Museum

Hertford Museum was originally founded in 1903 and is today located in an early 17th-century town house with a recreated Jacobean-style knot garden of intertwined hedges of box and lavender. The displays depict Hertford's historic past as a royal borough and the collections include material related to the Hertfordshire Regiment. Objects cover archaeology, coins and medals, costume and textiles, decorative and applied art, fine art, social history and world cultures.

The Japanese collections number around 80 objects and include arms and armour, costume and personal accessories, toys and tools. The two founders of the Museum were the local businessmen and brothers Robert Thornton Andrews and William Frampton Andrews. Their youngest brother, Walter, travelled to Japan in 1878; he became rector of Middleton St. George and was appointed Bishop of Hokkaido in 1909. One of the Andrews sisters also travelled to Japan and met and married Dr. John Batchelor, the renowned scholar/missionary of the Ainu culture. The suit of armour, (which is generally on display), was a gift from the collection of Dr. John Batchelor.

**Hertford Museum**
18 Bull Plain
Hertford
SG14 1DT

Tel: 01992 582686

www.hertford.net/museum

# Ipswich

## Ipswich Museum

Ipswich Museum was founded on the Victorian objective of "uniting art and science". The Museum building bears the date 1880 and one wing of the Museum has a large cartouche bearing the words "Science and Art Schools" – much as the Victoria & Albert Museum in London, also founded on the twin principles of art and science has these two words inscribed on parts of the building.

The Museum's collections include archaeology, costume and textiles, science and technology and world cultures. There is a small collection of Japanese objects that includes a few carvings (netsuke and *okimono*), personal accessories (smoking sets), some ceramics, hair adornments and arms and armour. It is in this last area that the strengths of the collections lie. There are two full sets of armour plus a further two helmets (one by a maker of the Myochin family) as well as swords and sword-fittings. The swords are not in the best of polish, but there is an interesting oversize dedicatory sword in the collection.

Ipswich Museum
High Street
Ipswich
Suffolk
IP1 3QH

Tel: 01473 213761

museums.service@
ipswich.gov.uk
www.ipswich.gov.uk/
tourism/guide/museum.
htm

# Long Melford

## Melford Hall

Melford Hall has been the home of the Hyde Parker family since 1786. The exterior of the house has changed little since 1578 when Queen Elizabeth I was entertained here and it retains its original panelled banqueting hall. There is a Regency library, Victorian bedrooms, good collections of furniture and porcelain and a small display of items connected with Beatrix Potter, who was related to the family. Melford Hall contains a collection of Chinese and Japanese porcelain, especially Japanese Imari ware and there is a large charger with a central coat of arms that was probably intended for the Dutch market of around 1710.

Melford Hall
Long Melford
Sudbury
Suffolk
CO10 9AA

Tel: 01787 880286

melford@
nationaltrust.org.uk
www.nationaltrust.org.uk

Norwich Castle Museum and Art Gallery
Castle Meadow
Norwich
Norfolk
NR1 3JU

Tel: 01603 493625
Fax: 01603 493623

museums@norfolk.gov.uk
www.norfolk.gov.uk/leisure/museums/castle.htm

# Norwich

## Norwich Castle Museum and Art Gallery

Norwich Castle Museum and Art Gallery has collections of archaeology, natural history and fine art. The collections of paintings are, not surprisingly, strong in the East Anglian schools with paintings by artists such as Cotman. The decorative arts are well represented with Lowestoft porcelain and Norwich silver being predominant. In 1956 Norwich Castle Museum donated its entire ethnographic collection (including a significant number of Japanese items) to the Liverpool Museum; consequently there is little remaining today apart from a small collection of arms and armour that includes a few interesting swords.

## Sainsbury Centre for Visual Arts

The Sainsbury Centre for Visual Arts is one of the UK's leading galleries and is situated just outside Norwich on the campus of the University of East Anglia. The Robert and Lisa Sainsbury Collection was given to the University of East Anglia in 1973 and is housed in two buildings designed by Norman Foster. The collection combines modern Western art with fine and applied arts from Africa, the Pacific, the Americas, Asia, Egypt, medieval Europe and the ancient Mediterranean. The collection is particularly well-known for works by Francis Bacon, John Davies, Alberto Giacometti and Henry Moore.

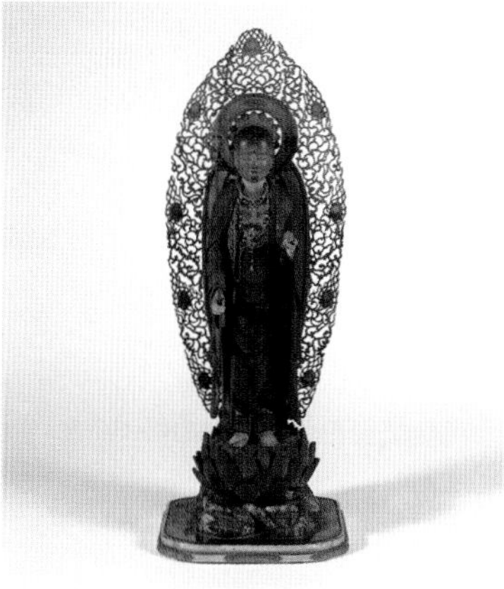

*Standing Jizo Bosatsu, Kamakura period*

There are now over 1,200 items in the collection and around 450 objects are on permanent display; of this collection some 140 are Japanese objects. Lord and Lady Sainsbury began to seriously collect Japanese art from the early 1960s and have been acquiring ever since. The strengths of the Japanese collections lie in the prehistoric, Buddhist and Shinto objects that have been so generously given and acquired for the Centre. *Jomon* pottery features in the collections as do sculptures in wood, bronze and clay. There are also fine examples of lacquer ware (a superb Negoro vase comes to mind) and paintings. Religious works are an important feature of the collection. The Sainsbury Collection's most recent acquisition is an elegant 12th-century wooden statue of a standing Jizo Bosatsu.

**Sainsbury Centre for Visual Arts**
University of East Anglia
Norwich
Norfolk
NR4 7TJ

Tel: 01603 593199

scva@uea.ac.uk
www.uea.ac.uk/scva

### Sainsbury Institute

In 1999 the Sainsbury Institute for the Study of Japanese Arts and Cultures (SISJAC) was founded by Lord and Lady Sainsbury with the aim: "To promote the study of the material and visual cultures of the Japanese archipelago, and in doing so act as a catalyst for international research in the field". Linked to both the University of East Anglia and the School of Oriental and African Studies in London, SISJAC has one of the best libraries devoted to Japanese art studies in Europe. SISJAC also has its own study collections in the form of a large collection of Japanese and European maps of Japan on long-term loan – with a view to donation – from Sir Hugh Cortazzi, a former ambassador to Japan who has already made a generous donation of over 1,000 books to the SISJAC library. This collection includes several unique maps, the earliest dating from 1528, as well as some rare ceramics.

**Sainsbury Institute**
64 The Close
Norwich
Norfolk
NR1 4DW

Tel: 01603 624349
Fax: 01603 625011

sisjac@
sainsbury-institute.org
www.sainsbury-institute.
org

# Saffron Walden

## Audley End House and Gardens

Audley End House was built in 1614 for Thomas, first Earl of Suffolk, on the scale of a royal palace, to entertain King James I who joked that it was too big for a king, but not for a Lord Treasurer. Charles II bought the house in 1668 and used it as a base when he attended the races at Newmarket. During the 18th century the fortunes of the house's owners declined and in 1745 it was bought by the Countess of Portsmouth for her nephew and heir, Sir John Griffin Griffin (4th Baron Howard de Walden and first Baron Braybrooke). He immediately began changes to the house and by the time of his death in 1797, he had added a suite of neo-classical rooms and a Gothic chapel designed by Robert Adam. The ever-busy Capability Brown had also been employed to remodel the grounds. The house was inherited by the 3rd Baron Braybrooke in 1825 who installed his extensive picture collection and filled the rooms with furnishings.

**Audley End House and Gardens**
Saffron Walden
Essex
CB11 4JF

Infoline: 01799 522399

customers@english-heritage.org.uk
www.english-heritage.org.uk

The Japanese holdings at Audley End are not extensive and there are less than 40 objects in the collection, which is not well documented. There are a few examples of export lacquer furniture to be found in the public rooms, as well as ceramics. The ceramics include a mix of 17th-century export porcelain as well as what appear to be late 19th-century tourist pieces.

## Saffron Walden Museum

The Saffron Walden Museum was first opened in 1835 by the Saffron Walden Natural History Society. The Museum's collections include displays about local history and archaeology as well as collections of natural history, furniture, decorative arts and anthropology. The main building is in the medieval centre of the town next to the ruins of the castle.

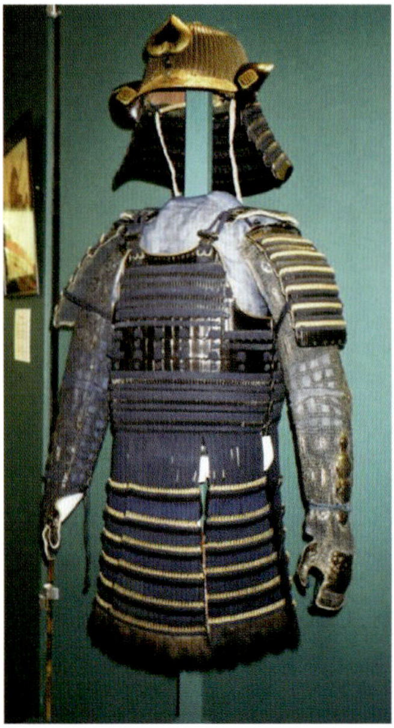

Composite suit of armour

**Saffron Walden Museum**
Museum Street
Saffron Walden
Essex
CB10 1JL

Tel: 01799 510333
Fax: 01799 510550

museum@
uttlesford.goc.uk
www.uttlesford.gov.uk

There are more than 50 Japanese objects in the collection, which includes decorative bronzes, arms and armour, mirrors, lacquer ware, graphic works, domestic and personal items (including clothing). There have been donations from local benefactors and the earliest object to enter the collection appears to be a lacquer box acquired around the time of the Museum's opening in 1835. There is no special display of Japanese objects as such, but the armour and other objects are used in temporary exhibitions.

## Sandringham

### Sandringham

Sandringham was built in 1870 by the Prince and Princess of Wales, later King Edward VII and Queen Alexandra and is now the private country house of Her Majesty The Queen and His Royal Highness The Duke of Edinburgh. The main ground-floor rooms, regularly used by the royal family, are open to the public during the summer months.

Sandringham
Norfolk
PE35 6EN

Estate Office:
Tel: 01553 772675
Fax: 01485 541571

www.sandringhamestate.co.uk

Both Queen Alexandra and later Queen Mary were great collectors and there is a large collection of porcelain, jade and crystal oriental figures. Members of the Russian and European royal families were frequent guests at Sandringham and brought gifts of enamel, silver and silver-gilt. There is an important collection of oriental arms and armour that had been brought back from the Far East and India in 1876. Among the extensive display of sporting guns there is an interesting pair of signed Japanese carbines from around 1870 which are unusual in that they are modelled on Western patterns.

## Woburn

### Woburn Abbey

Woburn Abbey has its roots in the monastic buildings constructed around 1145 for a group of Cistercian monks. The north wing of the present building is on the site of the monastic church and the present courtyard is on the site of the original cloister. Edward VI granted Woburn Abbey to Sir John Russell in 1547 although it did not become a family home until 1619.

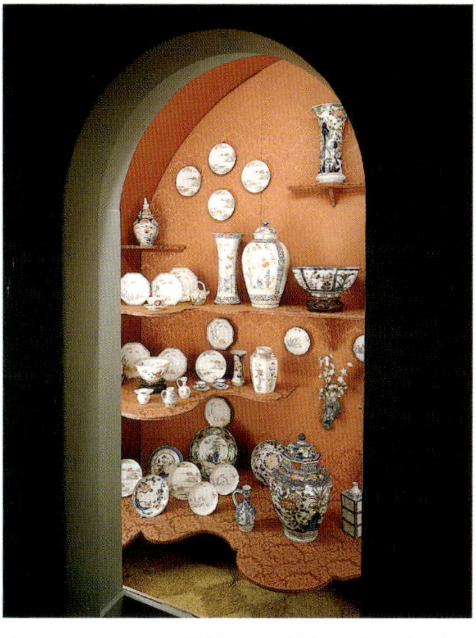

*Japanese alcore at Woburn Abbey showing kakiemon porcelain*

In 1747, the 4th Duke of Bedford commissioned the services of the Palladian architect Henry Flitcroft who rebuilt Woburn Abbey into most of what we see today. The next major building period was in 1786 under the direction of Henry Holland. In 1802 Humphrey Repton landscaped the park. Today Woburn Abbey is home to the Marquess of Tavistock, the son of the present Duke of Bedford.

Woburn has a superb collection of Venetian views by Canaletto; the 4th Duke visited Venice while on the Grand Tour in 1731. The paintings were subsequently commissioned and over the next few years arrived at Bedford House in London, where they remained until it was demolished in 1800; the paintings have been at Woburn Abbey since that time. There are also superb paintings by Van Dyck, Gainsborough, Reynolds and Velasquez as well as French and English furniture and silverware and a famous collection of Sèvres porcelain that had been presented to the 4th Duke by Louis XV of France.

The Japanese collection here is small, but contains a pair of lacquer export cabinets and a fine collection of Kakiemon porcelain most of which is displayed in the Japanese Alcove in Woburn Abbey crypt.

Woburn Abbey
Bedfordshire
MK17 9WA

Tel: 01525 290666
Fax: 01525 290271

enquiries@
woburnabbey.co.uk
www.woburnabbey.co.uk

# East Midlands

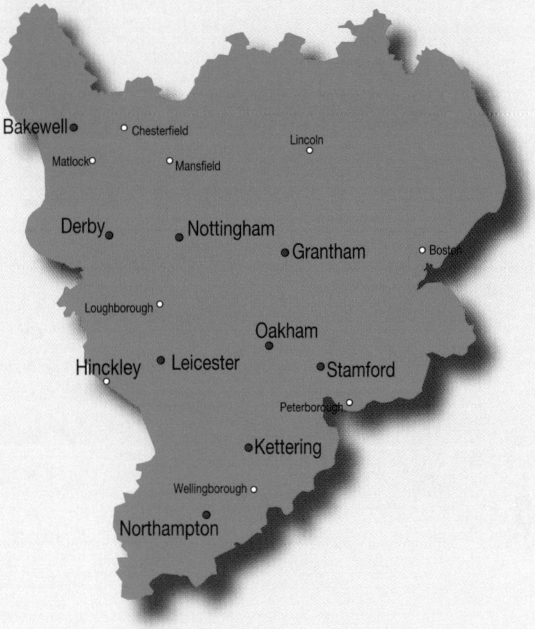

# Bakewell

## Chatsworth

Chatsworth was first built by Bess of Hardwicke in 1552 and has been owned and lived in by the Cavendish family ever since. The first Duke of Devonshire rebuilt Chatsworth in the classical style between 1686 and 1707, with the Library and North Wing added by the 6th Duke between 1790 and 1858. The park was landscaped by the 4th Duke (1720-1764), who engaged Capability Brown to reshape the formal garden. There are some 26 rooms open to the public and they contain paintings by artists such as Rembrandt, Tintoretto, Landseer and Sargent as well as superb painted ceilings and fine furniture and tapestries.

Chatsworth
Bakewell
Derbyshire
DE45 1PP

Tel: 01246 565300
Fax: 01246 583536

visit@chatsworth.org
www.chatsworth-house.co.uk

There is an outstanding collection of silverware and European and Oriental porcelain. There are nearly 100 examples of Japanese art held at Chatsworth and most are on display in the public rooms. These include Japanese export furniture, fine porcelain and some examples of metalwork. The current Duchess of Devonshire is the granddaughter of Algernon Bertram Mitford (1837-1916) who served with the British legation in Japan during the turbulent years 1866-1870.

# Derby

## Derby Museum and Art Gallery

Derby Museum and Art Gallery houses a wide range of important collections that include porcelain (especially Derby porcelain that has been produced in the city since around 1750), paintings and local archaeology and history. There are also many paintings by the celebrated 18th-century Derby artist Joseph Wright, A.R.A. (1734-97), which include portraits, landscapes, subjects from literature and scenes of industry and scientific equipment. The Archaeology Gallery contains local material from the Stone Age

Derby Museum and Art
Gallery
The Strand
Derby
DE1 1BS

Tel: 01332 716659

to the Middle Ages, with several fine Anglo-Saxon crosses and a splendid sarcophagus. There are also two Egyptian mummies.

Within the collection are about 30 Japanese objects including ceramics, prints and armour – none of which are on permanent display.

## Grantham

### Belton

Belton is an Anglo-Dutch Restoration house built in the last years of Charles II's reign between 1685 and 1688. In the 1770s the house was altered by the architect James Wyatt. The Brownlow and Cust families have had a long association with Belton House. They were the descendants of a wealthy Elizabethan lawyer who bought the estate in 1617 and family portraits are displayed in nearly every room, including one by Sir Joshua Reynolds of Sir John Cust, Speaker of the House of Commons from 1761 to 1770.

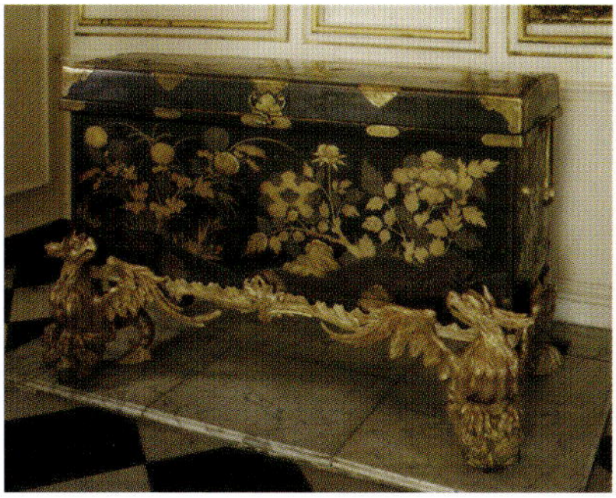

*Lacquer chest at Belton House*

Belton
Grantham
Lincolnshire
NG32 2LS

Tel: 01476 566116

belton@
nationaltrust.org.uk
www.nationaltrust.org.
uk/main

The interior holds a collection of good-quality furniture, outstanding wall mirrors, tapestries, silver and the remnants of a collection of old masters. There is also a collection of oriental porcelain including many examples of Japanese Imari and other export pieces. There are a few examples of export lacquer including a most splendid Namban chest on a European stand.

## Kettering

### Boughton House

**Boughton House**
Kettering
Northamptonshire
NN14 1BJ

Tel: 01536 515731
Fax: 01536 417255

llt@boughtonhouse.org.uk
www.boughtonhouse.org.uk

Since 1528 Boughton House has been home to the Duke of Buccleuch and Queensbury KT and the Montagu family, his ancestors. The early Tudor monastic building was added to over the years with the final major addition being in the French-style around 1695. Boughton has been described as "England's Versailles". The main collections are French and English porcelain, textiles and furniture of the 17th and 18th centuries along with paintings by artists such as El Greco and sketches by Van Dyck. There are some examples of 17th-century Japanese export furniture to be found around the house as well as some swords (including a *katana* apparently dated to the 15th century) in the armoury.

## Leicester

### New Walk Museum and Art Gallery

New Walk Museum and Art Gallery is situated within the historic New Walk area of Leicester. In 1849 the Literary and Philosophical Society formally presented to the town its various collections, which have grown and developed over the last 150 years. The Museum has extensive collections that cover both the natural and cultural world.

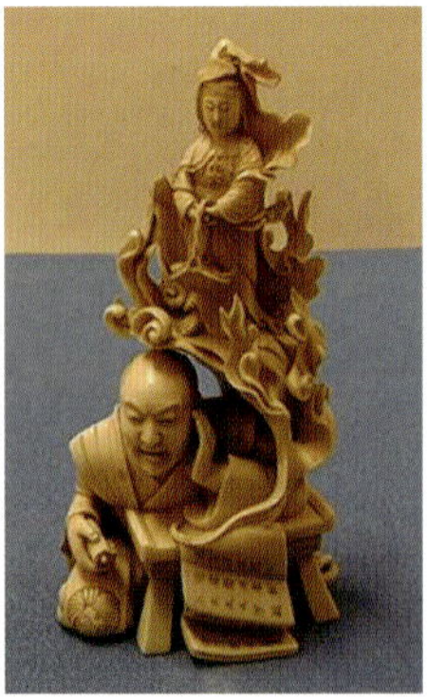

*Ivory okimono*

The main galleries of the Museum include works by Bacon, Degas, Lowry, Pissaro and Spencer. Other notable collections are those of European art dating from the 15th century to the present day. The Museum has an internationally recognised collection of 20th-century German art and one of the finest collections of German Expressionist art in the UK. Leicester is one of the most culturally diverse cities in the UK and has space for different cultures and faiths to present their own interpretations of life in Leicester and to interact with the collections.

There are about 400 Japanese objects in the Museum's collections and these include netsuke, *okimono*, lacquer (including inro), swords and sword furniture, pipe cases and personal accessories, metalwork, baskets, textiles, and ceramics. The Museum has had several significant bequests of objects; in 1924 and 1927 it received the George and Mary Hodge bequest of mostly 19th- century objects such as ivory carvings, lacquer and swords, many of high quality. The Livingstone bequest of ivory carvings and the Dryad collection of folk art and crafts also contributed interesting objects. There is usually a small selection of Japanese objects on display at any time although at the time of writing the gallery is closed for building work but due to open some time in 2004.

**New Walk Museum and Art Gallery**
53 New Walk
Leicester
LE1 7EA

Tel: 0116 225 4900
Fax: 0116 225 4927

www.leicestermuseums.ac.uk

## Nottingham

### Castle Museum and Art Gallery

The original Nottingham Castle was almost completely destroyed after the Civil War but was replaced by a mansion in 1674 which, in 1875, was converted into a municipal museum and art gallery for fine and applied arts. The museum contains objects relating to Nottingham's history and has collections of ceramics, silver and glass, and military displays as well as a fine art collection.

The Nottingham Museum collections include approximately 700 objects that have been catalogued as Japanese. These items are housed at three of the Nottingham Museum sites: Nottingham Castle Museum, the Museum of Costume and Textiles and Brewhouse Yard Museum. These collections include metalwork (mainly arms and armour including complete armours and parts) *tsuba*, *kozuka*, polearms, bow, quivers and arrowheads; about 200 19th- and 20th-century prints; around 20 ceramics and more than 30 examples of costume and textiles.

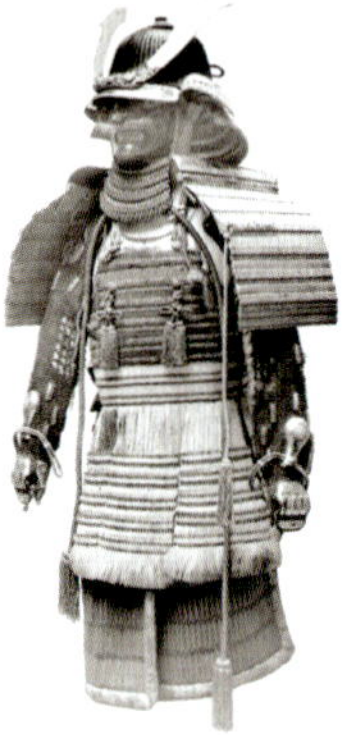

*Composite suit of armour*

Perhaps the most significant gift of Japanese art to the Museum was the Bowden collection of Japanese arms and armour, made in 1921 by Sir Frank Bowden, the first director of Raleigh Cycles in Nottingham. "His [Sir Frank Bowden's] interest in the Orient led him in 1915 to acquire the Japanese arms and armour collection of Renier de Bourbon who had inherited it from a relation, the Comte de Chambord. It is not known how the Comte de Chambord amassed the collection but it was probably through dealers after the Japanese imperial edict of 1876 abolishing the Samurai. A few pieces were given to Sir Frank's grandson, the present Sir Frank Bowden, who gave a Japanese Officer's sword in 1963." (From *Nottingham City Museum & Art Gallery Collecting Policy 1995-2000*.)

At the Castle Museum there is a suit of armour on display as well as at least one sword and some sword-fittings. There are occasional displays of prints at the castle and the Museum of Costume and Textiles has included Japanese objects in its displays.

**Castle Museum and Art Gallery**
Nottingham
NG1 6EL

Tel: 0115 915 3700

castle@ncmg.demon.co.uk
www.nottinghamcity.gov.uk/whatson/museums/castle.asp

# Northampton

## Central Museum and Art Gallery

Northampton Museum and Art Gallery has an extremely good collection of boots and shoes. There are also collections of ceramics, paintings and archaeology. There are only some 60 examples of Japanese art in the collections and these include swords, armour, metalwork and ceramics, as well as ethnographic objects including what appears to be an *ema* – a votive board. Documentation states that this was bought from a temple in Kyoto in 1892 by one E.F. Noel. Very little of the collection is on display.

There is a second collection in Northampton at the Abington Museum.

**Central Museum and Art Gallery**
Guildhall Road
Northampton
NN1 1DP

Tel: 01604 838111

museums@northampton.gov.uk
www.northampton.gov.uk/museums

## Abington Museum

This is a museum housed in a 15th-century manor house and has collections of local interest including galleries of Northampton's military history and houses the collections of the Northamptonshire Regimental Museum. These collections contain a considerable amount of World War II material associated with the regiment's time in the Far East and include many surrender swords, Japanese rifles, Japanese military insignia, captured flags and some sketches of scenes in Changi Gaol. While not 'art objects' as we may consider them they are, nevertheless, of some poignant interest.

**Abington Museum**
Abington Park
Northampton
NN1 5LW

Tel: 01604 631454

# Stamford

## Burghley House

Burghley House is regarded as one of the finest Elizabethan buildings in England and has been the home of the Cecil family for over 400 years. The house was completed in 1587 by Sir William Cecil, later Lord Burghley, who was principal adviser and Lord Treasurer to Queen Elizabeth I. Some of the interiors of the house were remodelled in the late 17th century by John, 5th Earl of Exeter who was a collector on a grand scale and visited Italy on three occasions and established a huge collection of art treasures at Burghley. The 9th Earl went on four Italian tours and added to the already vast collection of paintings, furniture, porcelain and furniture. He also commissioned Capability Brown to landscape the park from 1756.

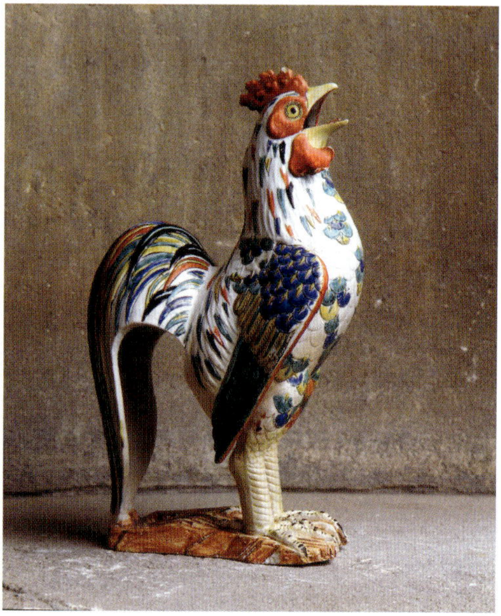

*Kakiemon cockerel*

The house includes the work of the wood carvers Grinling Gibbons and Jonathan Maine and plasterer Edward Martin. There are paintings by Kneller, Lely, Gainsborough, Giordano, Guido Reni, Pieter Breughel, Joos van Cleve, Giordano and Antonio Verrio. Burghley's collections of furniture and sculpture are equally impressive and reflect the taste of the 17th and 18th centuries. The European pottery and porcelain collection is extensive with examples from many important ceramic centres in Europe. There are a number of exceptional pieces, particularly the superb examples of majolica collected by the 9th Earl in the 1760s.

**Burghley House**
Stamford
Lincolnshire
PE9 3JY

Tel: 01780 752 451
Fax: 01780 480 125

info@burghley.co.uk
www.burghley.co.uk

As well as examples of Japanese export lacquer there is, perhaps more importantly, a superb collection of late17th-century Japanese porcelain, much of which features in an inventory of the Burghley House collections made in 1688. The Japanese collection today numbers in excess of 500 objects, most of which is porcelain and a considerable number of these pieces are on display in the public rooms. The collection was once much larger but two sales from the collections (in 1888 and 1959) certainly reduced the number of Japanese objects in the house. There are exceptional examples of Kakiemon porcelain, particularly figural pieces (for example, pairs of elephants, dogs, birds and sumo wrestlers).

# West Midlands

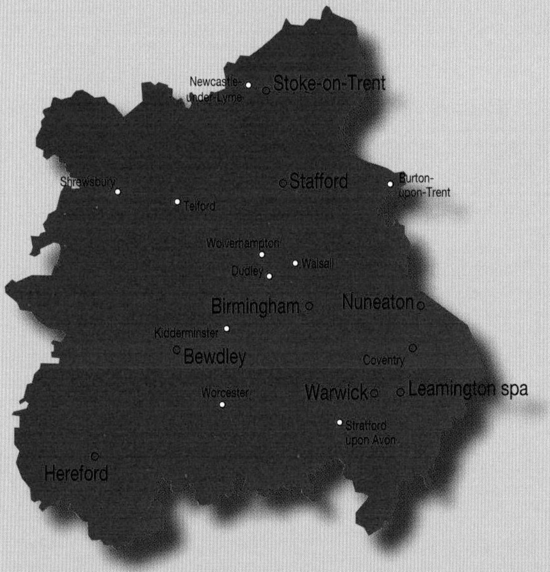

# Bewdley

## Bewdley Museum

The Japanese collections of the Bewdley Museum all came from the Kidderminster Museum and Art Gallery, which closed in 1990. There are more than 100 ivory carvings in the collection including netsuke and *okimono*, mostly dating to the 19th century. There is a potentially interesting group of late 19th-century hanging paintings as well as a few examples of weaponry, ceramics, lacquer and some items of footwear. There is, unfortunately, no permanent display of the Japanese collection although, periodically, thematic displays might include Japanese objects. It is, of course, possible to view objects in storage by prior appointment.

**Bewdley Museum**
Load Street
Bewdley
Worcestershire
DY14 9PA

Tel: 01299 403573
Fax: 01299 404740

bewdley.museum@wyreforestdc.gov.uk
bewdleymuseum.tripod.com

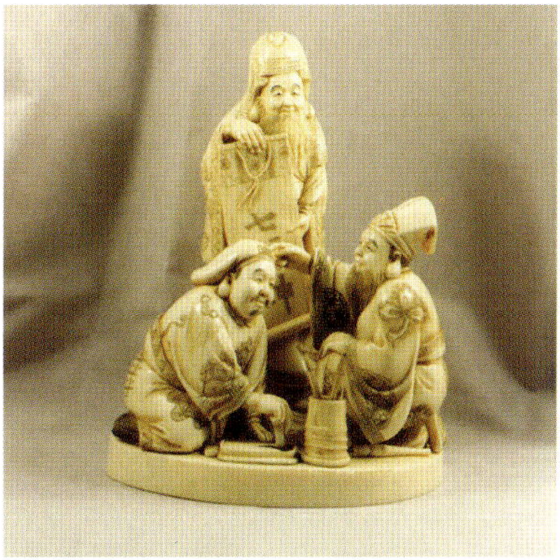

*Ivory okimono*

# Birmingham

## Birmingham Museum & Art Gallery

Birmingham Museum & Art Gallery was founded in 1885 and its collections cover fine and applied arts, archaeology and ethnography as well as local and industrial history. Prior to the opening by the then Prince of Wales (later Edward VII) there had been various small private collections open to the public. By the middle of the 19th century Birmingham's prominent citizens argued that what was needed was a city museum showing the best industrial design from around the world, "a local collection to rival South Kensington or the collections of continental European cities". As with the founding principles of the South Kensington Museum (the V&A) so the city's leading industrialists thought that exposure to good design and art education could only improve manufacturing quality in the 'City of a Thousand Trades' and philanthropists argued that the fortunes of the working man would be bettered by exposure to art and natural history. The current building houses a Japanese gallery and special exhibitions are often held in the adjacent restored Gas Hall.

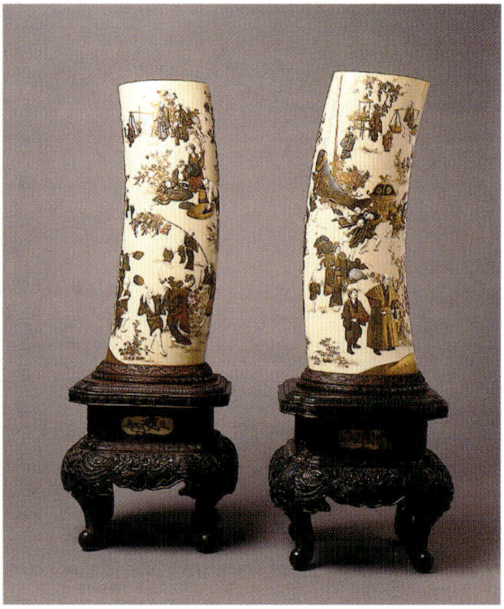

*Shibayama decorated ivory tusks; 1890 M 108.1&2*

The Japanese collection of Birmingham Museum & Art Gallery is certainly one of the finest regional collections in the UK. There is an extensive and important collection of sword furniture that was created partly in response to the Museum's early priority for the establishment of an international metalwork collection. Birmingham's industrialists were fascinated by the extensive and creative use of alloys by traditional Japanese metalworkers. The collection includes over 500 *tsuba*, ranging in date from the 16th to the 20th centuries. There are also several complete suits of armour, swords and other fittings.

Other Japanese material comprises lacquer (including inro), some textiles, and ivory carvings (including netsuke, *okimono* and tusks) as well as ceramics. One of the Museum's glories is the collection of well over 600 prints, illustrated books and albums, most of which were collected by the donor, Henry Watson Smith, in 1926. It would appear from records that he had himself collected around 1900, with the help of at least one leading dealer in Paris. The collection includes early masters such as Moronobu and Masanobu as well as later exponents of *ukiyoe* such as Utamaro and Toyokuni: there are also works by Hiroshige and Hokusai. A recent discovery in the collections has been an album of 81 oban-size kabuki actor prints, all in excellent condition. These have all been recently catalogued and a small exhibition was mounted in 2002.

**Birmingham Museum & Art Gallery**
Chamberlain Square
Birmingham
Warwickshire
B3 3DH

Tel: 0121 303 2834
Fax: 0121 303 1394

www.bmag.org.uk
www.bmag.org.uk/museum_and_art_gallery

## Coventry

### Herbert Art Gallery and Museum

In 1834 the minutes of the Coventry Mechanics Institute recorded that "the want of such an institution [art gallery and museum] in this city has long been experienced". It was not until 1938 that Sir Alfred Herbert (whose company was once the world's largest machine tool manufacturer) presented Coventry city with a donation of £100,000 for the erection of an art gallery and museum. Building work began in 1939, but at the outbreak of war all work was suspended and the basement, which was all that had been completed, was used as an air raid shelter.

When the war was over most of the city centre lay in ruins. As a result a new site was allocated for the Art Gallery and fresh plans drawn up for a building which, in design, would be more in keeping with the new city centre. Building work recommenced in July 1955 and Sir Alfred gave a further £100,000 towards the project. Finally, in March 1960 Lady Herbert, Sir Alfred's widow, declared the Art Gallery and Museum open.

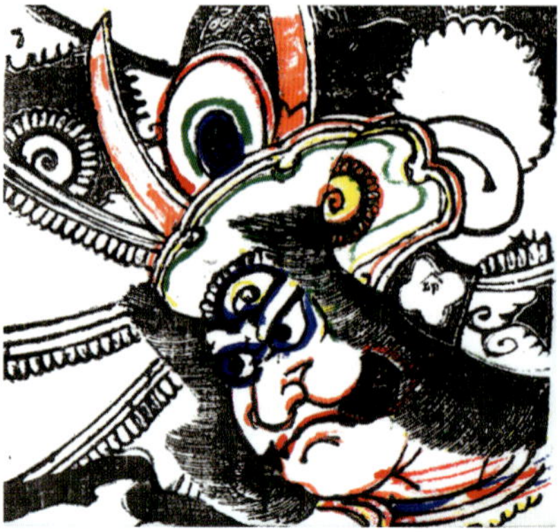

*Preparatory study for a kite, Kanno Yuji, 1995*

**Herbert Art Gallery and Museum**
Jordan Well
Coventry
Warwickshire
CV1 5QP

Tel: 024 7683 2381
Fax: 024 7683 2410

artsandheritage@coventry.gov.uk
www.coventrymuseum.org.uk

The Art Gallery and Museum has displays from the permanent collections that include natural history, social history and art. The Herbert Art Gallery and Museum reflects Coventry city's heritage through industry, culture and arts. The Japanese holdings are small with only some 30 objects; these include examples of Seto ware, *ukiyoe* prints (Kunisada, Eishi, and Toyokuni) as well as 20th-century prints by Urushibara and Hiroshi Yoshida. The largest part of the collection consists of contemporary works on paper (preparatory drawings for kites) by Kanno Yuji that were given to the Museum in 1995.

## Hereford

### Hereford Museum

Hereford Museum first opened in 1874, when many wealthy and philanthropic businessmen and enlightened local authorities, perhaps influenced by the works of Prince Albert, were realising that education was one route out of grinding poverty. Consequently movements such as that headed by the wealthy local Hereford landowner, James Rankin, raised money and worked with the local council to create the Free Library and Museum; the building opened on 10th October 1874 and in its decoration and the symbolism of the motifs used was an art work in its own right.

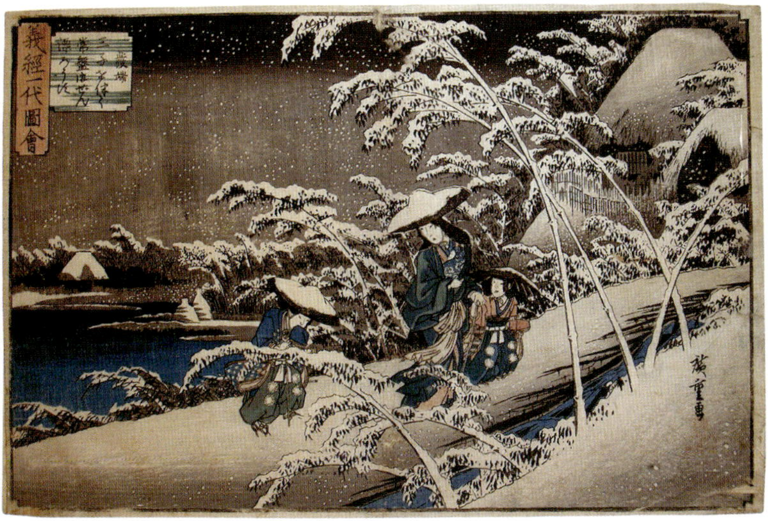

*Tokiwa's fight through the snow with her children, Ando Hiroshige, c. 1833*

The Hereford Library Committee noted in 1898: "A museum has become a necessity to modern education and no town professing to possess requisite educational means should be without one". In May 1915 proper cataloguing of the collections in an accession register began; because no lists were written before that time provenance of the collections has been difficult to establish.

Hereford Museum has only about 50 Japanese objects in the collection and as well as the few ceramics there is a collection of 32 prints, bequeathed in 1948 and including works by Hiroshige, Hokusai, Shunsho and Utamaro. Unfortunately none of the Japanese collection is on permanent display.

**Hereford Museum**
Broad Street
Hereford
Herefordshire
HR4 9AU

Tel: 01432 260692
Fax: 01432 342492

www.herefordshire.gov.uk

## Leamington Spa

### Leamington Spa Art Gallery and Museum

Leamington Spa was, until about 1800, a small village. The mineral springs to be found here were known in the Middle Ages, but it was not until 1784 that the village began to rediscover the springs and build baths around some of them.

In July 1814 The Royal Pump Room and Baths were officially opened. The Spa treatment was claimed to cure all manner of ailments. The Pump Room gardens were originally laid out and enclosed for the exclusive use of the patrons of the Pump Room "to afford them pleasant promenades". It was not until 1875 that the Pump Room Gardens became public.

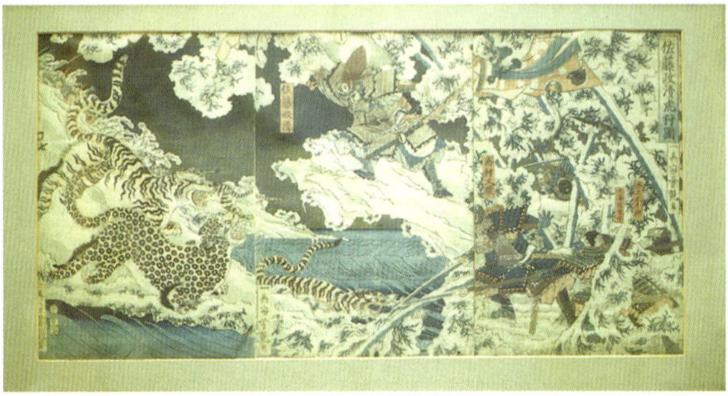

*Sato's Tiger Hunt, A580.1968.8*

**Leamington Spa Art Gallery and Museum**
Royal Pump Rooms
The Parade
Leamington Spa
Warwickshire
CV32 4AA

Tel: 01926 724700
Fax: 01926 742705

prooms@warwickdc.gov.uk
www.royal-pump-rooms.co.uk

Physiotherapy and hydrotherapy treatments remained available at the Pump Rooms until the late 20th century, but by the 1990s there were proposals from the council to relocate Leamington's Art Gallery and Museum to the Pump Rooms and the new building opened in 1999.

The collections include archaeology, ceramics and glass as well as paintings, drawings and sculpture, and the Japanese collections, of which only a few are on display, number only 43. They include prints, coins, ceramics and sword accessories.

## Nuneaton

### Arbury Hall

Arbury Hall is an Elizabethan house, built on the site of a 12th-century Augustinian Priory and has been the home of the Newdegate family for over 400 years. It was remodelled in the 18th century to become a splendid example of Gothic Revival architecture. The house contains fine collections of antique furniture,

**Arbury Hall**
Nuneaton
Warwickshire
CV10 7PT

Tel: 012476 382 804
Fax: 012476 641 147

**Nuneaton Museum and Art Gallery**
Riversley Park
Nuneaton
Warwickshire
CV11 5TU

Tel: 024 7635 0720
Fax: 024 7634 3559

museum@nuneatonandbedworth.gov.uk
www.nuneatonandbedworth.gov.uk/leisure/museum

pictures, glass and porcelain that can be seen in many of the rooms that are on view to the public.

Among the porcelain collection there are some good examples of Japanese Kakiemon and Arita ware, many of which can be seen in the dining room on (and under) the Jacobean furniture.

### Nuneaton Museum and Art Gallery

The Museum is perhaps best known for its displays relating to George Eliot who was born in Nuneaton. There is a small collection of World Culture objects that includes about 48 Japanese objects; these include swords and daggers, some ceramics, domestic objects, musical instruments and late 19th-century tourist pieces. None of these objects were acquired before 1945 and none are currently on display.

## Stafford

### Shugborough

In 1693 William Anson demolished the manor house on the site of Shugborough and built a three-storied dwelling that forms the centre of the house as we see it today. Between 1745 and 1748 further alterations were made under the architect Thomas Wright who added the pavilions either side of the 17th-century block. One of William's great grandsons, George Anson, joined the navy aged 14 and was created Lord Anson in 1747; in 1751 he was promoted to the first Lord of the Admiralty. He circumnavigated the world between 1740 and 1747 and brought back with him a splendid collection of Chinese porcelain (notably *famille rose* and *famille verte*), which is still displayed in the house today.

Beginning in 1794, the architect Samuel Wyatt further transformed the house into a fashionable neo-classical mansion. The second viscount was created First Earl of Lichfield in the coronation honours of William IV in 1831. This Earl led an extravagant life, entertaining lavishly at Shugborough, which led to his financial ruin in 1842. The entire contents of the house were sold in a sale lasting two weeks.

Shugborough
Milford
Staffordshire
ST17 0XB

Tel: 01889 881388
Fax: 01889 881323

shugborough.promotions@staffordshire.gov.uk
www.staffordshire.gov.uk/shugborough

It was the wish of the 4th Earl that the house be opened to the public. On the 4th Earl's death, the house, park and contents were offered to the National Trust in lieu of death duties. The property was then leased to Staffordshire County Council by whom it is currently administered. It is still the home of Patrick Lichfield, 5th Earl.

There are a few interesting Japanese objects at Shugborough: three Imari vases and two export lacquer cabinets on English gilt stands, which date from around 1710.

## Stoke on Trent

### Gladstone Pottery Museum

Gladstone Pottery Museum
Uttoxeter Road
Longton
Stoke-on-Trent
Staffordshire
ST3 1PQ

Tel: 01782 319232
Fax: 01782 598640

gladstone@stoke.gov.uk
www2002.stoke.gov.uk/museums/gladstone

Situated in the centre of the Potteries, the Museum has a collection of more than 650,000 objects. The collections include 20th-century British painting, costume and textiles, as well as examples of glassware, metalwork and dolls. The main collections are those of ceramics, particularly those of the Staffordshire ceramic manufacturers and the Museum has 39 examples of ceramics from the former Minton Museum collection. The Henry Bergen Collection of Studio Pottery includes over 600 pieces by potters including Bernard Leach, Hamada Shoji and at least one piece by Matsubayashi Tsurunosuke. There are also examples of Jomon-period ceramic shards in the collection.

## Warwick

### Charlecote

Charlecote Park was built in 1558 for Sir Thomas Lucy and there has been a home for the Lucy family on this site for some 700 years. There are strong associations with both Queen Elizabeth and Shakespeare, who apparently knew the house well – he is alleged to have been caught poaching deer on the Lucy estate and then fled to London. The house as viewed today certainly looks Elizabethan but is mostly Victorian as a result of the many changes made in 1823. The Great Hall has a plaster barrel-vaulted ceiling that has been painted to look like timber; other rooms have richly coloured wallpaper, decorated plaster ceilings and wood panelling. There are superb pieces of furniture and fine works of art, including a contemporary painting of Queen Elizabeth I. In 1946 Sir Montgomerie Fairfax-Lucy gave Charlecote Park to the National Trust.

**Charlecote**
Warwick
Warwickshire
CV35 9ER

Tel: 01789 470277
Fax: 01789 470544

charlecote.park@
nationaltrust.org.uk
www.nationaltrust.org.uk

There are few Japanese objects at Charlecote apart from a lacquer cabinet and table and a pair of square porcelain bottles.

## Wolverhampton

### Wolverhampton Art Gallery

Wolverhampton Art Gallery opened in May 1884 and was funded and constructed by local industrialist Philip Horsman. The gallery was designed by Birmingham artist Julius Chatwin. The characters on the frieze facing Lichfield Street represent the Arts and include sculpture, painting, architecture, pottery, glass-blowing and wrought iron work. The frieze on the St. Peter's Close side has figures representing sciences such as astronomy and navigation as well as local industries including blacksmithing and lock making. The man holding a scroll is modelled on a local stonemason who worked on the building in the 1880s.

Wolverhampton was a leading centre for japanning ---- the application of thick varnish as both protection and a base for decoration to tin, iron, papier-mâché and wood in imitation of Chinese and Japanese lacquered furniture. The collection contains many examples of such wares, mainly donated by local manufacturers and their descendants.

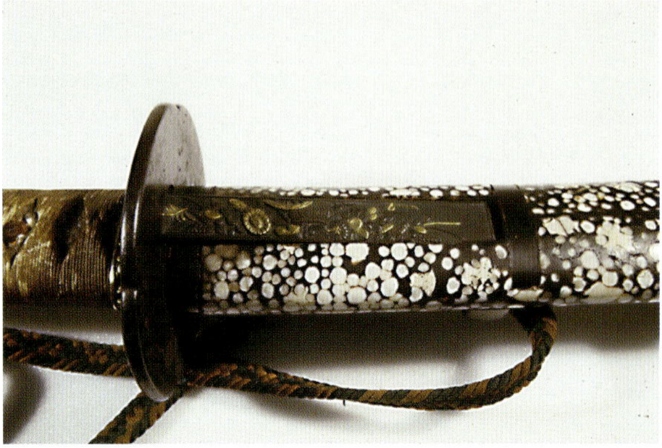

*Detail of tachi-style sword*

**Wolverhampton Art Gallery**
Lichfield Street
Wolverhampton
Staffordshire
WV1 1DU

Tel: 01902 552055
Fax: 01902 552053

info@wolverhamptonart.org.uk
www.wolverhamptonart.org.uk

The collection also includes Japanese material (also through gifts from local leading families) and includes swords and other edged weapons, sword-fittings, carved ivories (netsuke and *okimono*), bronze figures, dolls and lacquer ware (including inro). There is no permanent display of Japanese material but the collections are used in interpretative displays as appropriate.

# North West England

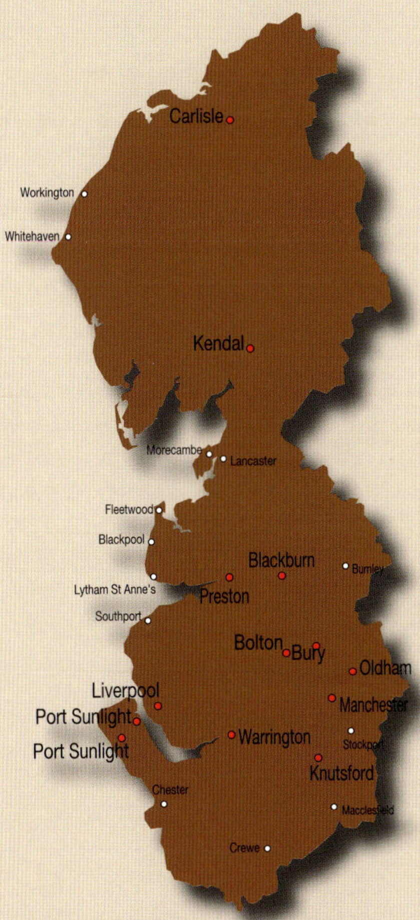

# Altrincham

## Dunham Massey

Dunham Massey
Altrincham
Cheshire
WA14 4SJ

Tel: 0161 941 1025
Fax: 0161 929 7508

dunhammassey@
nationaltrust.org.uk
www.nationaltrust.org.uk

Dunham Massey was built in the early 18th-century for the 2nd Earl of Warrington but the house was extensively reworked between 1905 and 1910. The house now presents one of the UK's most sumptuously ornate Edwardian interiors and contains outstanding collections of fine walnut furniture, paintings and Huguenot silver; there is also a splendid painting by Guernico.

The only Japanese objects to have been recorded (but as yet not verified) are some examples of Kakiemon porcelain and a large screen with the coat of arms of the 8th Earl of Rivers, which may have been acquired by the 2nd Earl of Warrington.

# Blackburn

## Blackburn Museum & Art Gallery

In 1871 the Free Library committee of Blackburn purchased land for £1,120 in order to create a Museum and Free Library. There was a competition for the best design that was won by the early French Gothic-style design of Messrs. Woodzell and Colcutt, Architects, of Finsbury Place, London. On July 18th 1872 the Mayor of Blackburn, Thomas Bury Esq., laid the foundation stone. The official public opening of the Blackburn Museum and Free Library was on June 11th 1874.

Blackburn Museum has an enormous collection of material relating to the history of the cotton industry but also has a ceramic collection that includes examples of Chinese and Japanese ceramics; there is also a small collection of netsuke. In addition, the Museum has a fascinating collection of artefacts that were brought back to Blackburn by local missionaries who went to work in Africa, China and Oceania.

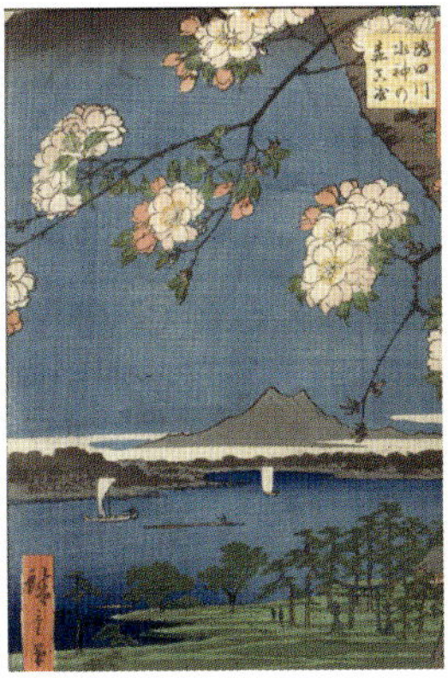

Cherry blossom on the Sumidagawa, Ando Hiroshige

Blackburn Museum & Art Gallery
Museum Street
Blackburn
Lancashire
BB1 7AJ

Tel: 01254 667130
Fax: 01254 695370

council.blackburnworld.com/services/museum/index.htm
www.cottontown.org/
(link to online catalogue of Hiroshige's *53 Stages of the Tokaido*)

The principal holdings of Japanese objects lie in the Lewis Collection of over 1,000 Japanese prints. Thomas Boys Lewis (1869-1942) was a mill-owner, antiquarian, poet and playwright as well as a great patron and benefactor to the Church and the Arts. It is unclear when exactly he began to collect Japanese prints but the collection is extensive and Lewis has annotated many of the prints himself with details of the title and the artist. The collection includes prints such as Hokusai's *The Wave at Kanagawa* as well as many other examples of *ukiyoe* including portraits of actors, pictures of famous courtesans, scenes of everyday life, landscapes and illustrations of myth and legend. Other artists represented in the collection include Utamaro, Hiroshige, Shunsho as well as *shunga* by Harunobu.

## Bolton

### Bolton Museum & Art Gallery

The first art gallery in Bolton was at Mere Hall Art Gallery and was presented to the town in 1890 by the MP, mayor and industrialist, John Pennington Thomasson. In 1939 a new Museum & Art Gallery was built by Bradshaw, Gass & Hope of Bolton. Shortly after the building opened, a significant bequest was received from the Bolton mill-owner, Frank Hindley Smith. Hindley Smith was an active patron of the arts who had acquired a large collection of 20th-

Bolton Museum & Art Gallery
Le Mans Crescent
Bolton
Lancashire
BL1 1SE

Tel: 01204 332211
Fax: 01204 332241

museum.customerservices@bolton.gov.uk
www.boltonmuseums.org.uk
www.ourtreasures.org

century paintings. On his death his collection was distributed amongst galleries throughout the UK with objects being donated to major galleries such as the Tate as well as to regional collections such as Bolton Museum & Art Gallery.

The Japanese collections in Bolton consist chiefly of the Editha Taylor bequest of 1959, which contains about 200 objects including inro and netsuke. Most of the other Japanese items in the collection have been donated by local people. Bolton has some examples of porcelain, cast bronze sculpture, inlaid ironwork, a small selection of weaponry and an Oyoroi suit of armour that was donated by the local Bolton firm of H. Murray and Co. in 1892. Very few pieces from the Japanese collection are on permanent display.

## Bury

### Bury Art Gallery and Museum

Bury Art Gallery originally opened in 1901 and was built as a result of the gift to the town of a collection of Victorian paintings that had been assembled by Thomas Wrigley, a local paper manufacturer. There were special conditions attached to the gift; Bury had to build a gallery to house the collection and also agree to display it separately from the rest of the collections. The Gallery was a thoroughly advanced building for its date, but this fact is disguised by its classical detailing. Underneath the stucco columns and swags is a framework of steel girders supporting concrete floors. The Museum was opened in the basement of the gallery in 1907 and is currently undergoing a major refurbishment as a Museum and Archive Centre, which will hopefully reopen in 2005.

In addition to the paintings collection there is a good selection of ceramics, particularly late 19th- and early 20th-century lustreware. The Japanese collections are minimal containing only "one woodblock print in two halves; 1 frame containing 30 portraits painted on silk of Japanese poets; 4 pieces of carved Ivory, all signed". However, the Museum does contain a magnificent monumental bronze standing more than three metres high! The bronze is signed, 'Cast by Seifusai, resident of the Eastern Capital, Japan'. This is most likely Terada Tetsugoro who used the art name Seifusai and whose work was exhibited at the Paris (1878) and Philadelphia (1876) expositions by Minoda Chojiro of Yokohama. Bury museum curators know that the bronze was given in 1901 by Henry Whitehead, one of Bury's most prominent businessmen. Whitehead was High Sheriff of Lancashire in 1903 and was noted for his philanthropy. Research into the splendid bronze is, at the time of writing, ongoing.

**Bury Art Gallery and Museum**
Moss Street
Bury
Lancashire
BL9 0DR

Tel: 0161 253 5878

artgallery@bury.gov.uk
www.ourtreasures.org

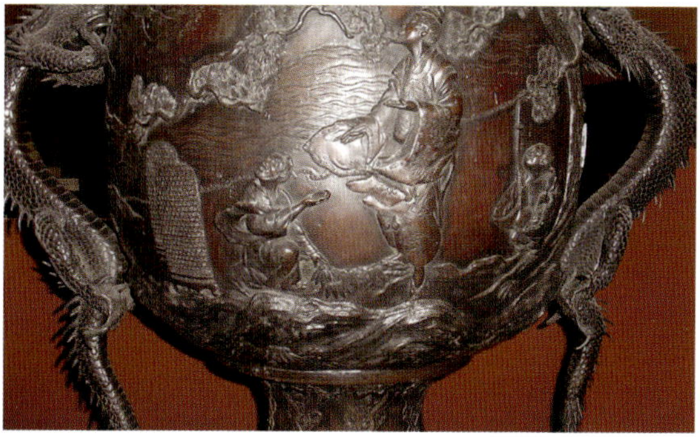

*Detail of bronze incense burner*

## Carlisle

### Tullie House Museum

Established by Carlisle Corporation in 1893, Tullie House Museum and Art Gallery houses considerable collections of fine and decorative art, human history and natural sciences. The Museum underwent a major redevelopment in 1990, involving expansion within existing buildings and the construction of a new wing housing the new Border Galleries, an Art Gallery, shop, lecture theatre and restaurant spaces. In 2001 an underground gallery was developed as part of a Millennium Commission Award.

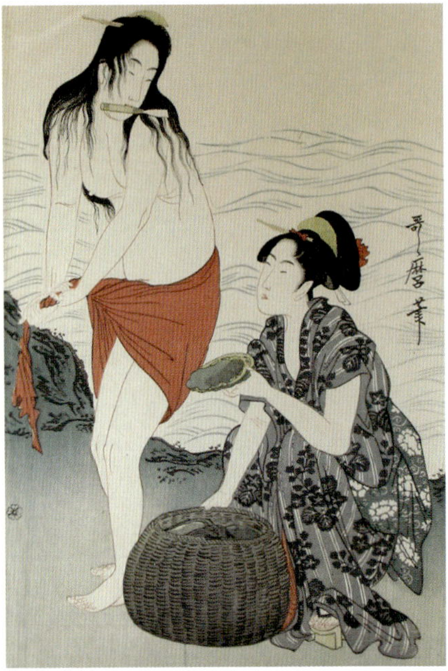


*Detail of triptych 'Shell-divers' by Kitagawa Utamaro, 1949.125.217*

Tullie House Museum
Castle Street
Carlisle
Cumbria
CA3 8TP

Tel: 01228 534781
Fax: 01228 810249

enquiries@tullie-house.co.uk
www.tulliehouse.co.uk

The Department of Fine and Decorative Arts has a collection of fine art, decorative art, costume and textiles produced or associated with Carlisle and Cumbria. The collections also contain nearly 40 Japanese prints, 29 of which were bequeathed by Emily and Gordon Bottomley who were personal friends of the great artist, collector and stage designer Charles Rickets (1866-1931) who saw the Noh theatre in Japan and with his companion Charles Shannon owned an exquisite collection of Japanese art, much of which is now in the British Museum. The collections are occasionally displayed in temporary exhibitions in the Special Exhibitions Gallery and the Art Gallery.

## Kendal

### Abbott Hall Art Gallery

The collection at Abbot Hall, a house built in the mid-18th century on the site of an earlier ecclesiastical building, includes works ranging in period from the 18th century (in period settings) to contemporary

**Abbott Hall Art Gallery**
Kendal
Cumbria
LA9 5AL

Tel: 01539 722464
Fax: 01539 722494

ws@abbothall.org.uk
www.abbothall.org.uk

work and includes examples by many of Britain's leading artists such as Ramsay, Lawrence, Ruskin, Turner, Nicholson, Schwitters, Spencer and Hepworth. There are also examples of arts and crafts metalwork, furniture, pottery and jewellery. There are approximately 50 Japanese objects in the collection, mostly woodblock prints, but also some examples of ceramics and bronzes. The majority of the Japanese collection is held in storage but can be seen on application.

**Sizergh Castle**
Nr. Kendal
Cumbria
LA8 8AE

Tel: 015395 60070
Fax: 015395 61621

sizergh@nationaltrust.
org.uk
www.nationaltrust.org.uk

### Sizergh Castle

Sizergh Castle was originally built in thc Middle Ages by the Strickland family that still lives here today. The castle has an outstanding sequence of Tudor oak-panelled rooms and the collections include portraits as well as furniture and ceramics that have been acquired by the family over the centuries. The collections contain a late 17th-century Japanese Kutani ware bowl mounted in silver, which, by tradition, was given to Theresa Strickland by Mary of Modena (1658-1718), Queen to James II.

## Knutsford

### Tatton Park

Tatton Park is an early 19th-century Wyatt house and is opulently decorated, providing an excellent setting for the Egerton family's collection of pictures, books, china, glass and silver. The theme of Victorian grandeur extends into the garden where there is an orangery, Tower garden, pinetum and Italian and Japanese gardens – for which Tatton is justly renowned. The garden was constructed between 1910 and 1913 for Alan de Tatton Egerton who had visited the Japan-British Exhibition at White City in 1910. The garden at Tatton is possibly one of the finest examples of Japanese gardens in Europe. From 2000 to 2001 the Japanese garden was fully restored by means of existing records of the garden's construction and research work undertaken by the Osaka University of Art.

Tatton Park
Knutsford
Cheshire
WA16 6NQ

Tel: 01625 534400
Fax: 01625 534403

tatton@cheshire.gov.uk
www.nationaltrust.org.uk
www.tattonpark.org.uk

The restoration project is well documented at this site: www.tattonpark.org.uk/attractions_restjapgarden.htm

In several rooms within the house there are examples of Japanese ceramics (Imari and Kakiemon), *cloisonné* enamels and one curious piece of furniture described as Japanese. There are also some woodblock prints and an interesting group of woodblock-printed albums (not on display). Although listed here as a National Trust property Tatton is in fact financed, administered and maintained by Cheshire County Council.

## Liverpool

### Liverpool Museum

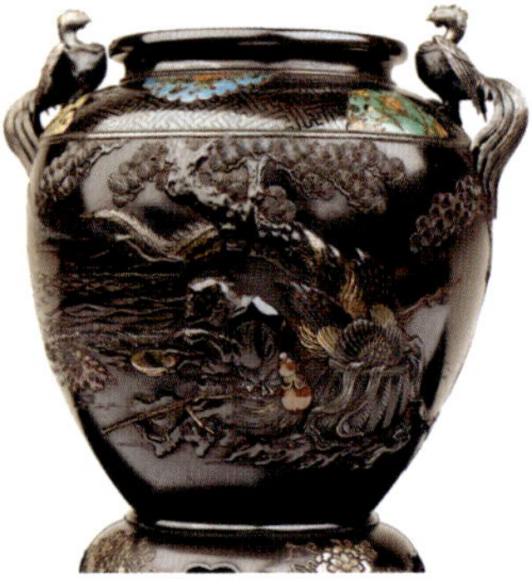

*Patinated bronze vase inlaid with cloisonné enamels, 43.22.03*

Liverpool Museum was founded in 1851 and was officially opened in 1860 by its benefactor, the wealthy local businessman William Brown MP. The Museum cares for approximately 2,750 items from Japan and of these some 1,189 are classified as arms and armour. Herein lies the strength of the collections. These Japanese collections reflect the enthusiasm for Japanese art in the late 19th and early 20th centuries and most of the items were donated by local collectors; many of the finest pieces are of the Meiji period. The fine collections of military objects include swords, sword-fittings and 13 suits of armour. There are fine collections of decorative metalwork – particularly of the Meiji period, including *cloisonné*. There are some equally fine examples of lacquer work (especially inro and decorative Meiji-period lacquer), as well as personal and domestic accessories, sculpture (including a large intriguing bronze Kannon figure), works on paper (including *ukiyoe*) and some Ainu material. In 1956 Norwich Castle Museum donated its entire ethnographic collection to Liverpool; this included a significant number of Japanese items.

Many of the Museum's pieces come from the collections of Randal Hibbert (1865-1942) and F.W. Mayor (d.1935), both local men who were collecting in the early part of the 20th century. From the Randal Hibbert collection there are 113 swords, 147 *tsuba*, 170 miscellaneous sword-fittings plus inro, netsuke and *okimono*, all ranging in date from the Nambokucho to the Meiji period. Some objects were acquired through agency of Yamanaka in Japan, with several items form the collections of Gilbertson, Huish, Behrens, Naunton and Hawkshaw, and some are believed to be ex-Bowes collection. Hibbert was particularly interesting as he never travelled to Japan and only acquired his collection from dealers in London and Paris but was known to have bought directly from dealers in Japan.

From the collection of Frederick W. Mayor there are nine swords with superb examples of Meiji-period sword mounts, 223 *tsuba* (mostly decorative works of the Meiji period), 132 *kozuka*, mostly Edo and Meiji period, 72 *fuchi-kashira*, all excellent quality examples of craftsmanship of the Bakumatsu period. There are also several high-quality decorative metalwork vases and lacquer boxes of the Meiji period and a large collection of netsuke and inro; some objects are from the collections of Naunton, Hawkshaw and G.G. Davies.

**Liverpool Museum**
William Brown Street
Liverpool
Merseyside
L3 8EN

Tel: 0151 478 4399

themuseum@
liverpoolmuseums.org.uk
www.liverpoolmuseums.
org.uk

At present there are no Japanese objects on display, but the Museum will be opening a major new gallery devoted to World Cultures in 2004. The gallery will then display over 100 Japanese objects; these will include arms and armour, *tsuba*, netsuke, inro and Buddhist sculpture.

## Manchester

### The Manchester Museum

The origins of the Manchester Museum lie in the great quest for knowledge and improvement in medicine, science and art, which was so typical of the 19th century. The first collections were acquired by the Manchester Society of Natural History, which was created in 1821, and subsequently, in 1850, the collections of the Manchester Geological and Mining Society were acquired. Owen's College (now the University of Manchester) took over responsibility for the collections in 1867.

The College commissioned Alfred Waterhouse, the architect of London's Natural History Museum, to design a museum to house these collections. The Manchester Museum was subsequently opened in 1885. In 1912 the 'pavilion' extension was erected to house the archaeological and Egyptian collections and in 1927 an extension was built to house the ethnographic collections. The Manchester Museum collections include natural history, archaeology, ancient Egyptian material as well as ancient pottery from America, ethnographic collections from Australia, Africa and Asia with a particularly good collection of armour and archery-related material from Asia.

The most significant number of Japanese objects comes from the collection of R.W. Lloyd and comprises some 1,000 items of sword furniture, swords, wood carvings, lacquer, ivories, metalwork and pottery. The collection arrived here because Lloyd was a keen entomologist, which brought him into contact with Dr.

Hincks, the Museum's then Keeper of Entomology. Hincks introduced him to Professor Canon, Chairman of the Museum Committee. Cannon was also a keen collector of Japanese objects and suggested Lloyd's collection be brought to Manchester. When Lloyd died his collection was bequeathed both to Manchester and the British Museum, Manchester acquiring additional items the BM did not require, such as the lacquer boxes. The Museum's Living Cultures gallery usually has Japanese objects such as armour, swords and fittings as well as netsuke on display.

The Manchester Museum
The University of Manchester
Oxford Road
Manchester
M13 9PL

Tel: 0161 275 2634
Fax: 0161 275 2676

museum.man.ac.uk
museumsunwrapped.man.ac.uk (covers all of Manchester's museums)

There is also a collection of over 4,000 objccts of archery-related material from all over the world. The nucleus of the collection was donated in 1946 by Ingo Simon, a lifelong researcher into the development of the bow, and a skilled and dedicated archer. The collection contains a significant representation of Japanese archery equipment including bows (such as an interesting steel example), arrows and arrowheads, quivers of various types and other accessories such as gloves. There is generally a small selection of Japanese material on display.

### Manchester Art Gallery

The Manchester Art Gallery has its roots in the Royal Manchester Institution for the Promotion of Literature, Science and the Arts. The current gallery was designed in 1824 by Charles Barry, who was later the architect of the Houses of Parliament. In 1882, the Institution's building and collections were given over to the city and became Manchester Art Gallery. In 1898, the City Council purchased land behind the gallery for a planned extension and in 1938 they bought Charles Barry's impressive Athenaeum building to provide additional display space. However, by the time the gallery closed in 1998 it was still only able to display a small amount of its fine and decorative art collections. Following a four-year refurbishment and expansion programme the Manchester Art Gallery re-opened in 2002.

The Gallery has an outstanding collection of 19th-century Pre-Raphaelite paintings including Dante Gabriel Rossetti's *Astarte Syriaca* and *Autumn Leaves* by John Everett Millais. There are also some paintings of the 18th century including works by Gainsborough and Reynolds. The gallery's new wing displays 20th-century British art including work by Francis Bacon, Bridget Riley, David Hockney and Henry Moore. Manchester Art Gallery also has a distinguished collection of decorative art including ceramics, metalwork, textiles and furniture from many periods.

The Japanese collections consist mostly of prints (largely by 18th- and 19th-century artists such as Eisen, Hiroshige, Hokusai, Shunsho and Utamaro), a good collection of arms and armour, other metalwork (including bronze objects and a silver and enamel incense burner), *cloisonné* enamel, ceramics, ivory carvings (including netsuke), lacquer (including inro and a picnic set), and an ivory, lacquer and mother-of-pearl shrine. There is also an interesting *norimono* (palanquin) bearing the *mon* (family crest) of the Tokugawa family. The arms and armour collection came from Lord Egerton of Tatton and there are some extremely interesting swords and complete sets of armour to be found in the collection. Manchester Art Gallery's collections are mostly held at the main gallery but some objects from the collections can also be found at Wythenshawe Hall and Heaton Hall.

**Manchester Art Gallery**
Mosley Street
Manchester
M2 3JL

Tel: 0161 235 8888
Fax: 0161 235 8899

www.manchestergalleries.org/index.html

**John Rylands University Library of Manchester**

The John Rylands Library houses a wonderful collection of rare books and manuscripts including the *St. John Fragment* (the earliest fragment of the New Testament in existence, dating from c.125AD) as well as some fine medieval manuscripts. Its grand neo-Gothic style building is a landmark in the centre of Manchester. The John Rylands Library merged with Manchester University Library in 1972 to form the John Rylands University Library of Manchester. The library building on Deansgate in the city centre houses the special collections of older material, and holds special exhibitions based on the collections.

**John Rylands University Library of Manchester**
Oxford Road
Manchester
M13 9PP

Tel: 0161 275 3764

special.collections@man.ac.uk
rylibweb.man.ac.uk
rylibweb.man.ac.uk/spcoll
rylibweb.man.ac.uk/data1/dg/exhibition/japan

The Japanese special collections of the library contain over 200 printed books and about 200 manuscripts as well as around 30 photographs. The earliest items in the collection are early 17th-century printed works but most of the collections are 18th or 19th century. The library is currently closed pending building works but will hopefully reopen in spring 2006.

### The Whitworth Art Gallery

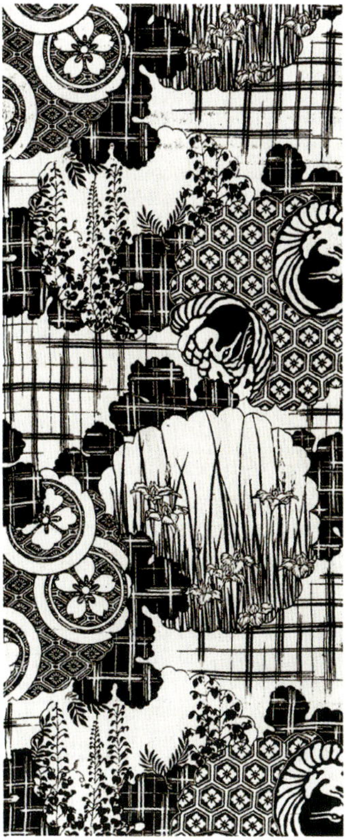

*Indigo resist dyed sash, T.11566*

The Whitworth Art Gallery has a collection of art and design that includes a remarkable range of watercolours, prints, drawings, modern art and sculpture, as well as the largest collection of textiles and wallpapers outside London. The gallery was originally founded in 1889 and has been part of the University of Manchester since 1958. It takes its name from Sir Joseph Whitworth (1803-87) a Stockport-born engineer, who left money in his will that was used to fund a number of local institutions.

**The Whitworth Art Gallery**
The University of
Manchester
Oxford Road
Manchester
M15 6ER

Tel: 0161 275 7450

whitworth@man.ac.uk
www.whitworth.man.
ac.uk/index.htm

The Japanese collections include over 1,000 examples of textiles including woven, embroidered and stencilled or resist-dyed pieces. There are eight books of textile samples, around 150 actual stencils and over 500 woodcuts. In addition there is an impressive bronze incense burner that had been shown at the Manchester Royal Jubilee exhibition in 1887.

## Oldham

### Gallery Oldham

Oldham has a long tradition of museums and collecting dating back to 1815 when a 'museum' of curiosities opened on Glodwick Lows. By the 1880s three eminent local industrialists (with an interest in natural history and fine art – the great Victorian vision of combining art and science) persuaded the local council to create a museum to hold their collections; as a result, the Free Library, Art Gallery and Museum opened in 1883. By the middle of the 20th century the collections had expanded beyond natural history to include ethnography, archaeology and antiquities and numismatics.

**Gallery Oldham**
Oldham Cultural Quarter
Greaves Street
Oldham
Lancashire
OL1 1AL

Tel: 0161 911 4653
Fax: 0161 911 4669

ecs.galleryoldham@
oldham.gov.uk
www.galleryoldham.org.uk

There are approximately 150 examples of Japanese art in the collections and these include swords and sword-fittings (including *tsuba* and *kozuka*, some of which were donated as early as 1888), carvings (including figurative works, ivory netsuke and *okimono*), ceramics (including a reasonable quantity of Satsuma ware), mirrors, coins and some silk embroideries (most likely of the Meiji period).

# Port Sunlight

## Lady Lever Art Gallery

The collection at the Lady Lever Art Gallery represents the personal taste of William Hesketh Lever, 1st Lord Leverhulme. He first began buying art in the late 1880s to use as advertising material for the Sunlight soap brand that his company produced. From this beginning Lord Leverhulme quickly grew into a discerning collector and he founded the Lady Lever Art Gallery in 1922 dedicating it to the memory of his wife. The gallery is set in the garden village of Port Sunlight, also created by Lord Lever and is famous for its British 18th- and 19th-century paintings, 18th-century furniture and an exceptional collection of Wedgwood ceramics. There is also a collection of Chinese porcelain, tapestries and embroideries, as well as classical antiquities and memorabilia relating to Lord Leverhulme's fascination with Napoleon. Among these objects there is a small Japanese collection that includes eight pieces of porcelain (Imari and Hirado ware), two *cloisonné* enamel pieces (one signed by Namikawa of Kyoto), one ivory box, one inro and one rather splendid Japanese saddle and trappings, which was bought by Lord Leverhulme in Kobe during a visit there in 1913.

**Lady Lever Art Gallery**
Port Sunlight Village
Wirral
Cheshire
CH62 5EQ

Tel: 0151 478 4136

ladylever@
liverpoolmuseums.org.uk
www.liverpoolmuseums.
org.uk/ladylever
www.portsunlight.org.
uk/gallery

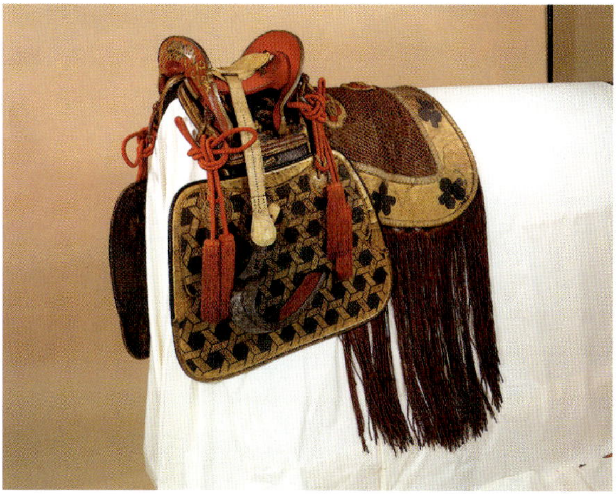

*Saddle and harness*

# Preston

## Harris Museum

The Harris Museum (originally the Harris Free Library, Museum and Art Gallery) was built and opened in sections between 1882 and 1896) and is located in the centre of Preston in a Grade I listed building. The Museum has large collections of paintings, sculpture, textiles, costume, glass and ceramics, as well as a gallery that deals with the history of the town. There is also a collection of contemporary craft. It is perhaps surprising that there is not more Japanese art to be found in Preston. The present curator of the Harris Museum has discovered that on 3rd April 1879 the local Avenham Institute held "an exhibition of Japanese curiosities and manufactures" to mark the 50th anniversary of the Institute for the Diffusion of Useful Knowledge. In 1882 the trustees of the late Edmund Robert Harris, a local solicitor who had died in 1877, endowed the Institute, which was then renamed the Harris Institute and this became a centre of excellence for the teaching of art and science.

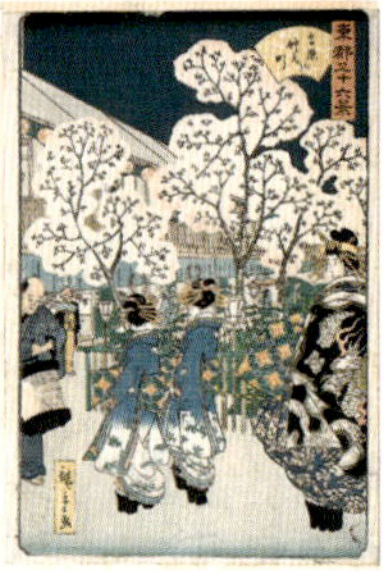

*Cherry blossom at Asakusa, Ando Hiroshige*

Today there are about 100 Japanese objects to be found in the Museum (as well as over 100 gaming counters) and the collection includes woodblock prints, lacquer, sword-fittings (including *tsuba* and *kozuka*), *cloisonné* enamels, ceramics, carvings (including netsuke and *okimono*), some contemporary textile art and one Noh mask. The history of the collection is poorly documented but it is known that some items arrived in 1883 as part of the Richard Newsham collection of fine and decorative art. The Museum has a pair of pierced metalwork vases that

**Harris Museum**
Market Square
Preston
Lancashire
PR1 2PP

Tel: 01202 258248

harris.museum@
preston.gov.uk
www.visitpreston.com
www.visitpreston.com/
whats_on/museums/
harris.htm

date back to around 1870, which may have been acquired around that time. There are usually some examples of metalwork and *okimono* on display at the Museum.

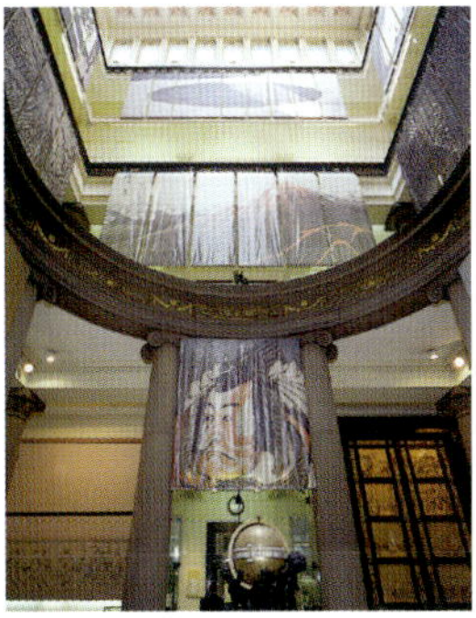

*Installation by Junichi Arai at the Harris Museum, Preston*

## Warrington

### Warrington Museum & Art Gallery

Warrington Museum and Art Gallery was founded in 1848 with specimens from the local Natural History Society. The Museum's collections have grown in excess of 200,000 objects covering natural sciences, antiquities, social history, numismatics, ethnology, fine and decorative arts and an extensive local photographic archive. The majority of the collections relate to Warrington and the surrounding areas.

**Warrington Museum & Art Gallery**
Bold Street
Warrington
Lancashire
WA1 1JG

Tel: 01925 442392
Fax: 01925 442399

museum@
warrington.gov.uk
www.warrington.gov.uk/
entertainment/Museum/
home.htm

The Museum's ethnographical collection contains over 3,000 objects from many world cultures including Africa, the Americas, Asia, India, Polynesia, Oceania and Australasia. In the Human History gallery, which was established in 1936, there are over 600 objects on display; the arrangement has remained largely untouched for over 60 years. Within the collection are nearly 400 Japanese objects, which include sword-fittings (including *tsuba*), textiles and costume, metalwork (including *cloisonné*), printed material and carvings including netsuke (these are generally on display). The earliest acquisition of Japanese material came into the Museum around 1850.

# Yorkshire and Humberside

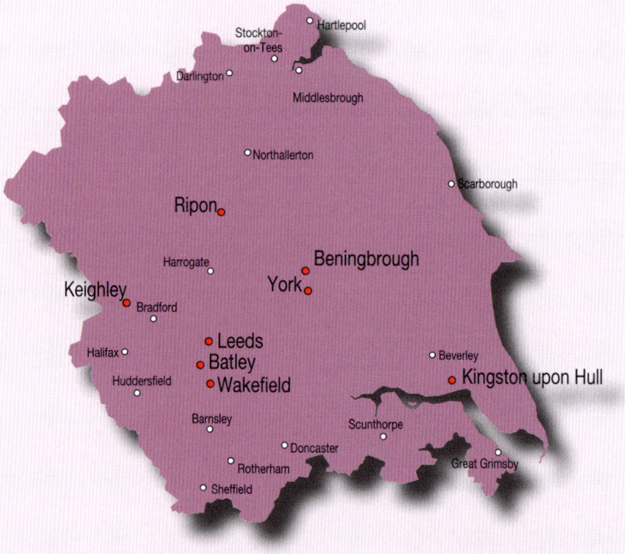

# Batley

## Bagshaw Museum

Bagshaw Museum is an extraordinary Gothic mansion set at the top of the wooded slopes of Batley's Wilton Park. It was built around 1875 for local businessman and mill-owner George Sheard, apparently for what was then an enormous sum of £25,000. In 1909 the estate was auctioned and sold to Batley Corporation for £5. Later that same year, local businessman Walter Bagshaw was asked to furnish one room as a museum. By 1911, when Wilton Park Museum was opened to the public, there were three completed rooms; by 1924, there were 12 rooms open. When Walter Bagshaw died, the museum was renamed The Bagshaw Museum and his children, Noel and Violet, continued his work, travelling widely collecting and donating items to the Museum.

There are currently some 70 Japanese objects in the collection including ceramics, metalwork (including arms and armour) as well as textiles. The strength of the collection lies in its decorative metalwork.

**Bagshaw Museum**
Wilton Park,
Batley
West Yorkshire
WF17 0AS

Tel: 01924 326155
Fax: 01294 326164

bagshaw.museum@
kirklees.gov.uk
kinfo@kirklees.gov.uk
www.kirkleesmc.gov.uk

# Beningbrough

## Beningbrough

Beningbrough was built around 1716 for John Bourchier and has a splendid baroque interior. It has an impressive collection of over 100 18th-century portraits on loan from the National Portrait Gallery, London, including Kneller's portraits of members of the Kit-Kat Club. There is an interesting collection of furniture and oriental porcelain that includes only three examples of Japanese Arita ware of the 17th and 18th centuries.

**Beningbrough**
York
YO30 1DD

Tel: 01904 470666
Fax: 01904 470002

beningbrough@
nationaltrust.org.uk
www.nationaltrust.org.uk

## Keighley and Bradford

Cliffe Castle Museum
Spring Gardens Lane
Keighley
West Yorkshire
BD20 6LH

Tel: 01535 618231
Fax: 01535 610536

www.bradford.gov.uk/tourism/museums/cliffe.htm

Cartwright Hall
Lister Park
Bradford
West Yorkshire
BD9 4NS

Tel: 01274 751212
Fax: 01274 481045

www.bradford.gov.uk/tourism/museums/cart.htm

### Cliffe Castle Museum and Cartwright Hall

The Japanese collections (that number around 600 objects) are divided between Cliffe Castle and Cartwright Hall in Bradford; those broadly classified as 'art' are at Cartwright Hall while those defined loosely as 'ethnography' are at Cliffe Castle. The collections include textiles, ceramics, fans and prints but the strengths lie in the collections of arms and armour. This part of the collection, which is at Cliffe Castle, includes complete suits of armour as well as bows, arrows and swords.

Cliffe Castle was built between 1875 and 1882, as an elaborate mansion for textile mill-owner, Henry Isaac Butterfield. In 1959 the house was converted into the local museum. Set in an attractive hillside park, this museum specialises in natural history and geology. There is also pottery, stained glass, fine furniture, local history, curios, dolls and toys.

Cartwright Hall opened in 1904 with an important collection of Victorian and Edwardian works following its donation to the city by Samuel Cunliffe Lister. It is here that prints and ceramics can be found.

## Kingston upon Hull

Wilberforce House Museum
25 High Street
Hull
East Yorkshire
HU1 1NQ

Tel: 01482 613 902
Fax: 01482 613 710

www.hullcc.gov.uk/wilberforcehouse

### Wilberforce House Museum

Wilberforce House is the birthplace of William Wilberforce, the 18th-century politician. The Museum holds unique collections relating to Wilberforce's campaign to abolish slavery. The house has been a museum to his memory since 1906. The main displays tell the horrific story of slavery and Wilberforce's struggle to abolish it. The Museum is included in this guide as, at the time of writing, there is a collection of Hina-Matsuri dolls and associated furniture (numbering about 90 pieces in all) on loan from the royal collection.

# Leeds

## Leeds Museums and Art Galleries'

The Japanese collections of Leeds Museums and Art Galleries fall under three main institutions: Leeds City Art Gallery, Lotherton Hall and Temple Newsam. There are more than 500 objects in these collections, including prints, costume, ceramics, ivory carvings, metalwork (including *cloisonné*), religious and festival items, everday objects and personal accessories as well as arms and armour. Most of these in the latter categories are held in the main museum reserve collection and can be seen by prior appointment.

**Leeds City Art Gallery**
The Headrow
Leeds
West Yorkshire
LS1 3AA

Tel: 0113 247 8248

www.leeds.gov.uk/artgallery

Leeds City Art Gallery is primarily a collection of works on paper featuring artists such as J.M.W. Turner, John Sell Cotman, Rembrandt, Cozens and Girtin. The collections also include more modern works by artists such as the Leeds artist Atkinson Grimshaw, shelter drawings by Henry Moore and work by contemporary artists such as Paula Rego, Mark Wallinger and Rose Garrard. There is a small collection of over 50 Japanese woodblock prints held by the gallery in the reserve collection store.

## Lotherton Hall

Lotherton Hall was acquired by the local Gascoigne family in 1825 when both house and park were purchased by Richard Oliver Gascoigne. In 1893 Colonel Frederick Gascoigne inherited the property and together with his wife Gwendolen extended and remodelled the house and gardens. In 1968 the Gascoigne family presented the Hall to the City of Leeds, together with its park, garden and art collections. These, along with items brought from Temple Newsam House and Leeds City Art Gallery and objects bought specially for the house since it opened as a museum in 1969 are what visitors to the house see today. The major part of Lotherton's collection is the Gascoigne bequest, which consists of splendid furniture, silver, china, paintings, sculpture and textiles.

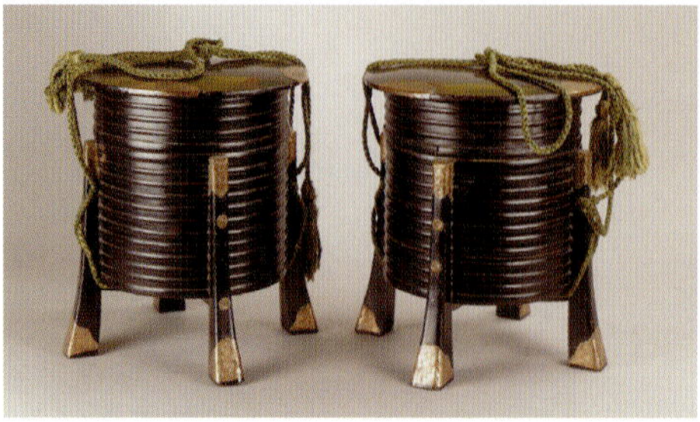

*Pair of lacquer picnic boxes*

The ceramics collection is extremely good and ranges from Chinese armorial pieces acquired by Sir Thomas Gascoigne in the 1770s, to contemporary pottery and porcelain by makers such as Bernard Leach, Lucie Rie and Liz Fritsch. Many potters have been influenced by the early Chinese ceramics bequeathed by Frank Savery to Leeds in 1965. These reflect the main types of Chinese wares from the Neolithic period to the 15th century that are shown alongside oriental screens, furniture and paintings acquired by Colonel Gascoigne on his numerous foreign trips.

Other members of the Gascoigne family visited Japan in the 1920s and from 1945 to 1951 Sir Alvary Gascoigne was head of the UK Liaison Mission to Japan with the rank of ambassador. The pair of screens at Lotherton was acquired by Lady Gascoigne in Japan around 1950. Other Japanese objects at Lotherton include ceramics, furniture and prints.

**Lotherton Hall**
Lotherton Lane
Aberford
Leeds
West Yorkshire
LS25 3EB

Tel: 0113 281 3259

www.leeds.gov.uk/lothertonhall

### Temple Newsam House

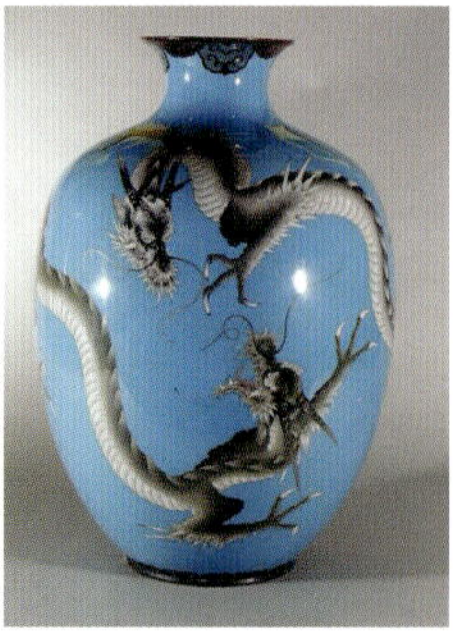

*Cloissone vase with dragons*

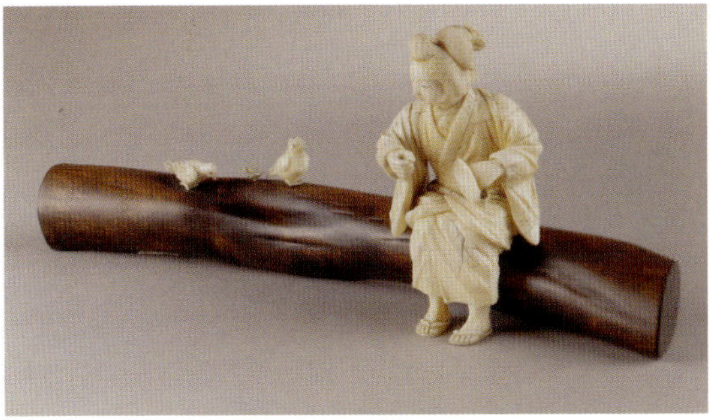

*Ivory and wood okimono of a Bijin on a tree trunk with birds, c.1890*

**Temple Newsam House**
Temple Newsam Rd.
Leeds
West Yorkshire
LS15 0AE

Tel: 0113 2641358

www.leeds.gov.uk/templenewsam

Originally a Tudor house, Temple Newsam has been extensively remodelled over the centuries. The collections consist of decorative arts displayed in their original room settings including one of the largest collections of Chippendale furniture in the country. There are over 350 old masters including examples by Reynolds and Gainsborough. There is silver by Paul de Lamerie and other great craftsmen, together with exceptional pottery, textiles and wallpapers. Among the Japanese objects at Temple Newsam is a superb pair of export lacquer cabinets (c.1690) mounted on English frames (c.1730) that were brought to Temple Newsam in 1758 by Frances, Viscountess Irwin.

### Leeds University Art Collections and Gallery

**Leeds University Art Collections and Gallery**
The Brotherton Library
University of Leeds
Leeds
LS2 9JT

Tel: 0113 343 2777
Fax: 0113 343 5561

special-collections@library.leeds.ac.uk
www.leeds.ac.uk/gallery

The University of Leeds Art Collection is recognised nationally as an important research resource and source of reference across a wide range of significant artists. The collection consists mainly of European (principally British) paintings, drawings and prints, dating from the 16th century up to the present day, with small collections of sculpture and photographs. There is also a collection of Yorkshire Pottery, as well as a small group of Chinese and Japanese art works. This collection includes at least 30 woodblock prints by artists such as Utamaro, Hiroshige and Kunisada. Works are periodically exhibited and, at the time of writing, an exhibition on the work of Kawamura Bumpo is being planned for late 2004 – although it is unclear as to how many, if any, of these works are from the University's own collection.

## Royal Armouries Museum

The Japanese collections of the Royal Armouries Museum in Leeds (formerly the collections at the Tower of London) have the privilege of containing the first documented Japanese objects to arrive in the UK. These are the two suits of armour given to Captain John Saris who had arrived in Japan in 1613 to establish a trading factory on behalf of the East India Company. Saris returned bearing gifts from the shogun for King James. These included two suits of armour, a *katana* and a *waggadash* (*wakizashi*) for himself. He also had a large private collection of *shunga* – Japanese erotic prints, which were burned by the company and he was dismissed for this and for excessive private trading.

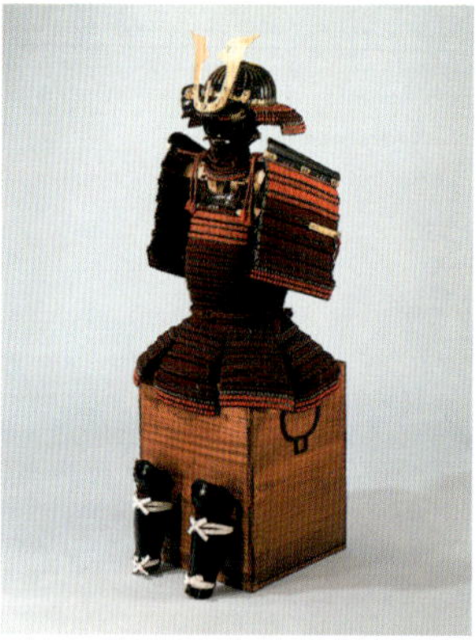

*Japanese armour given to James I*

The armours have had a chequered history and in 1660, one of the two armours, the "armour sent to his now Majesty, Charles the second, by the great Mogull, consisting of backe, breast, taces headpiece, vizor and pieces of the greaves" appeared in the *View and Survey of the King's Majesty's Armoury* and excited considerable public interest. In July 1662, "many persons of quality went to the armoury in the Tower of London to see that most noble and strong defence for the body, the suit of armour sent from the Emperor Mougul, which suit was presented to His Majesty the King of England". In 1688, a valuation of £5 was placed upon the armour. From being the first recorded

Japanese object to arrive in Britain the fact that the armour was Japanese was disregarded until the 19th century and the Tower of London remained both an armoury and a visitor attraction for centuries.

From the original collections held at the Tower of London it was decided to create a dedicated museum for the arts of warfare and in 1996 the Royal Armouries Museum in Leeds opened to the public. The Museum was built to display and interpret the national collections of arms and armour, for which function the Tower of London had been deemed no longer appropriate. In addition to display galleries the Museum has a tilt-yard where demonstrations of jousting and other forms of mounted martial sport are given. There are also demonstrations of falconry and the use of hunting dogs, a menagerie for the horses, dogs and birds and a craft court where gunsmiths, leather workers and other traditional craftsmen can be seen at work.

Among the five main galleries of the Museum there is one dedicated to the arms and armour of China and Japan. There are close to 600 Japanese objects in the collections that include mainly Edo period arms, armour and equestrian equipment (and a small collection of woodblock-printed books), but also 20th-century firearms, ammunition and armour. There are approximately 170 objects on display in the galleries. Behind this gallery is a dojo in which various demonstrations of Asian and European martial arts (some in full armour) are performed.

Since 1991 the Museum has been twinned with the Nikko Toshogu Shrine in Japan. The Shrine was built in 1623 as the final resting place of the Shogun Tokugawa Ieyasu and is celebrated for its *yabusame* (horseback archery) contests. There is a figure of a man and horse wearing the equipment used today in the *yabusame* festival at Nikko in the centre of the gallery. Demonstrations of *yabusame* have been given both at Leeds and in the moat of the Tower of London itself.

**Royal Armouries Museum**
Armouries Drive
Leeds
West Yorkshire
LS10 1LT

Tel: 0113 220 1999

enquiries@
armouries.org.uk
www.armouries.org.uk

## Harewood House

Harewood House is the home of the Earl of Harewood, cousin to Queen Elizabeth II and has been the home of the Lascelles family for over 200 years. Harewood House was designed by John Carr of York in 1759, the interiors were the work of Robert Adam and the grounds were developed by Capability Brown. Much of the furniture at Harewood was designed especially for the house by Thomas Chippendale who was born nearby in Otley.

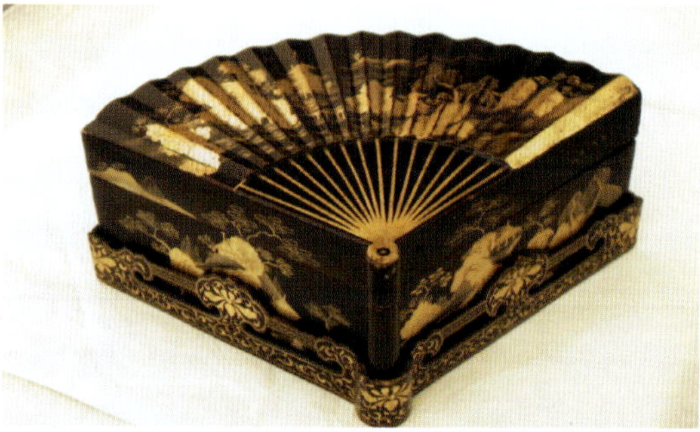

*Fan-shaped lacquer box*

Successive generations of the family have added their own taste in fine art to the collections currently to be found in the house. The 1st Viscount Lascelles collected French porcelain and Chinese celadon (many in French ormolu mounts) and commissioned watercolours by the foremost artists of the day. The collection of paintings includes works by Veronese, Bellini, El Greco, Reynolds, Gainsborough and Turner.

There are nearly 30 examples of Japanese art to be found at Harewood; these include the types of export lacquer ware one might expect to find as well as some large Imari plates, smaller lacquer vases and three swords. The latter include at least one sword surrendered in 1945. There is also an interesting small lacquer box given to HRH Princess Mary and the 6th Earl of Harewood as a wedding present from the then Crown Prince of Japan in 1922.

**Harewood House**
Harewood
Leeds
West Yorkshire
LS17 9LQ

Tel: 0113 218 1010
Fax: 0113 218 1002

business@harewood.org
www.harewood.org

# Ripon

## Newby Hall

Newby Hall was built in the 1690s by Sir Christopher Wren's assistant, John Etty. In the 1760s one William Weddell, a relation of the Compton family who currently lived at Newby Hall, acquired a large collection of classical sculptures and Robert Adam was commissioned to alter some of the interiors of the house; Thomas Chippendale made some of the furniture.

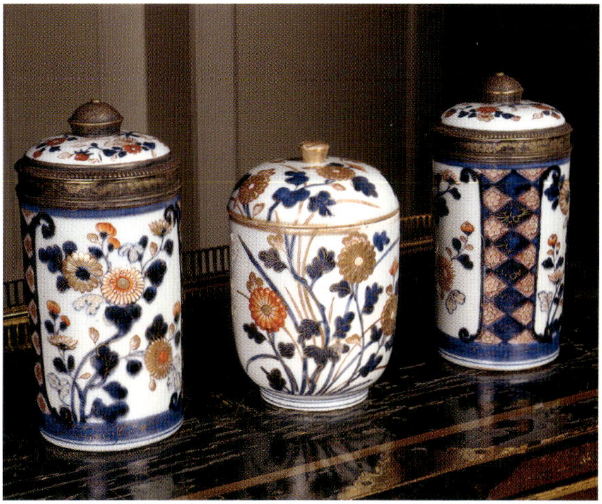

*Arita ware on export lacquer cabinet*

There are approximately 40 Japanese objects at Newby Hall and the collection includes ceramics, 19th-century bronze vases and several excellent examples of export lacquer cabinets. The ceramics are represented by some splendid Arita, Imari and Kakiemon porcelain including garnitures from around 1700 as well as late 19th-century chamber pots. Most of the Japanese collection is on display in the public rooms although there are a few objects currently undergoing conservation work. It is unclear as to when the Japanese objects were acquired but research is ongoing into the provenance of the collection.

Newby Hall
Ripon
North Yorkshire
HG4 5AE

Tel: 01423 322583
Fax: 91423 324452

info@newbyhall.com
www.newbyhall.com

# Wakefield

## Nostell Priory

In 1733 Nostell Priory was built on the site of a medieval priory for Sir Rowland Winn, 4th Baronet. Robert Adam was commissioned to complete the state rooms that are among the finest examples of his interiors. The State Bedroom is decorated with a rococo ceiling and Chinese wallpaper, which was introduced by Robert Adam. The Priory and its contents were given to the National Trust in 1953 by Lord St. Oswald, however, it remains the family home of Lord and Lady St. Oswald.

Nostell Priory contains a superb collection of Chippendale furniture that was designed especially for the house by the great cabinet-maker. The collection also includes paintings by Pieter Brueghel the younger, Holbein, Van Dyck and Hogarth, a remarkable 18th-century doll's house complete with its original fittings and Chippendale-style furniture; there is also a long-clock by John Harrison with its extremely rare movement made of wood. The collection includes an important lacquered Arita porcelain garniture; there are two covered vases and two beakers. They are, however, not original to the house having been bought in 1998.

Nostell Priory
Doncaster Road
Nostell
Nr. Wakefield
West Yorkshire
WF4 1QE

Tel: 01924 863892
Fax: 01924 865282

nostellpriory@
nationaltrust.org.uk
www.nationaltrust.org.
uk/nostellpriory

# York

## Sutton Park

Sutton Park is the home of Sir Reginald and Lady Sheffield and was built in 1730 by Thomas Atkinson. The house contains 18th-century furniture, paintings mostly from Buckingham House (now Buckingham Palace) and a notable collection of porcelain. There are a few examples of Japanese porcelain within the collection including 17th-century Imari ware and 19th-century Imari and Arita ware. These objects are always on display in the rooms open to the public.

Sutton Park
Sutton-in-the-Forest
York
YO61 1DP

Tel: 01347 810249
Fax: 01347 811251

info@statelyhome.co.uk
www.statelyhome.co.uk

## York Art Gallery

The gallery has its origins in a temporary wooden building that was erected in 1879 for the second Yorkshire Fine Art and Industrial Exhibition. The architect Edward Taylor was retained by a group of York citizens after the exhibition to design a more permanent gallery. A site was secured within the grounds of St. Mary's Abbey, a design was agreed and the building as we see it today was erected; it became the City Art Gallery in 1892.

The gallery has a collection that shows the development over 600 years of western European art and includes works by Parmigianino, Bellotto, Hogarth, Reynolds, Gwen John, Lowry, Barbara Hepworth and David Hockney. There is a collection of watercolours, drawings and prints with a local emphasis; artists represented in the watercolour collections are John Piper, Rowlandson, Turner and Cotman. The graphic collection includes approximately 150 Japanese woodblock prints by artists such as Utamaro, Hokusai, Hiroshige and Sukenobu.

An important feature of the collections is the group of pioneer studio pottery assembled by the Very Reverend Eric Milner-White (1884-1963), former Dean of York Minster. This collection includes examples of pottery by Staite Murray, Bernard Leach, Hamada Shoji and Kawai Kanjiro. The majority of the ceramics are on permanent display.

York Art Gallery
Exhibition Square
York
YO1 7EW

Tel: 01904 551862
Fax: 01904 551866

art.gallery@ymt.org.uk
www.yorkartgallery.org.uk

# North-East England

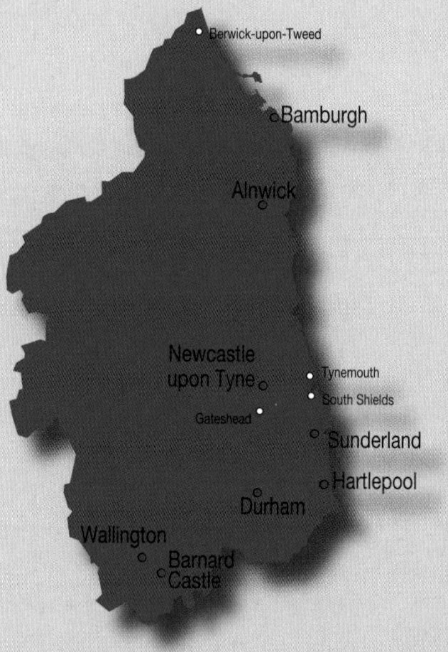

## Alnwick

### Alnwick Castle

Alnwick Castle has been the home of the Earls and Dukes of Northumberland since 1309. It has a few interesting examples of Japanese export art including a 17th-century Kakiemon jar and a pair of Imari covered bowls. The castle also has some fine examples of export lacquer ware cabinets including a pair on English stands, circa 1770, which are at the time of writing on loan to Syon House, Syon Park, West London – the London home of His Grace, the Duke of Northumberland. At Alnwick there is also a 19th-century lacquer cabinet given by King George V and Queen Mary to Helen, 8th Duchess of Northumberland.

**Alnwick Castle**
Alnwick
Northumberland
NE66 1NQ

Tel: 01665 510777
Fax: 01665 510876
Infoline (24 hr):
01665 511100

www.alnwickcastle.com

## Bamburgh

### Bamburgh Castle

Bamburgh Castle has an ancient history having been first fortified in the 6th century. The castle took shape after the Norman invasions but the present castle was much restored by the first Lord Armstrong in the early 19th century. It is still the home of the Armstrong family. It has a small but varied Japanese collection including 19th-century Satsuma ceramics, *cloisonné*, bronzes, two *yari* and two *aiguchi* and a "pair of lacquered table stands, Japanese late 19th-century". Its strongest link to Japan is that in 1953 the present Japanese Crown Prince Akihito, now Emperor of Japan, visited Bamburgh Castle while on a tour of the UK and as the Emperor Showa's official representative at the coronation of Queen Elizabeth II. The visit was detailed in the *Japan Society Bulletin 10*, dated June 1953. It is unclear whether any of the Japanese objects at Bamburgh were in fact gifts from the then Crown Prince.

**Bamburgh Castle**
Bamburgh
Northumberland
NE69 7DF

Tel: 01668 214515
Fax: 01668 214060

bamburghcastle@aol.com
www.bamburghcastle.com

# Barnard Castle

## The Bowes Museum

The Bowes Museum first opened in 1892 as a purpose-built public art gallery founded by John and Josephine Bowes to house their art collection. It was designed by the French architect Jules Pellechet and is built on a grand scale in the manner of a French château. It lies in beautiful grounds in the market town of Barnard Castle in Teesdale. Pevsner described Barnard Castle as "that bold incongruity, looking exactly like the town hall of a major provincial town in France. In scale it is just as gloriously inappropriate for the town to which it belongs (and which it gives some international fame) as in style". Despite Pevsner's reservations the Museum actually lies discreetly in its own grounds and does not dominate the town and is surrounded by a spacious park which is at present being returned to its original 19th-century form.

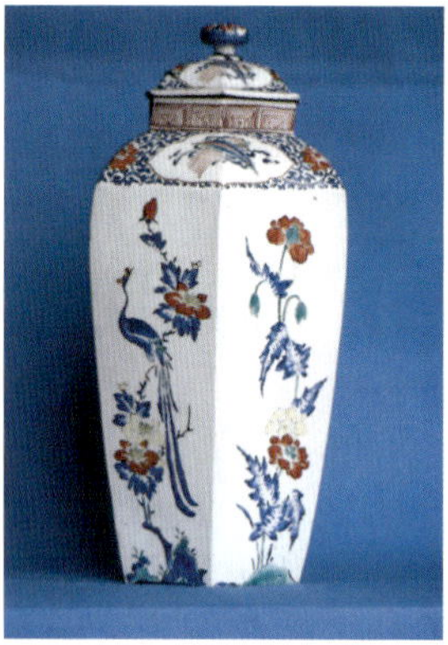

*Kakiemon vase*

The Japanese collections number some 200 objects and comprise mostly ceramics (Imari, Kakiemon, Arita etc.) and include both vessels and figures. There are also examples of lacquer and furniture including some very impressive 19th-century marquetry pieces with lacquer decoration as well as an export lacquer chest and a full-size *norimono* (palanquin). The collections are well described in Sue Thompson's article *Japanese Export Art at the Bowes Museum* in *The Arts of Asia*, September/October 1991.

The Bowes Museum
Barnard Castle
Durham
DL12 8NMP

Tel: 01833 690 606
Fax: 01833 637 163

info@bowesmuseum.org.uk
www.bowesmuseum.org.uk

# Durham

## The Oriental Museum

The Museum was founded in 1950 and the present building was opened to the public in 1960; it was created with funds from the Calouste Gulbenkian Foundation and is part of the University of Durham. The current name was adopted in 1982 to avoid any confusion with the Gulbenkian's own art collections. The Museum serves as a teaching and research resource for the university teaching staff and students but is also open to general visitors and for more serious researchers into the collections. The Oriental Museum displays collections of oriental art and archaeology from modern-day China to Ancient Egypt, Japan, South-East Asia and the Islamic lands.

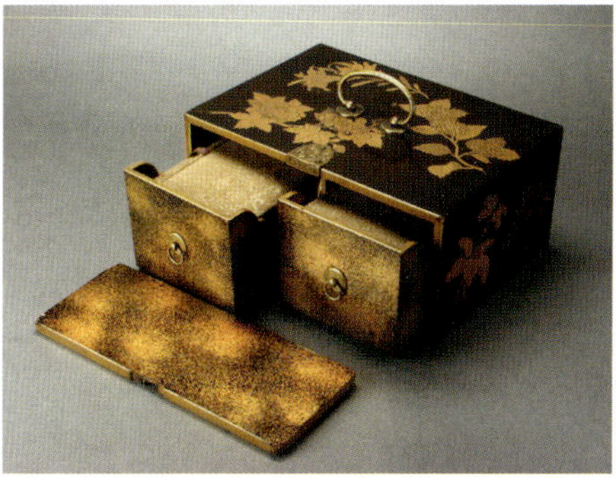

*Laquer box with cards*

The Japanese collections comprise around 1,300 objects that include bronzes (and other metalwork), ceramics, lacquer (including inro), carvings (including netsuke and wooden objects), textiles, coins, weaponry and over 450 graphic works. At any one time around 200 objects might be found on display in the galleries. Major strengths of the collection lie in its holdings of Kakiemon and Imari porcelain and its netsuke and inro collections. It has an exquisite album of woodblock prints *Shin Bijin*, by the Meiji-period artist Toyohara Chikanobu. There is an interesting article about the Oriental Museum's Japanese collections in *The Arts of Asia*, November/December 1983.

**The Oriental Museum**
Elvet Hill
Durham
DH1 3TH

Tel/Fax: 0191 374 7911

Oriental.Museum@
durham.ac.uk
www.dur.ac.uk/oriental.
museum

# Hartlepool

## Hartlepool Art Gallery

The original Hartlepool Museum had been located in Sir William Gray House since the 1920s but the collections moved to the new Hartlepool Art Gallery that opened in 1996. The Gallery is in a beautifully restored old Victorian church; it holds mostly temporary contemporary exhibitions (including the works of Antony Gormley and Anish Kapoor), photography and work of regional, national and local interest.

Hartlepool Art Gallery
Church Square
Hartlepool
Durham
TS24 7EQ

Tel: 01429 890000

Reserve collections are held at:
Sir William Gray House
Clarence Road
Hartlepool
TS24 8BT

Tel: 01429 523438

www.thisishartlepool.co.uk/attractions/artgallery.asp

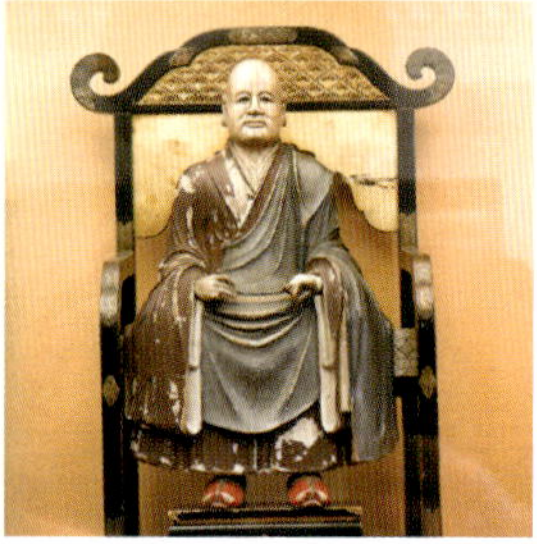

*Portrait figure of a priest*

There are about 100 Japanese objects in the collection, which includes netsuke, fans, prints, *okimono* and armour. There is also an extremely interesting (possibly a 19th-century copy) half-life-size sculpture of a seated priest, which came from the collection of one Colonel W. Thomlinson, a local businessman and philanthropist, who had travelled the world widely including the Far East.

# Morpeth

## Cragside

Cragside was the home designed and built for the industrialist and armaments magnate, William Armstrong. He wanted somewhere to entertain and impress his eminent business contacts and it was important to him that the house should use the latest available technology. Cragside was the first house in the world to be electrically lit by hydro-electricity. By the 1880s it contained extremely advanced forms of heating and lighting.

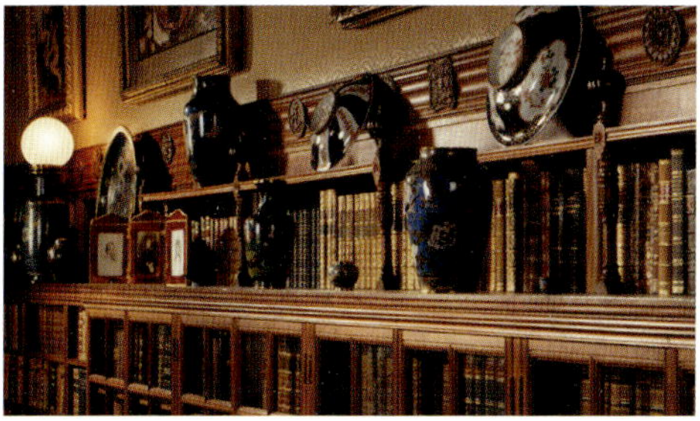

*Cloissone at Cragside*

**Cragside**
Rothbury
Morpeth
Northumberland
NE65 7PX

Tel: 01669 620333
Fax: 01669 620066

cragside@
nationaltrust.org.uk
www.nationaltrust.org.uk

There are quite a number of Japanese objects (around 90 or so) in the collection and these include woodblock prints, *cloisonné*, some lacquer (including an interesting Edo-period *suzuribako*), ceramics, as well as some smaller pieces of furniture (mostly 19th-century) and photographs. Cragside has had many distinguished visitors including the present Japanese emperor (in 1953) and his son, the present Crown Prince (in 1991).

### Wallington

Wallington dates from around 1688 and was built on the site of a medieval castle that had been extended into a Tudor house. The house has been the home to many generations of the Blackett and then the Trevelyan families; in 1942 Sir Charles Trevelyan gave the house and its contents to the National Trust. There is a Palladian exterior and an interior of magnificent rococo plasterwork.

**Wallington**
Cambo
Morpeth
Northumberland
NE61 4AR

Tel: 01670 773600
Fax: 01670 774420

wallington@
nationaltrust.org.uk
nationaltrust.org.uk

Wallington has some unusual collections, which include dolls' houses, model soldiers, kitchen utensils and Lady Wilson's Cabinet of Curiosities. Among the paintings are William Bell-Scott's famous depictions of Northumberland and there is a splendid collection of ceramics, especially far-eastern porcelain. This collection, which includes many examples of Japanese porcelain, was formed in the 18th and 19th centuries and the present display was arranged in 1888.

# Newcastle upon Tyne

## Hancock Museum

The Hancock Museum is primarily a museum of natural history whose origins can be traced back to around 1780 when a private collection of ethnographic and natural history material was acquired by one Marmaduke Tunstall. This collection was eventually acquired in 1823 by the Literary and Philosophical Society of Newcastle and displayed in a small museum. In 1884 the new Newcastle Museum opened on its present site. In 1890 the naturalist John Hancock, who had been instrumental in setting up the new museum, died and the museum was renamed the Hancock Museum in his memory.

There are about 100 Japanese objects in the Hancock Museum collection. These include arms and armour, clothing and personal accessories such as smoking accoutrements and writing implements. There is also a small collection of typical late 19th- century souvenir items.

Hancock Museum
Barras Bridge
Newcastle upon Tyne
Tyne and Wear
NE2 4PT

Tel: 0191 222 6765
Fax: 0191 222 6753

info@twmuseums.org.uk
www.twmuseums.org.uk/hancock

## Laing Art Gallery

The Laing Art Gallery was founded in 1901 by Alexander Laing, a Scottish wine and spirit merchant. The gallery first opened in 1904 and today houses an extensive collection of British oil paintings, watercolours and decorative arts including ceramics, silver and glassware. In the late 19th and early 20th centuries there were strong links between Japan and North-East England as much of Japan's naval and merchant fleet was built in the shipyards of the North East.

One of the most notable acquisitions of Japanese art at the Laing was the gift of Albert H. Higginbottom, who donated more than 1,000 objects to the gallery. The gift included paintings, woodblock prints, ceramics, metalwork (including sword-fittings, stirrups and mirrors), porcelain and lacquer (including inro and at least one lacquered saddle).

Laing Art Gallery
New Bridge Street
Newcastle upon Tyne
Tyne and Wear
NE1 8AG

Tel: 0191 232 7734
Fax: 0191 222 0952

info@twmuseums.org.uk
www.twmuseums.org.uk/laing

# Sunderland

## Sunderland Museum

Sunderland Museum contains a wide range of collections of local and regional importance, particularly local history, including shipbuilding and coal mining, natural history, geology, glass and pottery made on Wearside (particularly Sunderland lustreware), and fine art collections that include 19th- and 20th-century paintings (including works by L. S. Lowry), archaeology and ethnography.

Within the ethnography collections are a group of about 50 Japanese objects including swords and a partial suit of armour. The collection has not yet been fully identified or well-documented and therefore there are currently no Japanese objects on display at the museum.

**Sunderland Museum**
Burdon Road
Sunderland
Tyne and Wear
SR1 1PP

Tel: 0191 553 2323
Fax: 0191 553 7828

info@twmuseums.org.uk
www.twmuseums.org.uk/sunderland

# Wales

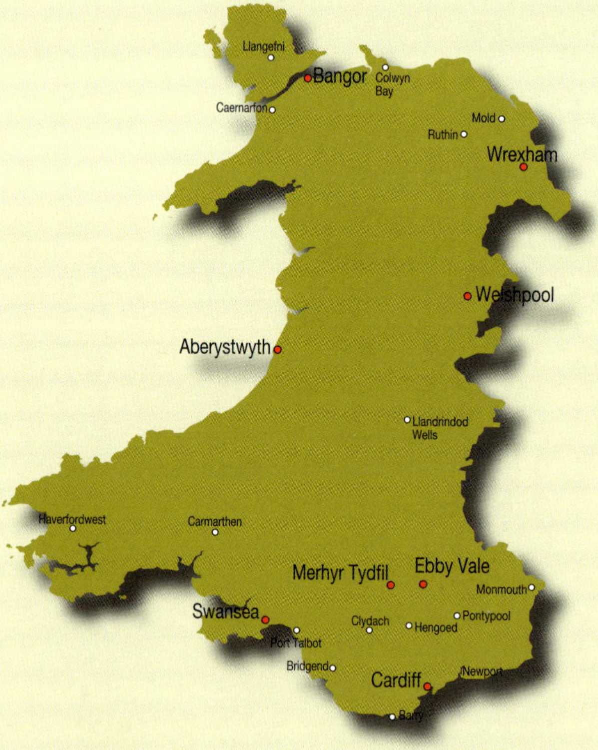

Llangefni
Bangor
Colwyn Bay
Caernarfon
Mold
Ruthin
Wrexham
Welshpool
Aberystwyth
Llandrindod Wells
Haverfordwest
Carmarthen
Merhyr Tydfil
Ebby Vale
Monmouth
Swansea
Clydach
Hengoed
Pontypool
Port Talbot
Bridgend
Cardiff
Newport
Barry

# Aberystwyth

## Aberystwyth School of Art, Gallery & Museum

The ceramic collection is one of the major collections of studio ceramics in Britain and is particularly noted for its studio pottery of the period 1920-1940. The collection has fine examples of pottery by many potters, including Bernard Leach. The main collection at the University was formed between 1920 and 1936; since 1974 there has again been an active policy to acquire contemporary ceramics. In 1986 the display area was extended and a purpose-built gallery was created on the ground floor of Aberystwyth Arts Centre. The principal parts of the collection are permanently on display in display storage in the back gallery while the front gallery is used for changing displays and exhibitions from the permanent collection and touring exhibitions.

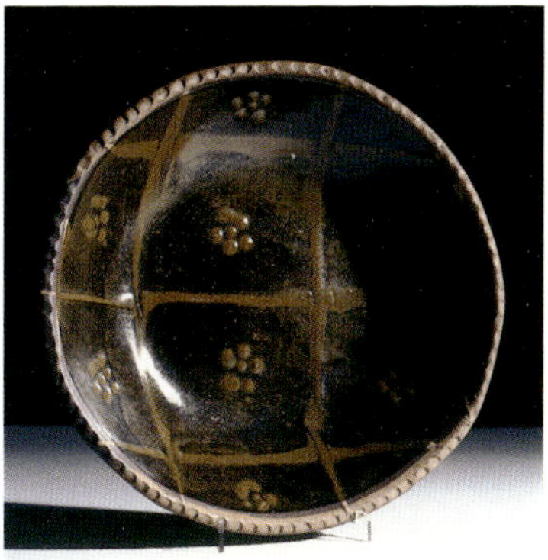

*Slipware dish by Hamada Shoji*

The University College of Wales was founded in 1872 and from an early date began to receive donations of objects and art works that formed the basis of the College Museum, conceived mainly as a teaching museum for science and ancient history. George Ernest Powell was a benefactor during his lifetime and on his death in l882 bequeathed his personal library and art collections to the College. The major part of this benefaction consisted of drawings, paintings and objects d'art, but also included some ceramics, mainly what were then contemporary examples of Japanese Satsuma and Imari ware imported into Europe on the wave of enthusiasm for things Japanese in the late 19th century. There were also examples of continental figurines and individual pieces of Islamic and pre-19th century European wares.

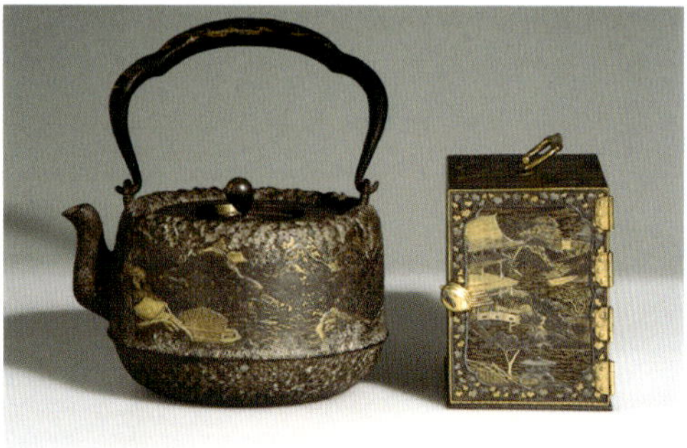

*Tea cattle and inlaid cabinet by Komai of Kyoto*

The lifelong friendship that was formed in the second decade of the 20th century between Bernard Leach, Shoji Hamada and Kanjiro Kawai was to be influential in affecting the direction of ceramics in both Britain and Japan. In the work of these potters, especially Bernard Leach, the theories of the Arts and Crafts Movement became fused with oriental ideas and philosophy. Their influence in Japan was also important in the craft revival known as Mingei, led by their philosopher friend Soetsu Yanagi. The ceramics that inspired them are not the sophisticated wares but the traditional ceramics of Japan. In l92l Hamada and Leach went to St. Ives where they founded the pottery that was to be the cradle for a number of young potters in the 1920s.

There are some 125 Japanese objects in the collections today, including 18th- and 19th-century Japanese ceramics such as Satsuma and Bizen ware. There are also some interesting examples of metalwork (inlaid iron decorative objects by Komai of Kyoto and inlaid decorated tea kettles) as well as examples of lacquer, woodblock prints and netsuke.

**Aberystwyth School of Art, Gallery & Museum**
University of Aberystwyth
Buarth Mawr
Aberystwyth
Ceredigion
SY23 1NE

Tel: 01970 622460

www.aber.ac.uk/ceramics/
www.aber.ac.uk/art/collect.html

# Bangor

## Penrhyn Castle

Thomas Hopper built Penrhyn Castle in the neo-Norman style between 1820 and 1845 for the wealthy Pennant family. The Pennant family made their fortune from trade in Jamaican sugar and Welsh slate. The castle is located between Snowdonia and the Menai Strait. Hopper also designed its interior with many elaborate carvings, panelling, plasterwork and furniture in a 'Norman' style. The castle contains many interesting objects such as a one-ton slate bed that was made especially for Queen Victoria: there is also a good collection of Old Master paintings. The stable block contains an industrial railway museum, a model railway museum and a wonderful dolls' museum with a large collection of 19th and 20th century dolls.

There are a few examples of Japanese ceramics but there are three Japanese export lacquer cabinets in the castle, one certainly of the late 17th century and of extremely fine quality that is displayed on a superb William Kent-style stand before some equally interesting painted Chinese wallpaper.

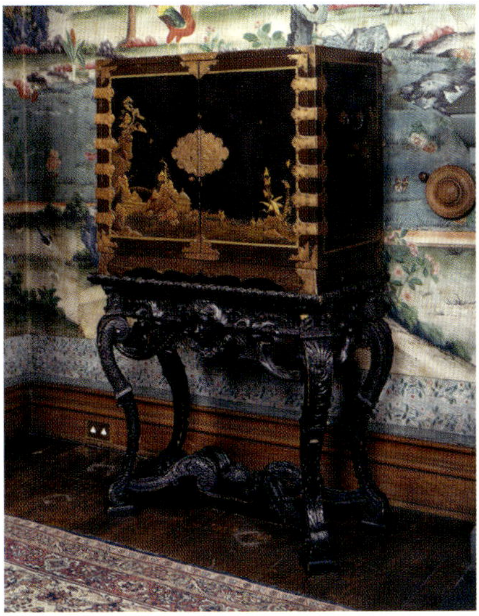

*Laquer cabinet at Penrhyn Castle*

**Penrhyn Castle**
Bangor
Gwynedd
LL57 4HN

Tel: 01248 353084
Fax: 01248 371281

penrhyncastle@
nationaltrust.org.uk
www.nationaltrust.org.uk

# Cardiff

## The National Museum & Gallery

The National Museum of Wales was founded in 1907, but it contains the art collection of the former Cardiff Museum of Natural History, Arts and Antiquities, begun in 1882. The first home for the new national art collection was in 11 police cells and a corridor in the Cardiff Law Courts. It was finally transferred to the present building during the 1920s.

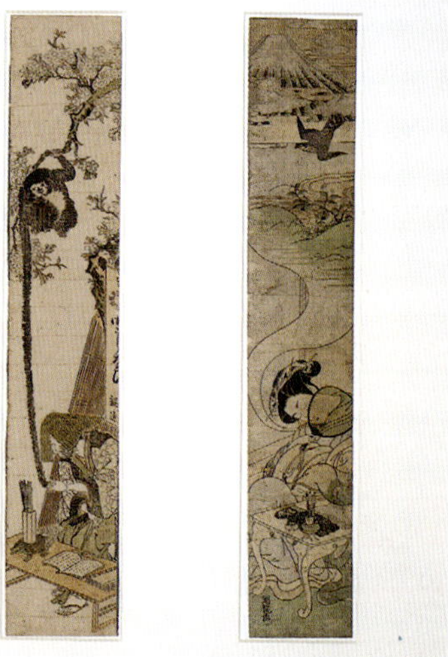

*Hashira-e by Koryusai*

"In July 1915 Dr. W.E. Hoyle, first Director of the National Museum of Wales, received from his nephew in Japan a long letter confirming that he had just shipped from Tokyo to Cardiff several crates of objects, including utensils for the tea ceremony, lacquer, textiles and woodblock prints. A detailed list appended to the letter has made it possible to identify at the Museum all but three of these objects, all of them previously undocumented and the purpose behind their acquisition totally lost. Hoyle's nephew was Bernard Leach, at that time a young artist just discovering the joys of Japanese pottery but soon to become the pre-eminent British potter of the 20th century. Leach was always as influential for his thinking as for his pots and it is fascinating now to be able to use his correspondence with his uncle and the Japanese collection that he sent to Wales to examine the early development of his ideas." Text courtesy Andrew Renton, Curator, Applied Art.

In all, between 1913 and 1915 Leach collected and sent back some 52 objects some of which still have their original Japanese boxes. In 1926 Miss Elizabeth Hughes (1851-1925) bequeathed 171 objects which included woodblock prints, ceramics, lacquer, textiles, metalwork (including *tsuba* and *cloisonné* enamels). Miss Hughes had held a chair at the Japan Women's University, Tokyo some time between 1899 and 1905.

**The National Museum & Gallery**
Cathays Park
Cardiff
CF10 3NP

Tel: 029 2039 7951
Fax: 029 2057 3321

www.nmgw.ac.uk/nmgc

In addition to these collections the Fine Art Department of the Museum has some 470 Japanese woodblock prints (although it is unclear whether this figure includes items from Miss Hughes' bequest). Works by many *ukiyoe* artists are represented in the collections.

## Llandudno

**Llandudno Museum**

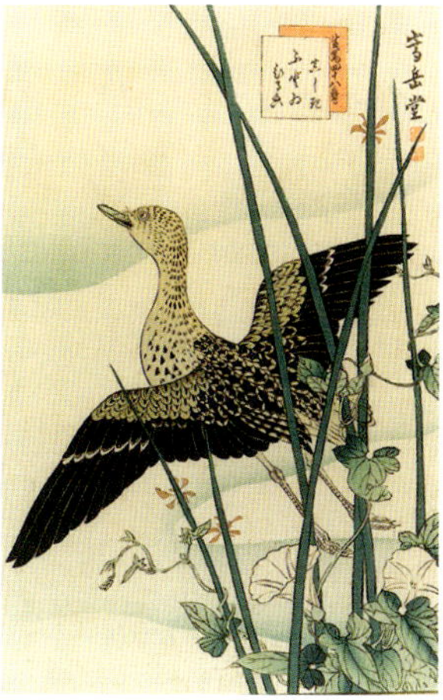

*Woodblock print: from birds and flowers of the four seasons*

Llandudno Museum opened in 1927 at Rapallo House, Craig y Don. The house and its contents had been left to the town of Llandudno by Francis Edouard

Chardon, "for the benefit of the inhabitants of, and visitors to, Llandudno". Chardon was a keen collector of paintings, sculptures and objets d'art from all over the world and much of his collection was displayed at the Museum. The collections moved to their current location in the 1980s.

In addition to Chardon's collections, which included some netsuke, there are about 60 Japanese objects in the collection including woodblock prints, carvings (ivory and wooden netsuke and *okimono*), bronzes and a Boys Festival armour from the then Prince of Wales (later Edward VIII), acquired on his visit to Japan in 1922.

**Llandudno Museum**
Chardon House
17-19 Gloddaeth Street
Llandudno
North Wales
LL30 2DD

Tel/Fax: 01492 876517

www.llandudno-tourism.co.uk/museum

## Merthyr Tydfil

### Cyfarthfa Park

William Crawshay, owner of the Cyfarthfa Ironworks, commissioned Cyfarthfa Castle in 1824. The Gothic-styled castellated mansion and grounds overlooked his immensely successful ironworks and has been called the most impressive monument of the Industrial Iron Age in South Wales. The castle was sold to the local council in 1909 and the collection traces the social history of the town, and includes family portraits, fine art, porcelain, Egyptology and costume. There are around 20 to 30 Japanese objects in the collection, mostly bronzes (flower vases for the most part) but also a few prints. Most of the bronzes are on display in the galleries.

**Cyfarthfa Park**
Brecon Road
Merthyr Tydfil
CF47 8RE

Tel/Fax: 01685 723112

museum@cyfarthapark.freeserve.co.uk

## Swansea

### Glynn Vivian Art Gallery

The Glynn Vivian Art Gallery was founded in 1911 as a purpose-built civic art gallery through the benefaction of Richard Glynn Vivian (1835-1910), the fourth son of the copper industrialist family. He was a seasoned traveller and art collector whose wish was to pass on his love of art. His collections included work by old

**Glynn Vivian Art Gallery**
Alexandra Road
Swansea
Wales
SA1 5DZ

Tel: 01792 516900
Fax: 01792 516903

glynn.vivian.gallery@
swansea.gov.uk
www.swansea.gov.uk/
glynnvivian

masters as well as porcelain and Swansea china. The ceramic collections today include British, European and Oriental wares and a growing representation of 20th-century fine art by Welsh and Welsh-based artists such as Ceri Richards as well as Augustus and Gwen John. There are also works by artists such as Gustave Doré, Epstein, Hepworth, Nicholson, Nash, and Spencer.

There are about 20 Japanese works on paper (mostly woodblock prints by Kuniyoshi and Hiroshige) and the (approximately) 35 ceramics were mostly acquired in 1931 and seem to be early 20th- century examples of coffee sets and tea ware in a very western, almost art deco style.

## Welshpool

### Powis Castle

Powis Castle was originally built around 1200 by Welsh princes and was subsequently adapted and embellished by generations of the Herbert and Clive families, who furnished the Castle with a wealth of fine paintings and furniture. Extensive building work was carried out from about 1772 and a ballroom was built and other rooms were redecorated in the fashionable classical style. George Herbert died in 1801 but his sister had married Clive of India's son. Their son was heir to both the Castle and the Clive fortune, which allowed it to be properly maintained. A collection of Clive mementoes from India is on display in part of the old ballroom. The Castle underwent further extensive refurbishment in 1815-18, and again from 1902. The Castle was bequeathed to the National Trust in 1952 although it remained partly a private home until 1988.

The collections include a group of Japanese black lacquer boxes and export furniture associated with Clive of India and may be the "two Japan knife cases" mentioned in Clive's 1775 inventory. There is also a lacquer chest with the monogram 'W.P' which may be for William, 2nd Marquess and titular Duke of Powis (1665-1745). There is a large set of 18th-century covered Imari vases and beakers described as Chinese, but these may be Japanese.

**Powis Castle**
Welshpool
Wales
SY21 8RF

Tel: 01938 551929
Fax: 01938 554336

powiscastle@
nationaltrust.org.uk
www.nationaltrust.org.uk

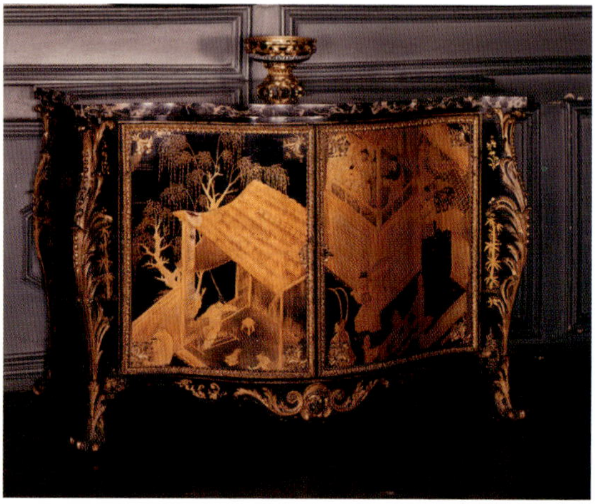

*Laquer commode at Powis Castle*

## Wrexham

### Chirk Castle

Chirk Castle was completed in 1310 and occupies a commanding position in the Welsh Marches. It has been lived in continuously since that time. The Castle has an austere exterior that contrasts with the elegant state rooms within; the rooms contain elaborate plasterwork, tapestries, portraits and superb Adam-style furniture. Chirk Castle was purchased in 1595 by Sir Thomas Myddelton who was a son of the governor of Denbigh Castle and a successful London merchant. He was also a founder of the English East India Company and in the Long Gallery there is an extremely fine Japanese lacquer chest that has long been associated with him. Dating from the early 17th century the chest is covered in shagreen and is decorated with panels of lacquer and mother-of-pearl.

**Chirk Castle**
Wrexham
Denbighshire
North Wales
LL14 5AF

Tel: 01691 777701
Fax: 01691 774706

chirkcastle@
nationaltrust.org.uk
www.nationaltrust.org.uk

# Scotland

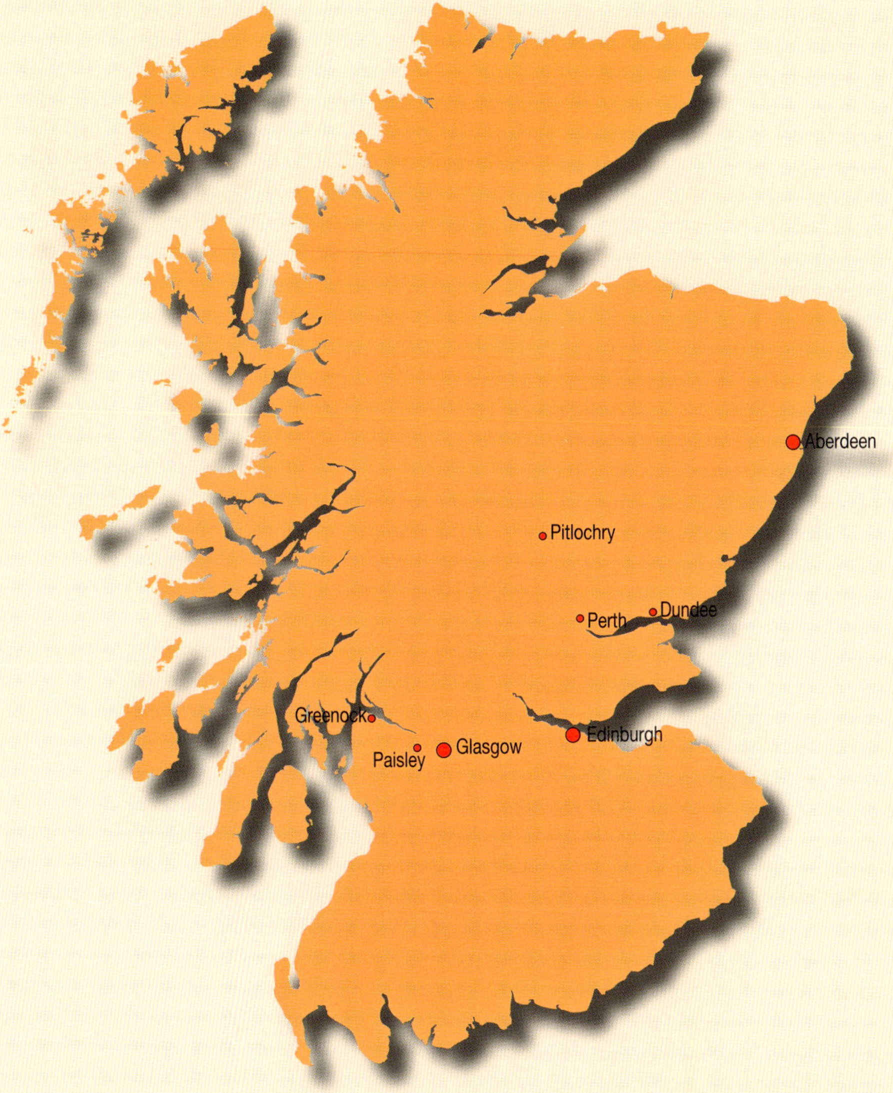

Aberdeen
Pitlochry
Perth
Dundee
Greenock
Edinburgh
Paisley
Glasgow

# Aberdeen

## Aberdeen Art Gallery & Museums

Aberdeen Art Gallery was designed by local architect Alexander Marshall McKenzie and opened in 1885. The Gallery has a diverse collection of works of art and includes celebrated examples of modern and contemporary art as well as work by the Impressionists and the Scottish Colourists.

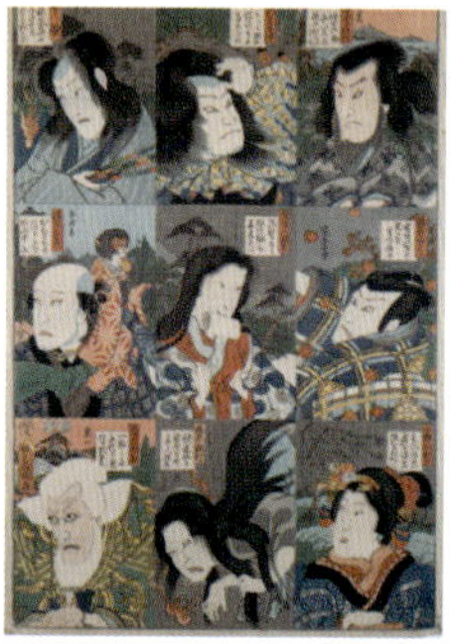

*Print by Kunisada*

The Gallery's permanent collections include painting, sculpture, costume and textiles, metalwork and silver (especially examples of silver by 18th-century Aberdeen silversmiths), ceramics (including some early Chinese ceramics) and some lacquer ware. The temporary exhibition programme includes contemporary art from the UK and overseas. 20th-century British art includes work by Stanley Spencer, Ben Nicholson and Francis Bacon and there are works by the French Impressionists and Post Impressionists including Monet, Renoir, Sisley, Bonnard, Toulouse-Lautrec and Degas.

The Japanese collections include about 30 woodblock prints that range in period from the 19th century (including Kunisada, Toyokuni, Kunichika) through to the 20th century (including Urushibara and Kiyoshi Saito). There are usually a few prints on display. There are also around 30 examples of applied arts: ceramics, sword-fittings, carvings (netsuke and *okimono*), lacquer ware and textiles (including a door-hanging by Serizawa Keisuke).

**Aberdeen Art Gallery & Museums**
Schoolhill
Aberdeen
Scotland
AB10 1FQ

Tel: 01224 523700
Fax: 01224 632133

info@aagm.co.uk
www.aagm.co.uk

# Dundee

## McManus Galleries

The McManus Galleries are housed in a splendid Victorian Gothic building designed in the 1860s by Sir George Gilbert Scott. The building was expanded in 1873 to house the Museum and Art Galleries; the Victoria Galleries were added between 1887 and 1889. In 1984 the building was renamed The McManus Galleries in honour of Dr. Maurice McManus, CBE, Lord Provost of Dundee (1960-67).

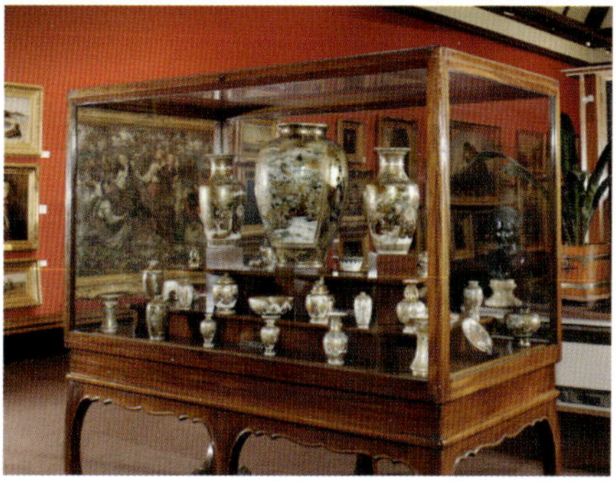

*Display of Satsuma ware at the McManus Gallery*

The Galleries contain Dundee's collections of art, history and the natural sciences; objects include material relating to local archaeology, Egyptology, local history (including a large photographic collection) and industrial history, costume, Scottish silver, glass and ceramics. There is a collection of some 400 paintings and watercolours once owned by the 19th-century industrialist James Guthrie Orchar.

There is a large ethnographic collection, which contains around 200 Japanese objects; these include textiles and costume, masks, lacquer ware, carved ivories, metalwork (including weapons, mirrors, and figures), woodblock prints and ceramics – including a large collection of Satsuma ware and a 41-piece 1920s tea service in eggshell porcelain. These impressive Satsuma pieces (38 in all) were given in 1943 by John Robertson, a jute merchant, and are on permanent display in a splendid specially designed case.

McManus Galleries
Albert Square
Dundee
Scotland
DD1 1DA

Tel: 01382 432350
Fax: 01382 432052

mcmanus.galleries@dundeecity.gov.uk
www.dundeecity.gov.uk/mcmanus/index.html

# Edinburgh

## Royal Museum

The collections of the National Museums of Scotland have been built up over more than two centuries and cover archaeology, ethnography, decorative and the applied arts, numismatics, social and military history, the history of science and technology, agriculture, geology and zoology. The Industrial Museum of Scotland was founded in 1854 during the wave of museum building that followed the Great Exhibition of 1851. In the 1860s the Museum, until then housed in temporary rooms, acquired a new building designed by Francis Fowke. Work began in 1861 and the Museum opened in 1866.

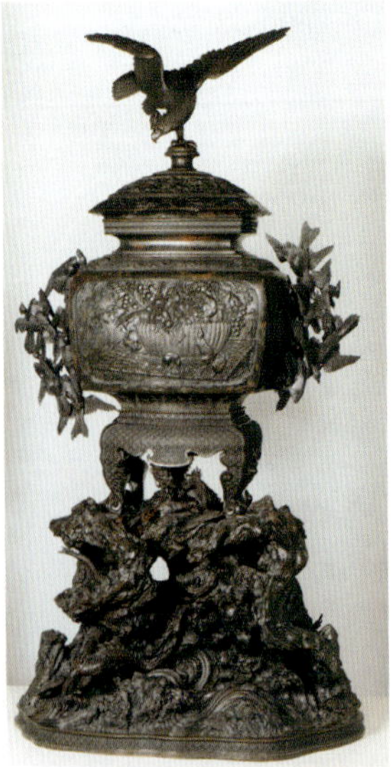
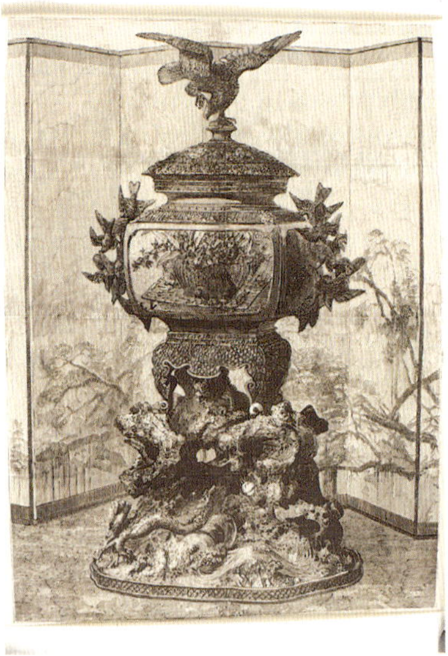

*Incense burner by Suzuki Chokichi, A.1877.4*

The Museum's holdings of Chinese, Japanese and Korean material include pieces of national and international importance. They include ceramics, glass, lacquer, costume, ivories, furniture, jade, bronzes, arms and armour. The earliest dateable pieces in the East-Asian collections are from Japan's Jomon period; the rest of the Japanese material mostly dates from the 18th to 20th centuries. The

Museum has maintained an active policy of collecting contemporary material, which has involved the acquisition of Japanese jewellery, modern prints and ceramics.

The Japanese collection comprises some 9,500 objects including a large collection of Japanese archaeology donated to the Museum around 1900 by Dr. Gordon Munro, a Scottish doctor who became Medical Director of Yokohama Hospital in Japan. Munro also donated a collection of about 350 Ainu objects, including ritual and domestic clothing and accessories. There are large collections of carvings (including netsuke), lacquer (including inro), swords and sword-fittings (including 260 *tsuba*), armour and other examples of metalwork (including *cloisonné* and Meiji-period bronzes), ceramics, textiles and costume, musical instruments and arms and armour. In addition there is a collection of around 4,000 woodblock prints, many in albums made up in Japan at the end of the 19th century.

Some of the earliest Japanese objects acquired by the Museum were part of the gift to Queen Victoria from Tokugawa Iemochi in 1860. The gift was sent to the V&A in London but then many objects were distributed to Edinburgh in 1866. Many examples of Japanese art can be seen in the Ivy Wu Gallery of Eastern Art, which opened in 1996.

**Royal Museum**
National Museums of Scotland
Chambers Street
Edinburgh
EH1 1JF

Tel: 0131 247 4219
Fax: 0131 220 4819

www.nms.ac.uk/royal

## Glasgow

### Hunterian Art Gallery

In 1783 William Hunter bequeathed his substantial and varied collections to the University of Glasgow. Hunter also bequeathed £8,000 for the construction of a suitable museum. Designed by William Stark, the building, classical in style with a dome on top, was erected in the gardens of the College behind the High Street and the Gallery was opened to the public in 1807.

**Hunterian Art Gallery**
82 Hillhead Street
University of Glasgow
Glasgow
G12 8QQ

Tel: 0141 330 5431
Fax: 0141 330 3618

hunter@museum.gla.ac.uk
www.hunterian.gla.ac.uk/index.html

In 1870 the Hunterian collections were transferred to the present site within Sir George Gilbert Scott's neo-Gothic building. At first the entire collection was housed together, and displayed in the packed conditions common in museums of that time. The art collections are housed in the Hunterian Art Gallery and include the Whistler Collection. This collection contains a particularly large number of Whistler's works as well as furniture, silver and ceramics, an extensive holding of the artist's materials and a varied group of personal effects. These include about 20 examples of Japanese ceramics as well as woodblock prints and a mid-19th-century screen.

### Kelvingrove Art Gallery & Museum

The International Exhibition of 1888 was held in Kelvingrove Park and the profits (over £40,000) helped fund the new Art Gallery, Museum and School of Art. The main temporary building of the Exhibition stood more or less on the site now occupied by the Art Gallery & Museum, facing the River Kelvin and the University. The Association for the Encouragement of Art and Music in the City of Glasgow then raised additional funds through public subscription to over £120,000 and in 1891 launched an open architectural competition for the new building.

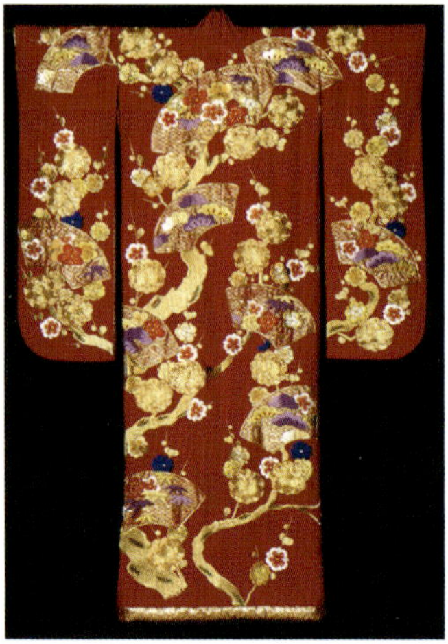

*Japanese wedding gown*

In 1892 the adjudicator, Alfred Waterhouse RA declared the winners to be John W. Simpson and E.J. Milner Allen, joint architects, of London. Although the building combines an assortment of styles, the best description is Spanish Baroque; the two main towers are said to have been inspired by those of Santiago de Compostela. The building opened in 1901 and hosted the International Exhibition, (which included a Japanese Pavilion).

**Kelvingrove Art Gallery & Museum**
Argyle St
Glasgow
G3 8AG

Tel: 0141 287 2699

museums@cls.glasgow.gov.uk
www.glasgowmuseums.com

(NB: Kelvingrove is closed for refurbishment and is scheduled to re-open in 2006.)

The earliest object acquired by Glasgow Museums was a Japanese sword presented by a Mr. Young in 1870. In 1878 the Japanese government gave to the City of Glasgow a remarkable collection of over 1,000 contemporary art works, which included architectural pieces, furniture, wood and lacquer ware, musical instruments, ceramics, metalwork, textiles and costume and paper samples. This gift was part of an exchange that promoted cultural understanding and awareness between Glasgow and Japan. There are a further 1,087 Japanese objects within Glasgow museums that were mostly collected by missionaries, engineers, soldiers, seamen or members of the British Civil Service. The collection today therefore holds over 2,000 Japanese objects and the founding collections have been expanded upon to include *ukiyoe* woodblock prints.

**Burrell Collection**

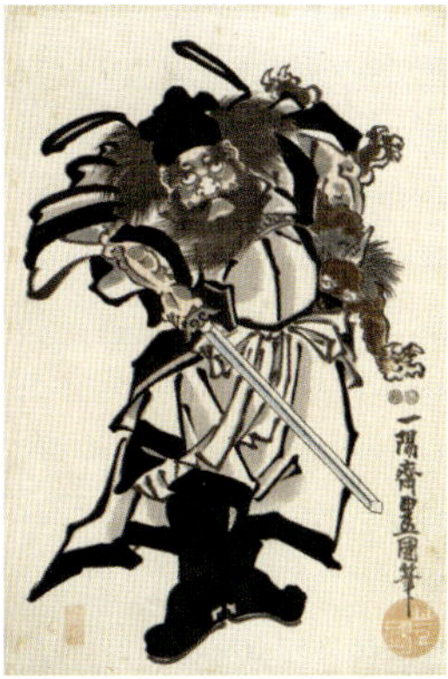

*Shoki the Demon Queller, 37/4*

In 1944 Sir William Burrell and his wife, Constance, Lady Burrell, gifted his collection of over 9,000 works of art to the City of Glasgow; the city acquired one of the greatest collections created by one person. William Burrell had been an art collector since his teens, and the collection is made up of works of all periods and from all over the world. The collection includes medieval art, tapestries, alabasters, stained glass and English oak furniture, European paintings, including works by Degas and Cézanne, an important collection of Islamic art, and modern sculpture including works by Epstein and Rodin. There are also collections of objects from China, Egypt, Greece and Rome.

Sir William wanted the collection to be housed in a building 16 miles from the centre of the Glasgow to show the works of art to their greatest advantage and to avoid the damaging effects of air pollution. No suitable site had been identified by Sir William's death in 1958, but Mrs. Anne Maxwell Macdonald and her family gifted Pollok House and 360 acres of Pollok Estate to the City of Glasgow in 1967. The Burrell was purpose built and opened to the public in 1983. The Burrell Collection houses a large collection of excellent *ukiyoe* woodblock prints and the curator of Chinese and Oriental Civilisations (responsible for Glasgow's Japanese art collections) is based at the Burrell Collection.

**Burrell Collection**
Pollok Country Park
2060 Pollokshaws Rd.
Glasgow
G43 1AT

Tel: 0141 287 2550
Fax: 0141 287 2597

museums@
cls.glasgow.gov.uk
www.glasgowmuseums.
com

## Greenock

### McLean Museum and Art Gallery

The McLean Museum and Art Gallery contains collections of local history, James Watt, ship and engine models, natural history, ethnography and an excellent fine art collection. The ethnography collection has over 300 Japanese objects, which include arms and armour (including a good collection of sword-fittings), lacquer ware (including inro), woodblock prints and printed books, ceramics, carvings (including netsuke), and equestrian objects such as saddles and stirrups. The displays change periodically but will generally include examples of swords and armour.

**McLean Museum and Art Gallery**
15 Kelly Street
Greenock
PA16 8JX

Tel: 01475 715624
Fax: 01475 715626

www.inverclyde.gov.uk/Museum/Index.htm

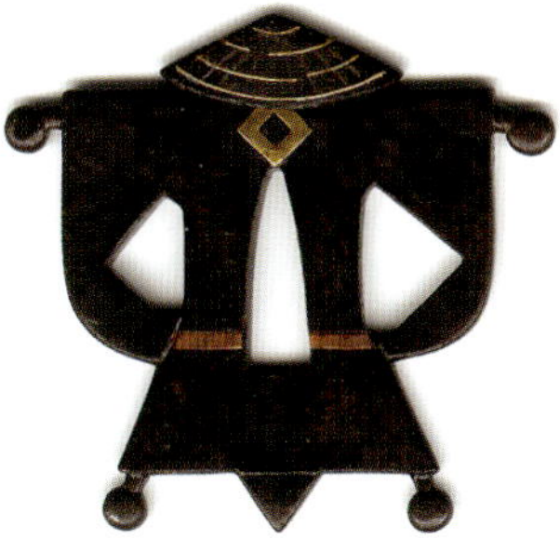

*Tsuba in the form of a scarecrow*

## Paisley

### Paisley Museum and Art Galleries

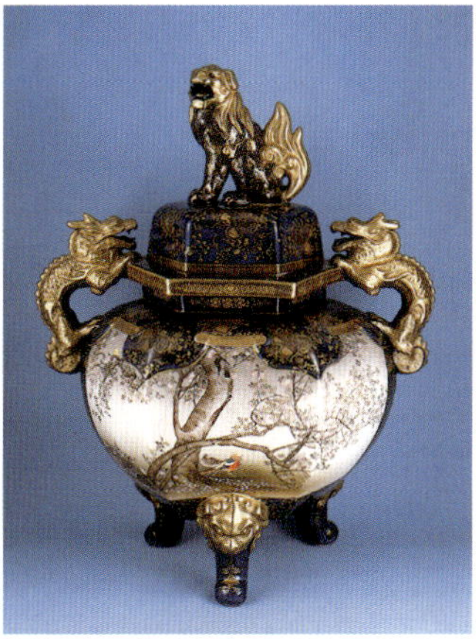

*Large koro by Kinkozan, c.1890, 1915-12f*

Paisley Museum and Art Gallery was Scotland's first municipally funded museum and opened in 1871. In 1882 art and sculpture galleries were added (paid for by Sir Peter Coats). The building was once more extended in 1901 and 1933 and included extensions for the library. Paisley is the home of the Paisley

**Paisley Museum and Art Galleries**
High Street
Paisley
Glasgow
PA1 2BA

Tel: 01418 893 151
Fax: 01418 899 240

museums-els@renfrewshire.gov.uk
www.renfrewshire.gov.uk

Pattern. Paisley shawls were woven here from 1805 onwards, although the pattern itself originates in the East. New shawl galleries were added in 1974. The Art Gallery contains many fine Scottish paintings and has a good collection of studio ceramics.

There are approximately 200 Japanese objects in the collections, which include ceramics, metalwork (including *cloisonné* enamels), textiles and costume, weapons, woodblock prints and printed books, some paintings, ivory carvings and photography. Only a small amount of Japanese material is on display at any one time.

## Perth

### Scone Palace

Scone Palace is the home of the Earl and Countess of Mansfield and has been the seat of parliaments and the crowning place of kings including Macbeth, Robert the Bruce and Charles II. Scone was given by James VI of Scotland (James I of England) to Sir David Murray in 1604 who in turn built a new palace in 1618; the castellated palace as it appears today dates from the early 19th century. The state rooms have a wonderful collection of paintings, furniture, ivory carvings, porcelain and objects d'art, including some pieces that once belonged to Marie Antoinette. There are 22 Japanese objects in the collection at Scone and all are on public display. They include ceramics (Imari and Kutani ware) and lacquer furniture, mostly of the 19th century. Scone Palace produces a guidebook in Japanese.

**Scone Palace**
Perth
Perthshire
PH2 6BD

Tel: 01738 552 300
Fax: 01738 552 588

visits@scone-palace.co.uk
www.scone-palace.net

## Pitlochry

### Blair Castle

Blair Castle has been home to the Earls and Dukes of Atholl for over 700 years. The Castle has been modified over the centuries, notably in the 1870s. Queen Victoria visited Blair Castle in 1844 and was so captivated by the royal bodyguard that she presented them with regimental colours. The Atholl Highlanders are the only private army in Europe and exist today as a private ceremonial bodyguard. The Castle has collections of paintings, arms and armour, costume as well as Jacobite memorabilia.

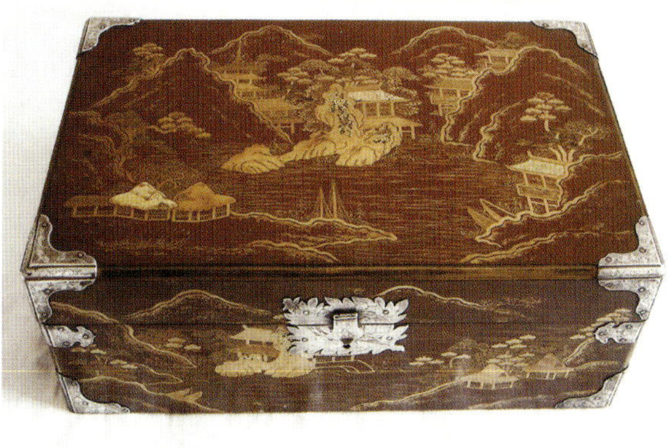

*Lacquer box presented by Crown Prince Hirohito in 1921 to the Duchess of Atholl*

There are around ten Japanese objects in the Castle's collections, some of which have an interesting history. There are ceramics, mostly 19th-century but with two large 17-th-century Imari vases. In 1883, as part of a tour of the Far East, the 7th Duke of Atholl travelled to Japan and between 1st and 23rd April visited Nagasaki, Kobe, Osaka, Kyoto, Yokohama and Tokyo. The Castle has an extensive inventory of what he purchased at each location but sadly many of these items cannot be located today. The objects purchased included large bronze figures, ivory carvings, sword-fittings, ceramics and bamboo carvings. On May 21st 1921 Crown Prince Hirohito visited Blair Castle and presented the Duchess with a lacquer box that can be seen at the Castle, as can a suit of armour, a late 17th-century lacquer cabinet and two pairs of *naginata*, which are all believed to have been bought in 1883.

**Blair Castle**
Blair Atholl
Pitlochry
Perthshire
PH18 5TL

Tel: 01796 481207
Fax: 01796 481487

manager@
blair-castle.co.uk
www.blair-castle.co.uk

# Northern Ireland

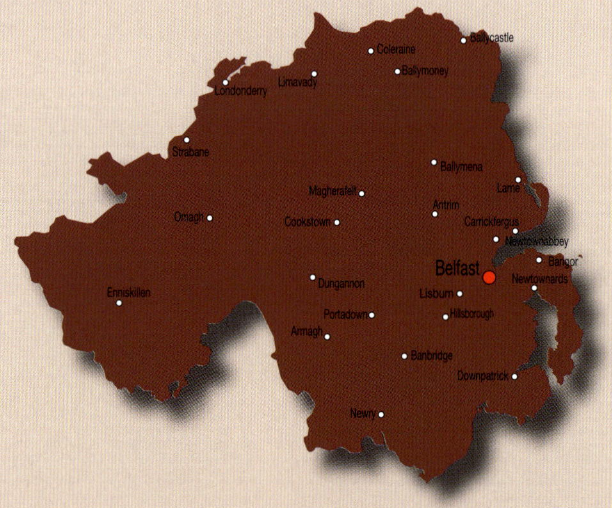

# Belfast

## Ulster Museum

The origins of the Ulster Museum can be traced back to 1821 when a society for the study of natural sciences was formed. The Belfast Natural History Society put its collections on public display in a new building, "the first ever museum erected in Ireland by voluntary subscription," which opened to the public in 1833. The range and quality of the collections was expanded to include ethnographic items, then archaeological specimens. The collections did not then include the visual arts. In 1888 the Belfast Free Public Library was established and an art gallery was added in 1890. A site in the Botanic Gardens was chosen for the building of a new, free Belfast Museum and Art Gallery and in 1924 the foundation stone was laid; in 1929 the new neo-classical building opened.

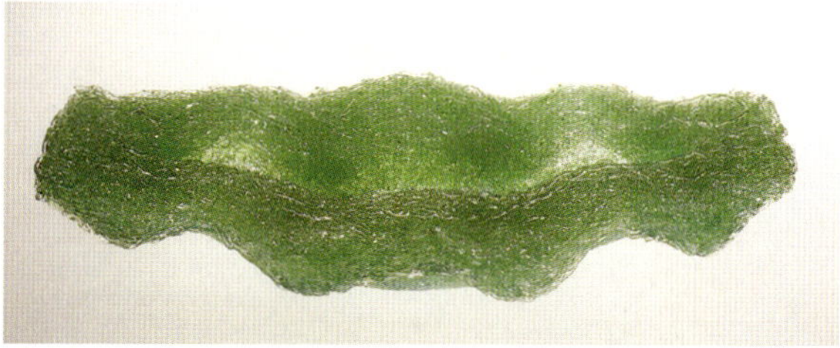

*Green wavy hexagonal bowl*

The collections gradually expanded and in the 1950s the Keeper of Art laid the foundations of the present fine art collections and recommended the enhancement of the modern and old masters collections. The collections departments today include Fine and Applied Art, Archaeology and Ethnography, Treasures from the Armada, Local History, Numismatics, Industrial Archaeology, Botany, Zoology and Geology.

The Japanese collections fall between the department Archaeology and Ethnography and the department of Fine and Applied Art. The former has some 68 Japanese objects including carved ivories, arms and armour, textiles and costume, lacquer ware and metalwork. The collection has a full-sized palanquin (acquired in 1891), which bears the *mon* (family crest) of the *daimyo* of southern Hokkaido. There is also a splendid Edo-period replica of a bronze lantern from Shittenoji in Osaka; the original is dated equivalent to 1274 and the copy also bears this date. The lantern is on permanent display outside the museum building. The Fine and Applied Art Department has around 50 Japanese objects including textiles and costume (including contemporary fashion by Miyake, Kenzo and others), late 19th-century jewellery, ceramics, *cloisonné* and an embroidered silk screen, which were probably acquired at that time. There are also some prints and contemporary glass. Japanese objects can generally be seen in themed displays, although there are a few pieces on permanent display.

**Ulster Museum**
Botanic Gardens
Belfast
BT9 5AB
Northern Ireland

Tel: 028 9038 3000
Fax: 028 9038 3003

www.ulstermuseum.org.uk

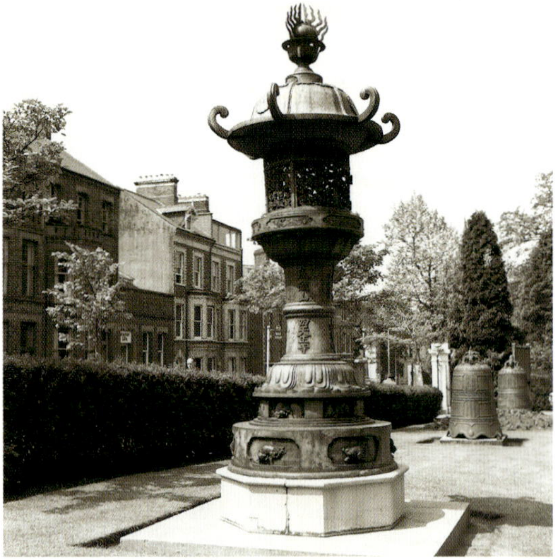

*Replica of a lantern at Shittenoji; in the grounds of the Ulster Museum*

# Republic of Ireland

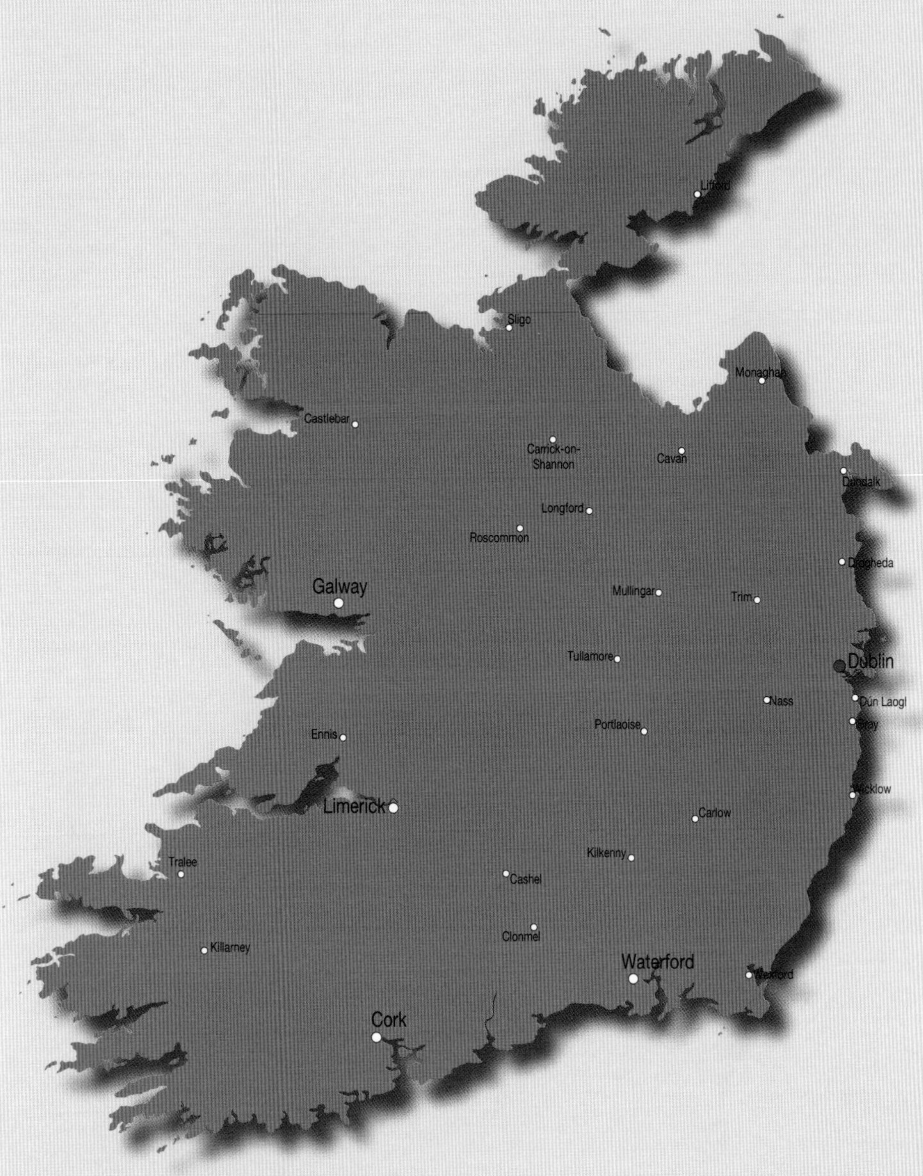

# Dublin

## Chester Beatty Library

Sir Alfred Chester Beatty was born in New York City in 1875. He initially attended Princeton University but transferred to Columbia from which he graduated as a mining engineer. Beatty's entrepreneurship had made him a wealthy man and his mining interests extended to Africa, Eastern Europe and his company was established virtually worldwide. From an early age he was a collector and he already had a library of note when, in 1910, his first wife died. He decided to move to London where, by 1911, he had taken up permanent residence. In 1917 he travelled to the Far East and expanded his collecting interests more widely into Chinese and Japanese works of art; in particular for *Nara Ehon* (Nara picture books) and he built up an extremely important collection of these works.

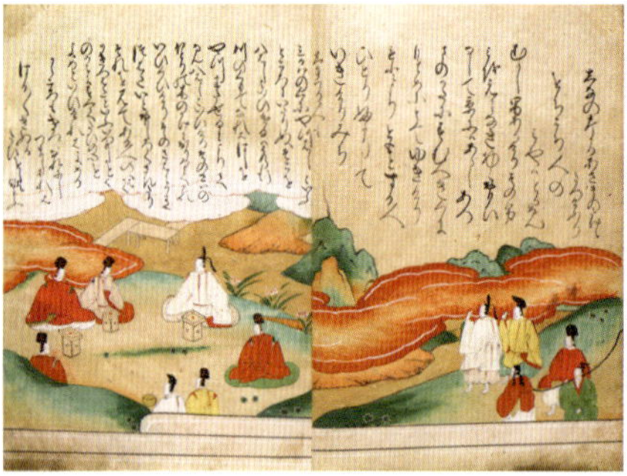

*Table of Ise; J.1050*

Beatty decided to leave his home in Britain and in 1950 he established his collection in a fashionable suburb of Dublin. He created a small purpose-built library that was opened to researchers in 1953 and, later, in a limited way to the public. In 1957 a purpose-built exhibition gallery was added to the library and this was expanded in the 1970s. The remarkable Chester Beatty Collections were moved from their original home to a new purpose-built museum and library at Dublin Castle in 1999. They opened to the public on the 125th anniversary of Chester Beatty's birth, 7th February 2000.

**Chester Beatty Library**
Dublin Castle
Dublin 2
Ireland

Tel: +353 1 407 0750
Fax: +353 1 407 0760

info@cbl.ie
www.cbl.ie

The Japanese collection is particularly renowned for its painted handscrolls and albums of the type known as *Nara Ehon*. These include a rare 16th-century copy of the *Tales of Ise* and several versions of the *Tale of Genji*. The Japanese paintings are complemented by a fine range of *ukiyoe* woodblock prints, with an outstanding set of over 700 *surimono*. A very early example of Japanese printing is the *Hyakumanto Darani*, a Buddhist charm housed in a wooden stupa and dates back to AD 768. Japanese decorative arts in the Library include a number of fine netsuke belt toggles, inro and *tsuba*.

## National Museum of Ireland

The National Museum of Ireland today consists of four separate museum buildings; three are situated in Dublin and one in Castlebar, Co. Mayo. The National Museum of Ireland – Archaeology and History was the original home of the Dublin Museum of Science and Art that opened in 1890. The National Museum of Ireland – Decorative Arts and History opened in 1997 and is the administrative headquarters of the National Museum of Ireland. The National Museum of Ireland – Natural History, originally belonged to the Royal Dublin Society and has been open to the public since 1857.

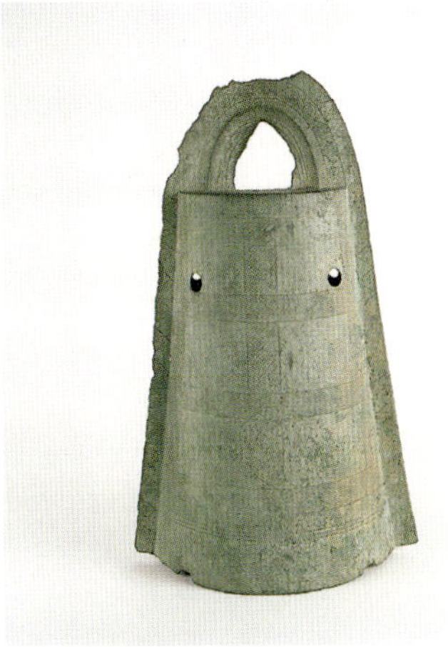

*Bronze dotaku, 1887.360*

The origins of the National Museum of Ireland lie with the enactment of The Dublin Science and Art Museum Act of 1877. This led to the transfer of the buildings and collections of the Royal Dublin Society to state ownership. These were further enhanced by the transfer of other notable collections from institutions such as the Royal Irish Academy and Trinity College Dublin. The original museum opened to the public in 1890 and housed coins, medals and Irish antiquities from the Royal Irish Academy including the Tara brooch and Ardagh chalice, ethnographical collections with material from Captain Cooke's voyages on loan from Trinity College Dublin and the collections of the Geological Survey of Ireland. These were joined by material from the decorative arts and ethnographical collections of the Royal Dublin Society and their Irish collections of antiquities, minerals and plants.

In 1988 the closure of Collins Barracks in Dublin eventually led to the buildings being assigned to museum use in 1994. The National Museum of Ireland – Decorative Arts and History opened at the former Collins Barracks in 1997. Its collections reflect Irish history over the last three centuries and also include collections of European and Oriental decorative arts. There are some 1,500 Japanese objects within the collections and they include woodblock prints, ceramics (some as early as Momoyama period), arms and armour, other metalwork (including a very good collection of *cloisonné* enamels), lacquer ware, carved ivories and a palanquin. The earliest acquired object came into the Museum's collections in 1878 and the earliest object is a fine example of a *dotaku*.

**National Museum of Ireland**
Decorative Arts & History
Collins Barracks
Benburb Street
Dublin 7
Republic of Ireland

Tel: +353 1 6777444
Fax: +353 1 6777450

marketing@museum.ie
www.museum.ie

# Index

# Illustration rights

| *page* | *Illustration* | *Copyright* |
|---|---|---|
| *11* | *Lacquer bowl in ormolu mounts* | *© HM Queen Elizabeth II* |
| *14* | *Bijin figure, Arita porcelain with overglaze enamels, c. 1680-1700, C.3-1961, Given by the Friends of the Fitzwilliam* | *© Fitzwilliam Museum, University of Cambridge* |
| *15* | *Tiger by Ganku c. 1784-96, 1931.4-27.01* | *© Trustees of the British Museum* |
| *17* | *The Japanese Court at the International Exhibition London, 1862* | *Illustrated London News* |
| *18* | *Japanese objects acquired by the V&A from Samuel Bing* | *© V&A Picture Library* |
| *18* | *Japanese objects originally bought by Londos & Co. Christopher Dresser's company, acquired the* | *© V&A Picture Library* |
| *19* | *Japanese Room at the Royal Bath Hotel, Bournemouth* | *Russell-Cotes Art Gallery & Museum* |
| *22* | *Ivory okimono* | *© Holbourne Museum, Bath* |
| *23* | *Natsume and box* | *By kind permission of the Museum of East Asian Art, Bath* |
| *25* | *Silver elephant by Nakagawa Yoshizane* | *© Russell-Cotes Art Gallery & Museum, Bournemouth* |
| *26* | *Plaque by Komai of Kyoto* | *© Russell-Cotes Art Gallery & Museum, Bournemouth* |
| *28* | *Fashion Produce (L), Yuji Hiratsuka* | *© Bristol Museums & Art Gallery* |
| *29* | *Viewing autumn maple leaves, c. 1890-1900. Mb4391-10* | *© Bristol Museums & Art Gallery* |
| *30* | *Japanese armour at Snowshill Manor* | *National Trust Photo Library/Andreas von Einsidel* |
| *34* | *Sudden shower on the Ohashi, Ando Hiroshige* | *Cheltenham Art Gallery & Museum; from the Trustees of the R E Summerfield Charitable Trust* |
| *36* | *Kagura mask* | *© Royal Albert Memorial Museum, Exeter City Council* |
| *39* | *Ivory netsuke of a foreigner* | *© Plymouth City Museum* |
| *40* | *Porcelain at Saltram* | *National Trust Photo Library/Andreas von Einsidel* |
| *41* | *Rectangular slab vase by Hamada Shoji* | *© A Gillam, Leach Pottery* |
| *43* | *Stonehenge, by Yoshijiro Urishibara* | *Salisbury and South Wiltshire Museum* |
| *44* | *Kakiemon bottle* | *© Sherborne Castle Estates* |
| *45* | *The Shibayama collection at the Royal Cornwall Museum, Truro* | *© Gregory Irvine* |
| *45* | *Metal dish with Shibayama-style decoration* | *Royal Cornwall Museum, photograph by Gregory Irvine* |
| *50* | *Meiji period shrine* | *© The Powell-Cotton Museum* |
| *51* | *Iron teakettle, 19th century* | *© Brighton & Hove Libraries and Museums* |
| *55* | *Print from the collection at Standen* | *National Trust Photo Library/John Hammond* |
| *58* | *Seto oil dish, Bernard Leach Source Collection, P.79.52* | *© Crafts Study Centre* |
| *59* | *Pair of Kakiemon hounds* | *© Firle Estate Trustees* |
| *59* | *Export porcelain in ormolu mounts at Clandon Park* | *National Trust Photo Library/Nadia Mackenzie* |
| *64* | *Kakiemon figure of a boy with a dog. Gift of Gerald Reitlinger, 1978.670* | *By kind permission of the Marquess of Tavistock and the Trustees of the Bedford Estates* |
| *67* | *Advertising material for the Miyako Hotel, Kyoto, 1908* | *© Pitt Rivers Museum, Oxford* |
| *69* | *Imari porcelain at Uppark* | *National Trust Photo Library/Geoffrey Frosh* |
| *70* | *Lacguer chest at Petworth House* | *National Trust Photo Library/Andreas von Einsidel* |
| *71* | *Detail of tachi and scabbard* | *© University of Durham, University Museums* |
| *78* | *Hyakumanto: Or.78.a.11* | *© The British Library* |
| *80* | *Ainu embroidered coat, donated by Dr John Anderson FRS, 1885, 12-19* | *The Trustees of the British Museum* |
| *81* | *Bodhisattva Monju by Koyu, c.1680, 1988.3-14.2 (left)* | *© Trustees of the British Museum* |

| | | |
|---|---|---|
| 81 | *Bodhisattva Fugen by Koyu, c.1680, 1988.3-14.1 (right)* | *© Trustees of the British Museum* |
| 84 | *Court fan, 19th century* | *© The Fan Museum Trust, Hélène Alexander Collection* |
| 86 | *Masks for Noh performance* | *© Horniman Public Museum and Public Trust, photograph by Heini Schneebeli* |
| 89 | *The Brittish Legation at Tozenji in Edo, Felice Beato, c.1863* | *© The Japan Society* |
| 91 | *Rice bowl, EBC 67821* | *© The Board of Trustees, Royal Botanic Gardens, Kew* |
| 92 | *Copy of the Chokushi-mon at the 1910 Anglo-Japanese Exhibition: now at the Royal Botanic ardens Kew* | *© V&A Picture Library* |
| 94 | *The Mazarin Chest, c. 1600, 415-1882* | *© V&A Picture Library* |
| 95 | *Bizen water jar c. 1600, 191-1882* | *© V&A Picture Library* |
| 95 | *Oyoroi armour presented to Queen Victoria by Tokugawa Iemochi in 1860: 362-1865* | *© V&A Picture Library* |
| 96 | *Tachi presented to Sir Harry Parkes by Emperor Meiji, M.13-1949* | *© V&A Picture Library* |
| 97 | *Art treasures from Japan: Exhibition at the Victoria & Albert Museum, 1958* | *© V&A Picture Library* |
| 97 | *Toys from the collection of the National Archive of Art & Design at the Victoria & Albert Museum* | *© V&A Picture Library* |
| 98 | *Japanese lacquer cabinet and French stand, c.1680* | *By kind Permission of the Trustees of The Wallace Collection* |
| 102 | *Kitagawa Utamaro, Act two from "The Chushingura parodied by famous beauties", P.349-1945, given by the Friends of the Fitzwilliam* | *© Fitzwilliam Museum, University of Cambridge* |
| 103 | *Haniwa figure, Kofun period, C.397-1991, given by Mr & Mrs Conrad Abrahams-Cureil, in memory of their daughter, Eleanora* | *© Fitzwilliam Museum, University of Cambridge* |
| 104 | *Seventeenth century export lacquer cabinet* | *Courtesy of the Marquis of Salisbury, Hatfield House* |
| 107 | *Standing Jizo Bosatsu, Kamakuza period* | *Robert and Lisa Sainsbury Collection, University of East Anglia, Norwich, NR4 7TJ. Photographer James Austin* |
| 110 | *Composite suit of armour* | *© Saffron Walden Museum, Uttlesford District Council* |
| 111 | *Japanese alcore at Woburn Abbey showing kakiemon porcelain* | *By kind permission of the Marquess of Tavistock and the Trustees of the Bedford Estates* |
| 115 | *Lacquer chest at Belton House* | *National Trust Photo Library/Mark Fiennes* |
| 116 | *Ivory okimono* | *© Leicester City Museums Service* |
| 118 | *Composite suit of armour* | *© Castle Museum & Art Gallery, Nottingham City Council* |
| 120 | *Kakiemon cockerel* | *Courtesy The Burghley House Collection* |
| 123 | *Ivory okimono* | *Courtesy of Bewdley Museum Service* |
| 124 | *Shibayama decorated ivory tusks; 1890 M 108.1&2* | *Birmingham Museums & Art Gallery* |
| 126 | *Preparatory study for a kite, Kanno Yuji, 1995* | *© Herbert Art Gallery, Coventry City Council* |
| 127 | *Tokiwa's fight through the snow with her children, Ando Hiroshige, c. 1833* | *The Hereford Museum, Herefordshire Heritage Services: bequeathed by Evelyn May Dill* |
| 128 | *Sato's Tiger Hunt, A580.1968.8* | *Reproduced courtesy of The Art Gallery & Museum, The Royal Pump Rooms, Leamington Spa, Warwick District Council* |
| 132 | *Detail of tachi-style sword* | *© Wolverhampton Art Gallery, Wolverhampton City Council* |
| 135 | *Cherry blossom on the Sumidagawa, Ando Hiroshige* | *Courtesy Blackburn Museum & Art Gallery, Thomas Boys Lewis bequest* |
| 137 | *Detail of bronze incense burner* | *© Bury Art Gallery & Museum* |
| 138 | *Detail of triptych 'Shell-divers' by Kitagawa Utamaro, 1949.125.217* | *© Tullie House, Museum and Arts Services, Carlisle City Council* |

| | | |
|---|---|---|
| 140 | *Patinated bronze vase inlaid with cloisonné enamels, 43.22.03* | *Courtesy of the National Museums Liverpool* |
| 145 | *Indigo resist dyed sash, T.11566* | *The Whitworth Art Gallery, The University of Manchester* |
| 147 | *Saddle and harness* | *© The Ashmolean Museum, Oxford* |
| 148 | *Cherry blossom at Asakusa, Ando Hiroshige* | *© Harris Museum and Art Gallery* |
| 149 | *Installation by Junicki Arai at the Harris Museum, Preston* | *© Harris Museum and Art Gallery* |
| 154 | *Pair of lacquer picnic boxes* | *Leeds Museums and Galleries (Temple Newsam House)* |
| 154 | *Cloissone vase with dragons* | *© Leeds Museums and Galleries (Lotherton Hall)* |
| 155 | *Ivory and wood okimono of a Bijin on a tree trunk with birds, c.1890* | *© Leeds Museums and Galleries (Temple Newsam House)* |
| 156 | *Japanese armour given to James I* | *© The Board of Trustees of the Armouries* |
| 158 | *Fan-shaped lacquer box* | *© Harewood House Trust* |
| 159 | *Arita ware on export lacquer cabinet* | *© Newby Hall Estate* |
| 164 | *Kakiemon vase* | *Courtesy The Bowes Museum* |
| 165 | *Laquer box with cards* | *© University of Durham, University Museums* |
| 166 | *Portrait figure of a priest* | *© Hartlepool Art Gallery, Borough of Hartlepool* |
| 167 | *Cloissone at Cragside* | *National Trust Photo Library/Andreas von Einsidel* |
| 171 | *Slipware dish by Hamada Shoji* | *The University of Wales, Aberystwyth* |
| 172 | *Tea cattle and inlaid cabinet by Komai of Kyoto* | *The University of Wales, Aberystwyth* |
| 173 | *Laquer cabinet at Penrhyn Castle* | *National Trust Photo Library/John Hammond* |
| 174 | *Hashira-e by Koryusai* | *© National Museums and Galleries of Wales* |
| 175 | *Woodblock print: from birds and flowers of the four seasons* | *Courtesy the Trustees of the Chardon Trust, Llandudno Museum* |
| 178 | *Laquer commode at Powis Castle* | *National Trust Photo Library/J Whitaker* |
| 180 | *Print by Kunisada* | *Aberdeen Art Gallery & Museums Collections* |
| 181 | *Display of Satsuma ware at the McManus Gallery* | *McManus Galleries, Dundee City Council Leisure and Arts* |
| 182 | *Incense burner by Suzuki Chokichi, A.1877.4* | *© Trustees of the National Museums of Scotland* |
| 184 | *Japanese wedding gown* | *© Kelvingrove Art Gallery & Museum* |
| 185 | *Shoki the Demon Queller, 37/4* | *© Burrell Collection* |
| 187 | *Tsuba in the form of a scarecrow* | *© McLean Museum and Art Gallery, Inverclyde Council* |
| 187 | *Large koro by Kinkozan, c.1890, 1915-12f* | *Paisley Museum & Art Galleries, Renfrewshire Council* |
| 189 | *Lacquer box presented by Crown Prince Hirohito in 1921 to the Duchess of Atholl* | *Blair Charitable Trust, Blair Castle, Perthshire* |
| 191 | *Green wavy hexagonal bowl* | *© Ulster Museum: reproduced with the kind permission of the Trustees of the National Museums and Galleries of Northern Ireland* |
| 192 | *Replica of a iantern at Shittenoji; in the grounds of the Ulster Museum* | *© Ulster Museum: reproduced with the kind permission of the Trustees of the National Museums and Galleries of Northern Ireland* |
| 194 | *Table of Ise; J.1050* | *Reproduced by kind permission of the Trustees of the Chester Beatty Library* |
| 195 | *Bronze dotaku, 1887.360* | *© National Museum of Ireland* |

## Gregory Irvine

Gregory Irvine is the curator in the Asian Department of the Victoria & Albert Museum, London, responsible for the collections of Japanese metalwork, particularly arms and armour. Formerly a curator in the Department of Japanese Antiquities of the British Museum, he joined the V&A in 1992. As well as extended periods of research into swords and armour in Japan, he is particularly interested in the philosophies and social background behind the use of weaponry in Japan's historical period.

He is the author of The Japanese Sword, the Soul of the Samurai, London 2000. He is currently working on a publication on Japanese cloisonné and is researching the history of collecting Japanese objects in Europe during the period 1850 - 1940. His other main area of research is in the use of masks in Japan's religious ceremonies and rituals, in folk performance and in the traditional theatre. He is preparing a publication and exhibition on this subject. He is a practitioner of kyudō, the Japanese 'Way of the Bow'.